William Arnold Spicer

History of the Ninth and Tenth Regiments Rhode Island Volunteers

And the Tenth Rhode Island Battery, in the Union Army in 1862

William Arnold Spicer

History of the Ninth and Tenth Regiments Rhode Island Volunteers
And the Tenth Rhode Island Battery, in the Union Army in 1862

ISBN/EAN: 9783744729147

Printed in Europe, USA, Canada, Australia, Japan

Cover: Foto ©ninafisch / pixelio.de

More available books at **www.hansebooks.com**

HISTORY

OF THE

NINTH AND TENTH

REGIMENTS

RHODE ISLAND VOLUNTEERS,

AND THE

Tenth Rhode Island Battery,

IN THE UNION ARMY IN 1862.

PROVIDENCE:
SNOW & FARNHAM, PRINTERS.
1892.

RHODE ISLAND

Ninth and Tenth Regiments,

AND

Tenth Battery.

WILLIAM A. SPICER,
Co. B, Tenth R. I. Vols.

CONTENTS.

	PAGES.
INTRODUCTION .	5
PRELIMINARY CHAPTERS:	
THE HIGH SCHOOL BOYS .	9
THE COLLEGE BOYS OF "BROWN"	21
THE RHODE ISLAND NATIONAL GUARD	37
THE CALL FOR VOLUNTEERS IN MAY, 1862	63
THE NINTH RHODE ISLAND VOLUNTEERS	67
THE TENTH RHODE ISLAND VOLUNTEERS .	121
THE TENTH LIGHT BATTERY RHODE ISLAND VOLUNTEERS	317
REUNIONS OF THE NINTH AND TENTH RHODE ISLAND VETERAN ASSOCIATIONS, .	334, 339
ROSTER OF NINTH AND TENTH RHODE ISLAND REGIMENTS AND TENTH BATTERY	301, 385
RESOLUTIONS	414–415

Introduction.

"NEVER in all history was so wonderful a scene as the sudden uprising of our people, and their quiet return to the pursuits of peace. We can only liken it to the poetic description of Sir Walter Scott, in the Lady of the Lake, when Roderick gives the shrill whistle through the copse and heath, that summons his men before the face of Fitz James.

> ' That whistle garrisoned the glen
> At once with full five hundred men,
> As if the yawning hill to heaven
> A subterranean host had given.'

"Then after his purpose was fulfilled, he bids them return again as silently as they had come.

> ' Short space he stood, then waved his hand,
> Down sank the disappearing band.
> It seemed as if their mother earth
> Had swallowed up her warlike birth.'

"In our land, not hundreds, but thousands and millions sprang to the call of liberty, and when their service was ended, after many of their comrades had perished on the field of honor, the survivors returned as quietly to the employments of peace and the delights of home." —*Rev. James G. Vose, D. D.*

Various veteran associations are wisely engaged in making a record of the personal experiences of their members in the War for the Union. Doubtless it will prove a most valuable and authentic record, and to it in generations to come, the historian will resort for the substance of his judgments.

The preparation of this book was undertaken at the unanimous request of the members of the Tenth Rhode Island Volunteers and Battery Association, at its thirtieth annual reunion, May 26, 1892.

Though the work assigned the Committee was entered upon with some reluctance, on account of business and professional duties, it has brought its own reward in the joy of living over old times again, and the days of youthful vigor, when at a moment's warning, we put on uniform and hurried to the defence of the capital.

This record professes to be, not a treatise on the war, but a modest, and we trust, truthful narrative of scenes and incidents of our three months' campaign in 1862, with such a description of the military situation in Virginia, as will enable the reader to form a correct estimate of the services rendered. Diligent inquiry has been made among the members for old letters, diaries and sketches, and one of the Committee, Comrade William A. Spicer, has consented to arrange the material collected and edit the history.

The Committee realize that the War for the Union is long since over, and that the years of peace and progress which have followed have made it only a memory. They still feel, however, that the rising generations which have grown up since the war, should become familiar with its history, and read enough of the details, to

INTRODUCTION. 7

know in what spirit it was carried on, and what of valor and devotion to country is still in our educated American youth.

"Prior to the late Rebellion," said Gen. Horatio Rogers, himself a gallant soldier, and an honored justice of the Supreme Court of our State, "it was a matter of speculation among us whether if opportunity offered, the young men of this generation would emulate the heroism of their patriotic ancestors. In those tranquil times, and to our inexperienced minds, the history of the great struggle for National Independence seemed like a romance. Our civil war has at length solved the problem, . . . and has proved that devotion to country has not withered in the hearts of American youth." And to-day, as we behold with patriotic pride our country's flag proudly floating over our public schools and colleges, we feel that it has a new meaning of freedom and blessing for this generation and the generations to come.

Certainly no class of our citizens exhibited a purer patriotism during the war, than the members of our high schools and colleges, and as a considerable part of the good material of the Ninth and Tenth Regiments and Battery, was drawn from the Providence High School and Brown University, we will introduce this history with brief sketches of those institutions at the time of the war of the Rebellion.

ALBERT J. MANCHESTER, Tenth R. I. Vols. ⎫
WILLIAM A. SPICER,   "   "   ⎪
WILLIAM A. H. GRANT,   "   "   ⎬ *Historical Committee.*
H. H. RICHARDSON,   Ninth "   ⎪
P. B. STINESS,   Tenth R. I. Batt. ⎭

PROVIDENCE, July 4, 1892.

THE HIGH SCHOOL IN 1862.

THE HIGH SCHOOL BOYS
OF PROVIDENCE.

"We are the boys, the gay old boys,
Who marched in sixty-one,
We'll ne'er forget old times, my boys,
When you and I were young."

— *Old song.*

OUR school days were cast in eventful times. Some of the Providence boys who met thirty years ago in the old High School on Benefit Street, can hardly have forgotten the stirring events which preceded the war, and the memorable presidential campaign of 1860. Joining the Lincoln wide awake army, they proudly shouldered their torches and marched on to victory, little heeding the threatening clouds of secession gathering in the Southern horizon. How few then, North or South, young or old, realized the nearness of the whirlwind of civil war, which was soon to burst forth and rage for four long years, carrying desolation into almost every family in the land. A struggle which killed six hundred thousand, and permanently disabled a million young men. But it abolished state rights and slavery, the causes of the conflict, and settled finally the great principle declared by Webster, that the Union is "now and forever, one and inseparable."

The first gun fired on Fort Sumter, April 12, 1861, aroused and excited the nation. President Lincoln at once called for 75,000 men. Rhode Island was ready, and looked to General Burnside for a leader. The ladies met in the church vestries and made uniforms for the volunteers. All classes were united in the determination to vindicate the honor of our flag. The excitement was fully shared, if not increased, by the High School boys. Every one was expected to show his colors, and it was voted to purchase and raise the national flag over the High School building. Hearing that the college boys were about to unfurl the "stars and stripes" over University Hall (where, eighty-eight years before, the old Revolutionary flag had floated), it was determined to anticipate them, if possible. Wednesday afternoon, April 17th, at five o'clock, being the time appointed for the exercises at the college, the following High School announcement appeared in the *Journal* of that day: "The 'stars and stripes' will be raised this afternoon over the High School, at *half past four!*" But the boys were finally induced to defer their public demonstration till the following morning, though they couldn't refrain from indulging in a little informal flag-raising at the hour first announced, thus securing the desired priority, and the following notice from the *Evening Press:* "High School Patriotism.—A splendid national flag, purchased by the subscription of over one hundred High School boys, was displayed from the High School building, this afternoon!" The formal exercises were of a most interesting character. At eleven o'clock, in the presence of teachers, scholars, citizens, and soldiers, who were about leaving for the war, the boys raised the flag, followed by the singing of the "Star Spangled Banner." The young ladies of the school carried small national flags. Mayor Knight delivered a brief opening address, and introduced Professor Chace, of Brown University, who responded with scholarly and patriotic sentiments. Bishop Clark related an anecdote of his great grandfather, who, after the battle of Bunker Hill, was obliged to sleep in a baker's oven, and added, "I am glad that he did not get *baked*, else I should not have been here to-day to address you!" and turning to the "Marines," who were soon to leave for Washington, with the First Rhode Island Regiment, he said, "some of *you* may have to sleep in a baker's oven before you get back, but I hope you will not get baked, but come home well bre(a)d men as you now are." They were indeed soon tried in the fiery furnace of Bull Run, and some never returned. Ex-Mayor Rodman, in his pleasant manner, referred to a conversation between Gen. Nathanael Greene and his mother, during the Revolution, in which she cautioned him "not to get shot in the back!" Dr. Caldwell made an impressive closing address, then "America" was heartily sung, followed by cheers for "the Union," "the young ladies of the High School," "Governor Sprague," the "First Regiment," and the "Marines." "Fifteen cheers and a Narragansett" were given by the boys for a dispatch, read by Bishop Clark, that Virginia had decided not to secede. But they found out, a few days later, that they had wasted their ammunition on the "Old Dominion."

It was now apparent that there was sufficient military spirit to warrant the formation of a High School company. A meeting was held in the hall, at which a committee of arrangements was appointed, who "pushed things," and in a few weeks the boys fell into line under the name of the "Ellsworth Phalanx," in honor of the youthful and gallant commander of the New York Zouaves. He had been shot at Alexandria, Va., a few weeks before (May

24th), while engaged in lowering a rebel flag from a hotel in that city. How it would have startled the members of the "Ellsworth Phalanx," could they have known that the next year, some of their number would be marching through that same rebellious city, and by the very hotel where Ellsworth fell! Yet so it proved, and as they marched, they sung the stirring strains of "Ellsworth's Avengers," quickly followed by that grand old marching song,

"John Brown's body lies mouldering in the grave
But his soul is marching on!"

The beautiful standard of colors presented to the Phalanx, was the gift of the young ladies of the High School.* Daniel W. Lyman, who was afterwards senator in the General Assembly, was chosen captain. The company averaged from seventy to eighty boys, according to the pressure of study at the High School. By an arrangement with the United Train of Artillery, their armory on Canal street became the headquarters of the corps, and under the direction of the veteran Col. Westcott Handy, of the Old Guard Continentals, it soon attained a creditable degree of proficiency.

The discipline was strict, and there was no levity, the boys thought, about the hot and hard marching. But who can forget those refreshing seasons after the long and toilsome drill or street parade, when good Colonel Handy marched us through his herb beer establishment, near the Great Bridge, and treated one and all, to a large glass of his celebrated beer, "compounded strictly from medicinal roots and herbs." May his memory *ever* remain

* This flag may still be seen at the High School on Summer Street.

as fragrant as his *beer!* What wonder that the corps rapidly advanced in discipline and spirits and soon attracted not a little public attention for its *steady* and soldierly bearing on parade. It was altogether, the boys thought, very serious business, but the discipline did much doubtless in kindling a warmer ardor of patriotism, and a stronger devotion to duty. An indulgent critic says, "that in point of marching, with all the legs going together, twisting itself up and untwisting, breaking into single file (for Indian fighting), forming platoons and wheeling with faultless line around the corner of North Main Street and Market Square ; getting out of the way of a wagon or omnibus, and circling the High Street liberty pole and town pump ; with ranks well dressed, and eyes 'right and left,' particularly in going by the High School, it was the equal of any military organization I ever saw."

It is needless for the writer to add that he was an ardent member of the "Phalanx," rising steadily from the grade of "private" to the rank of "corporal." Winning at the "target-shoot" the bright cockade of red, white and blue ribbons, to be worn on bayonet on parade, for making the lucky shot at two hundred yards. It was generally admitted that the "Phalanx" could drill better and execute the Zouave manœuvres in finer style than some of the older military companies. The exhibition drills of the corps, and the brilliant evening assemblies, with Lyman "potent to preside," will be pleasantly recalled. How they enlivened the long winter evenings of '61 !

But the Rebellion was not yet subdued. Brighter days were looked for with the opening of '62, but the situation seemed full of peril to the nation. As with men all over the land, so with the students of the High School, the condition of the country was the all absorbing topic of discussion. The following essay by "a corporal," and a member of the class of '62, illustrates the spirit of the school on

"The Coming Crisis."

"Our country is on the eve of a great crisis. From every appearance that we can discern, Liberty and Loyalty, and Rebellion and Slavery are about to grapple for the decisive struggle. The work of preparation, which has been energetically pushed forward during the past six months, is nearly completed. Our young general-in-chief has been employed with untiring energy in gathering his armies around the rebel capital, and hemming in the enemy on every side, and the command for the final advance seems almost now to echo along the whole line.

"We all know what a terrible shock must ensue, and can all estimate something of the magnitude of its results. Of course we expect our army to be victorious. It would seem as though the fruit of so much noble sacrifice, and of such gigantic preparation, must be victory. The people have given their money and treasure free as water, their lives even, as of little value in comparison with the great principles at stake. For these they have permitted their most sacred liberties to be invaded that success may be rendered more certain. We claim, too, and justly, the larger and better disciplined battalions; and military skill has been exhausted in placing in their hands the most destructive weapons of modern warfare. We suppose, therefore, our army to be invincible. But our confidence of victory lies not alone, or principally, in our physical strength, but in the moral strength of our cause. Best of all, we have 'God and the Right' upon our side. Truth and Justice are with us. The prayers of the millions of the enslaved throughout the world are with us. We are fighting to preserve the glorious Union for which our fathers fought and suffered so much. We are fighting for Freedom and Humanity everywhere.

"Truly it seems that with such a cause, and with such soldiers and generals, victory must rest upon our banners.

"Yet we must not be too sanguine of success. Although we know that the right must eventually triumph, yet our country may be called upon to pass through sterner trials, before it shall come forth from the flames of war purified and regenerated. We may again be destined to learn the terrible lesson of defeat. It seems now almost impossible, but we cannot tell.

"When our army was before Manassas last July, we supposed that victory would certainly be ours, and when the intelligence came of the panic and retreat to Washington, it fell upon the nation with a sudden shock that bowed it to the earth, and it has not recovered from the effect to-day.

"The tide of battle is so often turned by unforeseen and unexpected circumstances, that we can only hope and wait for the issue.

"While there is time, let us prepare for defeat as well as victory. For let the worst indeed come, we must never yield. Our most cherished principles, perhaps the national existence, are at stake. If we fail in this struggle for liberty and union, it will carry despair to the hearts of the oppressed and enslaved, and sound the death-knell of free institutions everywhere.

"Whatever sacrifice we may be called upon to make, let us stand ready to meet it. We are not too young to possess the spirit of true patriotism, the spirit of the gallant 'Ellsworth,' whose name we have chosen. Let us stand ready, therefore, so that if the safety of the country should demand it, we may rally with full 'Phalanx' in her defence, and give our aid, little though it may be, to the good cause."

The time was at hand. May 1862 came, and with it fresh news of disaster to the Union cause. Stonewall Jackson with 20,000 men, had sent Banks's little army whirling down the Shenandoah Valley, to the Potomac, and, at midnight, on the 25th, a dispatch came to Providence announcing the disaster, with an urgent appeal for troops for the protection of the capital. Just an hour later, the governor issued an order to immediately organize two new regiments, the Ninth and Tenth Rhode Island Volunteers, and the Tenth Light Battery, for three months' service. The response was prompt, and among other military organizations, the "Ellsworth Phalanx" of the High School furnished a liberal quota. The call found the boys "*volens et paratus,*" now our motto. At the head of Company B, Tenth Rhode Island Volunteers, recruited principally from the ranks of the High School and University companies, marched Capt. Elisha Dyer, formerly the governor of the state. The men are few who at his age (over fifty) would have left the comforts of home for the arduous position of captain in a volunteer regiment. And those High School boys, whose fortunate lot it was to belong to Captain Dyer's company, will hardly again find in life a day of such strange excitement, as that on which they first put on uniform and started for camp.

Many of the boys after completing their first term of service, re-enlisted, and as commissioned officers served through the war. Two hundred and twenty-five of the students of the High School served in the army and navy during the Rebellion. Seventeen died in the service.*

Let us pause for a moment, to honor the memory of one of our youngest comrades of Company A, Tenth Rhode Island Volunteers.

WILLIAM FREDERICK ATWOOD, class of 1862, son of William and Emeline P. Atwood, was born in Sing Sing, N. Y., in January, 1845. His father was engaged in the foundry business at that time, but soon after removed to Providence, R. I., where his grandfather, John Atwood, had been for many years a well-known resident and real estate proprietor. "Fred," as he was familiarly called at home, was educated in the public schools, and in 1859 entered the High School. He was possessed of a genial temperament and generous disposition, which drew around him a circle of personal friends. The opening of the war, in 1861, aroused and excited the High School boys, and when the urgent call for volunteers came in May, 1862, young Atwood (although but seventeen) enlisted, with many of his classmates, in Company A, Capt. William E. Taber, Tenth Rhode Island Volunteers.

As at home he had been a loving son and brother, so now he became an honored comrade, faithful in all his relations, as Captain Taber bears cheerful testimony. He was taken suddenly ill at Camp Frieze, in the latter part of June, and growing rapidly worse he was removed to Seminary Hospital, Georgetown, D. C.,

---

* See page 13, "In Memoriam."

where he died June 29, 1862, leaving the example of a brave and spotless manhood.

The career of young Atwood is one of the briefest recorded in the history of the war. But thirty days elapsed from the day of his departure from home to the day of his funeral. But those days, few as they were, signally illustrated his modest fidelity to every trust, and his cheerful surrender of the bright hopes of youth, to die in his country's service. In a retired and beautiful spot near the Soldiers' Home, overlooking the capital which his youthful footsteps had hastened to defend, he sleeps the sleep which no morning drum-beat shall break.

Strangely also, his father, who enlisted a few months later in the Eleventh Rhode Island Volunteers, sickened and died, and was buried at Arlington, only a few miles from his son's grave.

And we would not omit to mention, with honor, the name of our youthful and lamented comrade, Frederick Metcalf (son of Col. Edwin Metcalf), who, although but fifteen years old, enlisted with his other classmates in Company B. But Captain Dyer was unwilling to assume the responsibility of accepting so young a volunteer in the absence of his father (then in active service with his regiment at Hilton Head, S. C.) But this did not dampen the ardor of young Metcalf, and we find him in October of the following year, a second lieutenant in his father's regiment (the Third Rhode Island Heavy Artillery). He also creditably served as post adjutant at Fort Pulaski, Georgia, till May 27, 1864, when he was promoted to a first lieutenancy. But in the following August he was seized with the typhoid malaria, and died on the 28th, in the seventeenth year of his age.

In Memoriam.

ROLL OF STUDENTS OF THE PROVIDENCE HIGH SCHOOL
WHO
Died in the Service of their Country during the Rebellion.

MUNRO H. GLADDING,	Class of 1846.
FRANCIS B. FERRIS,	" 1848.
WILLIAM WARE HALL,	" 1848.
JOHN P. SHAW,	1850.
GEORGE W. FIELD,	" 1852.
JAMES H. EARLE,	1853.
HOWARD GREENE,	" 1855.
GEORGE WHEATON COLE,	1856.
SAMUEL FOSTER, 2D,	" 1856.
JESSE COMSTOCK,	" 1858.
J. NELSON BOGMAN,	1861.
PETER HUNT,	1861.
WILLIAM F. ATWOOD,	1862.
BENJAMIN E. KELLY,	" 1862.
CHARLES M. LATHAM,	1862.
FREDERICK METCALF,	" 1864.
EUGENE F. GRANGER,	" 1866.

NOTE.—The year given is in all cases, that of graduating.

BROWN UNIVERSITY IN 1862.

THE COLLEGE BOYS

OF "BROWN."

"For each of them considered that not for his father and mother only was he born, but also for his fatherland."—Demosthenes De Corona.

A LARGE number of the students of "Brown" left the "campus" for the camp, some at the very outbreak of the War of the Rebellion. During the winter of 1860, the political affairs of the nation assumed an aspect which no lover of his country could regard with indifference. The distant mutterings of the approaching storm were heard in Hope College and University Hall. The literary societies in their meetings discussed the questions of the day. These questions also furnished the chief topics in social intercourse, and studies correspondingly languished.

* In the spring of 1860, when Abraham Lincoln came to Rhode Island, he found no more attentive listeners to the two addresses that he delivered,—one in Providence and one in Woonsocket—than the students of "Brown," who flocked to hear him. One of them, William Ide Brown, the beloved class president of '62,—who gallantly served in the army from August 10, 1862, to March 29, 1865, when he was killed before Petersburg,—wrote March 8, 1860,

* This sketch is principally from the pen of Maj. S. L. Burrage, class of '64.

"Lincoln, of Illinois, speaks this evening at Woonsocket. There is to be an extra train, and ———— pays the expenses of eighty or ninety students." This occasion was one which few of the men who were in college can forget, so long as life shall last. Soon in the rapid march of events, the western orator became the President of the United States, and Brown saw him next in 1862, as in company with McClellan and Burnside the President passed along the lines in review of the army after the battle of Antietam.

Threatened violence at length appeared armed, and in April, 1861, the peal of hostile cannon filled the land. But the sound of the first gun which was fired at Fort Sumter did not die away when it reached the walls of the college. It would be impossible to set forth in words the state of feeling which was at once manifested throughout the university. The senior class procured a flag, and on the afternoon of April 17th, in the presence of the Faculty, the students, and a throng of the friends of the college, it was raised over University Hall. After the flag had been unfurled, and the band had played "The Star Spangled Banner," President Sears, standing on the steps of Manning Hall, delivered a brief address. He said he deprecated civil war. He regretted the necessity which it imposed on us as a people. But, he continued, the time for deliberation is past. Every man is now called upon to show himself worthy of the country of his birth. It is fitting, then, that to-day, the young men who have come to this university to learn—to learn to be patriots he would hope— and who have everything at stake in this crisis, should show that they appreciate the inestimable blessings which they have inherited from a brave and noble ancestry.

Bishop Clark said that eighty years ago the old Revolutionary flag waved over University Hall. It meant that our fathers were striving to establish the sacred institutions of a free government. The flag we raise to-day means that we intend to preserve those institutions. We deprecate war, he continued, especially civil war. All our interests, all our feelings are against it. But enemies have arisen among us. They have commenced the most wicked contest ever waged. We do not hate them, yet we cannot sit tamely by while they are endeavoring to destroy the very foundations of our political fabric.

Bishop Clark was followed by the Rev. Dr. Hall, who said it was not a time when any one should be silent who loves his country and his God. We are all men of peace, he added, but here is a thing inevitable. It is government or no government. The South does not wish to go peaceably. If we have erred at all we have erred on the side of forbearance, but the past is gone. Let us show by our action that we continue to love our whole country.

The hymn "My country, 'tis of thee," was then sung by the students.

The Rev. Dr. Caldwell said that on the previous Sabbath he could not but feel it was a time for praying rather than for preaching. The time for words was now past, the time for deeds had come. Be assured, he added, that what we see going on around us is going on everywhere, from Mason and Dixon's line to the lakes. A conflict is impending, but we go into it, not in passion; we simply seek to vindicate the honor of our country in restoring its rightful authority.

Ex-Governor Dyer delivered the last address. He commenced by saying that in the whole course of his experience he had never been subject to such conflicting emotions as were passing through his heart at that moment. Yonder is our country's flag, and the chimes of our city are ringing out the national anthems; but is it possible, he asked, that that flag and that music are needed to remind us that we are the citizens of one of the noblest nations of the earth? We are called to contend with traitors, the victims of delusion; all party distinctions, therefore, should be laid aside, and each man should be ready to make whatever sacrifices the honor of the country may demand.

Such is a brief outline of the addresses which were delivered on this interesting occasion. They did not float away on the soft winds, then laden with the freshness of returning spring. There were those grouped upon the chapel steps, who then, as never before, were "stirred with high hopes of living to be brave men and worthy patriots;" and to whom the words at that time spoken were an inspiration for good, as in the years which followed, when, weary from long marching, watching, fighting, they recurred to them for added strength in entering upon fresh trials of endurance.

Burnside had arrived in the city the day previous, and was already organizing the "First Rhode Island." While engaged in the business of his office in New York, he had received the following dispatch: "A regiment of Rhode Island troops will go to Washington this week. How soon can you come on and take command? William Sprague, Governor of Rhode Island." Both the answer and the answerer were ready. "At once," was the reply. Not a few from the several classes in the college entered its ranks. Brown, writing to his father that evening said, "To-night, as I see the streets thick with uniforms, it begins to seem like war. The excitement here is intense."

About the middle of May, a military company, the University Cadets, was organized at the college, and consisted of seventy-eight men, rank and file. It is a fact worthy of notice, that during the Rebellion eight of its fourteen officers served with distinction in the Union armies. The campus in rear of the university afforded a suitable drill-ground, and such was the proficiency to which the company soon attained, that the tri-weekly drill of the Cadets attracted not a little public attention.

Class-day occurred on June 13th. The class president, Mr. William W. Hoppin, was absent serving as a private in the First Rhode Island Volunteers. The president of the day, William W. Douglas, the class orator, Sumner U. Shearman, and the class poet, all afterwards entered the military service, and were mustered out with the same rank. In the afternoon of class-day, the University Cadets had their first public parade. The line was formed on the campus at three o'clock. Then preceded by Gilmore's (Pawtucket) full band, the company marched through the principal streets of the city, eliciting the praises of all for their soldierly bearing. Late in the afternoon, the Cadets visited the camp of the Second Rhode Island Volunteers, on Dexter Training Ground, where in the presence of Colonel Slocum (who was killed at the battle of Bull Run in July following), they went through the form for dress parade. After receiving the congratulations of Colonel Slocum and of his officers, among whom were two sons of President Sears, the company marched down

Westminster street "in four ranks open order," and returned to the college. Still later in the day, the Cadets escorted the senior class to the Aldrich House, where the class supper was served.

The year 1861 gradually wore away. Few expected that the Rebellion would long continue. But the disasters which in the months of May and June (1862) befell our army before Richmond, dissolved the dream of peace, and the question of duty became still more urgent to the students. Late in the month of May, 1862, almost as stirring scenes as those of April, 1861, were witnessed in Providence. Let us go back to May 25th, when, at midnight, a dispatch from the secretary of war was received by the governor of Rhode Island, announcing the defeat of General Banks and calling for troops. At one o'clock A. M., May 26th, an order was issued for the organization of the National Guards for active service, and the next day the regiment henceforth known as the Tenth Rhode Island Volunteers, left Providence for Washington under the command of Lieut.-Col. James Shaw, Jr. Company B, commanded by Ex-Gov. Elisha Dyer, was recruited almost entirely from the ranks of the several classes of the University and High School. Governor Dyer says, "The students could brook no restraint, and almost *en masse* came to our recruiting rendezvous for enrollment. It was a source of the deepest solicitude on the part of President Sears to know how far he was justified in resisting these resolute expressions on the part of the young men who had been placed under his protection and instruction. The offering would not have been too large had he consulted his own feelings alone. But it was the widow's son, and the orphan's brother, who desired release. He came to me in the conflict of duty and enthusiastic patriotism, and telling me of his embarrassment said, 'If you yourself will take these young men to the field, I can no longer refuse them.' I gave the pledge. The young men came, were enrolled, and without leaving the armory, entered upon the duties of soldiers. They all proved themselves worthy of their alma mater, and the sacred cause for which they enlisted. Always prompt, obedient and efficient, they won for themselves an honorable record. For no delinquency or misdemeanor did any name of theirs ever find a place on the morning report. On the muster out of the regiment, Sept. 1, 1862, many of these young men immediately reëntered the service, and as commissioned officers extended a record of which the University may well be proud."

In our admiration for President Sears and the young men of the University to whom reference is made in the words just quoted, let us not forget that other son of the University, whose pure, self-sacrificing patriotism appears in his tribute to the worth of others; who having received the highest honors in the gift of the people of Rhode Island, and when of an age which might claim exemption from military duty, cheerfully abandoned the quiet delights of home at the call of his country, and took upon himself the labors and responsibilities of a captain of infantry.

Class-day at Brown occurred June 12, 1862. Joshua M. Addeman, the class orator, was at the time a private soldier in the company and regiment to which we have just referred; but obtaining a short furlough he returned to Providence and delivered his oration on the appointed day. His theme was "The Alliance of Scholarship and Patriotism." He introduced his subject with the following earnest words:

"On this day, around which cluster memories and associations of the past, and fond hopes and anxious forebodings of the future, one thought transcends all others in importance. As if embodied in some fair form beseeching us for aid, our country rises before us, and excludes all minor and selfish considerations. No theme seems more appropriate to the day and of more vital importance in its bearing upon the future than "The Alliance of Scholarship and Patriotism." The orator accordingly proceeded to discuss the duties of the scholar with reference to the State, and then closed his address with the following eloquent words :

"This is an age when events follow each other more rapidly than in the prophet's inspired visions ; when years are heaping up more for history than centuries of the past ; an age which converts a nation devoted to peace into a vast army bristling with bayonets, and marching with serried ranks to the field of battle ; which summons men of science and of letters from their experiments and their books, the lawyer from his brief, the instructor from his pupils, the preacher from his desk, and bids them gird on the sword, and hasten to the defence of the best, the freest, the happiest country on which the sun ever shone. Obedient to the call, classmates have hastened on before us to discharge the patriot's duty. In thunder tones their example speaks to us of courage, of manliness, of devotion to country. Let us see to it that we faithfully discharge our duties as 'ever in our great taskmaster's eye.' The benedictions of a grateful country will then rest upon our labors, and above all, the satisfaction of an approving conscience will be our exceeding 'great reward.'"

The class poet, H. F. Colby, sang of the power that a nation possesses in the remembrance of a glorious past. The poem closed with these thrilling sentences:

> "But these fond memories in the present hour
> Became the instruments of wondrous power.
> The guns of Sumter sent a startling thrill
> Through hearts still mindful of Bunker Hill;
> And April's tears wept o'er a war begun,
> As in the trying days of Lexington.
> An unseen spirit caught the flaming brand,
> And swept on lightning wings the startled land.
> 'Come from your homes, ye free!' its trumpet cried,
> 'Preserve the country of your father's pride.'
> And from the North, where sighing forests rise
> In state primeval to the bending skies,
> From granite hills, and battle-fields whose sod
> The feet of patriot heroes once have trod,
> From the bright shores of Narragansett's bay,
> Along the silvery Mohawk's wending way,
> Soft as the rippling tide on Erie's shore,
> Loud as the tumult of Niagara's roar,
> From lakes majestic, from the Western plains,
> Rich in the billows of their ripening grains,—
> From every city's street and rural home,
> Came up that single answer: 'Yes, we come.'
> And they *did* come. Potomac's wooded banks
> Gleamed with the bristling steel of serried ranks:
> The sentinel's strange voice was echoed there,
> And blazing camp-fires lit the evening air.
> From the foul dragon's teeth of civil strife
> A numerous army sprung to active life."

"The patriotic history of Brown University during the War for the Union is one of which every student may well be proud, and in time to come her children will love her the more for what she was during the troublous times through which the nation has just passed."

We conclude this sketch of "Brown" with brief tributes to the memory of two of her loyal sons, who served in the Tenth Rhode Island Volunteers in 1862.

MATTHEW MCARTHUR MEGGETT,* class of 1864, son of Alexander and Sarah Meggett, was born in Chicopee Falls, Mass., July 24, 1836. The story of his life is but a simple record of the struggles of a poor boy, who desired the benefits of a liberal education, not so much for the sake of learning as to make it the means by which good could be accomplished. He early evinced an interest in the subject of religion, and deep religious feelings marked his whole life. It is natural that a young lad thus constituted, should look to the ministry of the Gospel as the proper sphere for his efforts in life, and that a Christian mother should hope to see such a son consecrated to the duties of the ministerial office. His father's death occurred when Matthew was but eight years old, . . . and his boyhood was necessarily devoted to manual toil, for the support of himself and of his aged mother. . . . In the year 1842, his family removed to Slatersville, R. I., where Matthew was employed in a mill. After some years he united with the Congregational Church in that place. At length, in 1854, he entered Phillips' Academy at Andover, Mass. His letters home always evince persevering effort, filial affection and religious zeal.

* Written by James W. Colwell, B. U., 1864.

"I am often discouraged," he says "when I see how much is to be done. I try, however, to look at the bright side, and am determined to struggle on. I have advantages beyond many others, and my trust is in God. I have been thinking of mother to-night. I hope she is not lonely. It often makes me feel sad to think that I have to leave her alone while I am here endeavoring to get an education." He entered Brown University in the fall of 1858. His limited means caused him much anxiety, and to increase them he gave instruction in the public evening schools of Providence during the first winter. But these supplies did not prove adequate to his wants, so that he remained in college hardly a year at this time. Two years were then passed in teaching, mostly in Woonsocket, R. I. In the autumn of 1861 he resumed his studies at Brown, entering now the class of 1864. As at school, so in college, whatever he did was accomplished by perseverance and industry.

From the first breaking out of the Rebellion Meggett felt it his duty to enlist in the army, and at length, near the close of his Sophomore year, when there came from the President another call for men, he decided to go. Saturday, May 24, 1862, he wrote in his journal: "I have been thinking a great deal to-day about entering the service with those who enlist for three months. Ex-Governor Dyer goes on with a fine company from Providence, and I should like to go with him. He will have none but moral men in his company, it is said. I look upon my going as a duty. I shall be ashamed to say that I contributed nothing by way of personal sacrifice toward restoring my country." A day or two later, having gained the consent of his mother, he enlisted in Company B, Tenth Regiment Rhode Island Volunteers.

On May 27th, the regiment left Providence, . . . and was assigned to garrison duty in the defences of Washington. Meggett writes to his brother: "Our 'mess' is mostly made up of college boys. We had a prayer-meeting Sunday afternoon, at which Captain Dyer and Lieutenant-Colonel Shaw were present and made remarks. It was an impressive meeting." In his last letter to his mother, written before he was taken sick, he speaks of his return home with pleasure, and lovingly plans what he will then do for her comfort and delight.

On Sunday, August 10th, he went into the hospital a sick man. In a few days the disease assumed a graver form, and was pronounced by Dr. Wilcox typhoid fever, and he grew rapidly worse till the 18th, when he died, and a telegram was sent to his mother at Pawtucket, R. I. His bereaved friends could hardly credit the startling intelligence that he who had left them strong and vigorous had been cut down by death just on the eve of his return to the loved ones at home. The sad news was soon verified by a letter from the chaplain, Rev. Dr. Clapp. The body of the dead soldier was embalmed and forwarded to his friends. In accordance with the request of his company, the funeral services in Pawtucket were delayed until their return home.

The regiment arrived in Providence on the morning of Aug. 28, 1862, and on the day following his funeral was solemnized in the Congregational Church, Pawtucket. His comrades in-arms were present to take part in those last sad offices of respect and affection. His pastor, Dr. Blodgett, President Sears, and the beloved chaplain of the Tenth Regiment, Dr. Clapp, all bore cheerful testimony to his faithful, earnest, devoted Christian life.

And yet one more we mourn on our regimental roll of honor, LEVI CAREY WALKER,* class of 1865. He was born in Hartford, Conn., Oct. 30, 1840. He was the son of Rev. William Carey and Almer L. Walker. His boyhood gave promise of a well moulded life. At seventeen he entered the Connecticut Literary Institution at Suffield, from which he graduated with the highest honors of his class. In the ensuing fall he entered Brown University with the class of "sixty-five." He at once advanced to a high rank in scholarship, and engaged as heartily in the sports of the campus as in the duties of the class-room; he also identified himself with the religious interests of the college.

Thus the months of the Freshman year rolled away till May, '62, came, bringing with it the sickening news of disaster to the Union army. On the 25th, at midnight, came the pressing summons for troops, and before the sun had set the Tenth Rhode Island was under marching orders.

Here was the long-sought opportunity for Walker. For him the call had no uncertain sound. We quote from his diary:

"Monday, May 26. A great struggle in my mind this morning. The country has called for men. I want to go. Cannot consult my parents. . . Have at length enlisted, with a prayer that God will help me. . . . While busy packing my knapsack father came. He made no objection to my going, but felt rather bad."

"Tuesday, 27. I have taken an important step, and am a soldier of the United States. Wrote mother. Started for Washington."

* Written by James McWhinnie, Jr., class of '67.

"My Dear Mother: There is no thought connected with my enlistment that gives me so much pain, as that I shall by thus doing increase your burden of anxiety and solicitude on my account. . . . I have studied to make myself worthy of your affection and your sacrifices. I know I have often erred, but as often have I repented. I do not wish to go to Washington without your full, free hearty consent. . . . Never would I stir one foot against your wishes. But mother, many parents have given up their dear ones to bleed, yes, die in their country's cause. Many have gone forth from the paternal roof as dear and better fitted for life or death than I; and can you hesitate? I should think your bosom would swell with pride at the thought that you were represented in your country's struggle for liberty."

On the morning of May 30th the regiment marched to Tenallytown, the sun pouring down its hottest rays. In his journal Walker writes: "Am somewhat lame after the long march. Spent the day hard at work pitching tents and throwing up embankments. Have been transferred with others to Company K, Capt. G. Frank Low."

We find the first record of illness on Thursday, June 5th, in which he speaks of having had a serious hemorrhage.

June 27th the regiment marched to Cloud's Mills, eighteen miles distant. Twelve miles Walker marched with the rest, but was then compelled to seek the ambulance. The regiment remained there for a short time, when it returned to the neighborhood of the forts on the northwest of Washington, marching nearly all night.

The fatigue of this weary march broke down Walker completely. The dreaded hemorrhages again commenced, and he began to fear for his life. We read in his journal :

"Monday, July 28. Reported at the hospital."
"Thursday, August 4th. I feel very sad! The doctor gives me no encouragement. Life with its bright prospects to be given up! I can hardly curb my feelings.   .   To be cut down so young! O, God, I look to Thee!"

In a few days the Tenth was on its way to Providence, bearing the sick, discouraged soldier to his yearning friends.

The last entry in his journal was on Thursday, August 28th :

" Arrived this morning at Providence, both glad and sad. Sad that I was not able to march with my company—a deep disappointment."

Such is the brief military career of Levi Carey Walker. He went to the field with as lofty a patriotism as ever inspired a Union soldier. He returned a mere wreck of his former self. Still he lived on, battling with a fatal disease, till Feb. 23, 1865, when the end came. The last words in his journal are: "How have my hopes been blasted! Yet I thank God my trust is still firm in Him." His remains were borne to the cemetery by his classmates, and tenderly committed to their last resting-place.
.   .   .   He had not been permitted to go down in the bloody strife, but he gave to the country a youth and life full of all noble promise as truly as the slumbering hero of Stone River or of the Wilderness.

RHODE ISLAND NATIONAL GUARD.

"THE people of Rhode Island are showing themselves to be eminently a military people. They have promptly done all that the government has asked of them for carrying on the war, and they have besides a large and efficient army organized for home service known as 'The National Guard of Rhode Island.' The martial spirit of the state is wisely encouraged and systematically directed by men of practical military ability, and, as the result, the State of Rhode Island is better able to furnish her quota of troops for service abroad, and altogether better prepared to meet possible emergencies at home than are any of her neighbors."

Nov. 21, 1861.   *New London Chronicle.*

Rhode Island National Guard.

> " For we will guard it with our lives,
> And keep our armor handy,
> And sing the song our fathers sang
> Of Yankee Doodle Dandy!"
> —*Ex-Mayor Wm. M. Rodman, 1861.*

THERE was a sad lack of military education and organization in 1861, when the President called for 75,000 men to serve for three months in the overthrow of the Rebellion. Yet the noble response showed that the heart of the nation was loyal and true. Rhode Island was the first to offer the services of her citizens, and, after furnishing her full quota, she was the first to organize her National Guard.

It is not surprising that with such a history as Rhode Island has, the idea should have early suggested itself of thoroughly organizing and arming the entire able-bodied population, and putting the State on a war footing, so that if, in crushing the Rebellion, disaster should come, the State could do what no other State has done, have every man capable of bearing arms, a soldier, ready for the emergency.

Standing in the armory of the First Light Infantry, the night before the departure of the First Regiment, James Shaw, Jr., a young officer who afterward distinguished himself both in the State and national volunteer service, said to William S. Hayward, of the Sixth Ward, and since mayor of the city, "We don't know how soon the rest of us may have to go; why not form ward companies, as they did in 1842, and learn to drill? Call a meeting in our ward and I will do what I can to help you." This suggestion, thus early made, was heartily approved, and acted upon, and a meeting of the citizens for organization, was held on Thursday evening, May 9th, who voted to form a company for military drill, appointed a committee to nominate officers, and adjourned to Tuesday evening, May 14, 1861. At that meeting Hon. Henry T. Grant, alderman of the ward, was elected captain; James Shaw, Jr., first lieutenant; James A. Winsor, second lieutenant; Thomas M. Brown, third lieutenant, and Hopkins B. Cady, first sergeant. Eighty men enrolled their names and a drill followed.

Meanwhile the following notice had been posted in the First Ward: "We, the undersigned, of the First Ward, feeling that the present state of the country demands that every man of suitable age should be prepared for any emergency, agree to meet two evenings in the week for the purpose of being thoroughly drilled by a competent military man, to be hereafter selected. All who wish to sign the above paper can do so by calling at Sweet & Angell's."

Wednesday, May 1, 1861, the First Ward Drill Corps organized with A. Crawford Greene as captain. Seventy men were in line who commenced drilling that night in "the school of the soldier."

April 23d. The Old Guard, Providence Artillery, was organized, 100 strong.

April 25th. The Old Guard, First Light Infantry, was formed.

April 26th. The "Cadets" invite all citizens who choose, to meet with them and become acquainted with "the school of the soldier."

The towns of the State also were prompt to move in the matter.

April 23d. The Narragansett Guards, of South Kingstown, were organized with 130 men. Colonel, Isaac P. Rodman; Lieutenant-Colonel, John N. Hazard.

April 27th. The Pawtucket Home Guard Company was started, followed May 1st by the Natick Home Company, and May 9th by the Smithfield Company.

May 10th the following Fifth Ward notice appeared in the *Journal*: "*Fifth Ward.*—Citizens desiring to organize a company for drill will meet in the Ward Room on Richmond street, on Monday evening next. Capt. James C. Hidden has consented to serve as drill-master. Mr. Stephen Horton desires to be the first 'high private.' All patriots between the ages of 14 and 65 are requested to come forward." The company was afterward organized with Stephen H. Hall as captain.

The same day the employés of the Corliss Steam Engine Works formed a company.

May 16th. The Home Light Guard, Capt. Jacob Dunnell, of Pawtucket, organized with one hundred solid men, consisting of citizens of middle age. Arms and uniforms have been supplied.

May 16th. The Slater Drill Corps, Capt. Henry F. Smith, Pawtucket, was formed with seventy-five members, mainly young men.

June 24th. Cudworth's Zouaves were organized in Pawtucket by a company of young men, who will exercise in the Zouave drill. Jesse Cudworth, Jr., captain.

June 11th. The Burnside Zouaves were organized in Providence. Colonel, S. Smith Wells; Lieutenant-Colonel, H. Herbert Sheldon; Major, George T. Paine; Captain, William W. Paine; Lieutenant, Nicholas B. Bolles; Adjutant, Thomas W. Chace; Quartermaster, George H. Potter; Clerk and Treasurer, Asa Lyman. Among the corporals appear the names of George A. Winchester and Charles F. Anthony. A uniform was adopted consisting of a blue jacket, trimmed with orange, full red pants, gathered at the ankle, with a drab gaiter, a blue mixed undershirt, faced with red, and a white forage cap, trimmed with red.

July 4th was celebrated with a spirit worthy of Independence Day. In Providence Col. A. Crawford Greene was chief marshal of the procession, which comprised, among other organizations the First Ward Home Guards, Major Burlingame; University Cadets, Captain Mason (Brown University); Ellsworth Phalanx, Captain Lyman (High School). In Warren, R. I., George Lewis Cooke, afterwards the genial quartermaster of the Ninth and Tenth regiments, and major of the Ninth, delivered an interesting address at the raising of "the Stars and Stripes" on the High School building.

Sunday, July 28th, marked the brilliant reception of the First Regiment returning with Colonel Burnside from the seat of war. Among the receiving companies were the Burnside Zouaves, Col. S. Smith Wells; Mechanics Rifles, Col. Jonathan M. Wheeler; First Ward Home Guards, Major Burlingame; Old Guard Light Infantry, Gen. James Shaw; Pawtucket Light Guard, Col. Olney Arnold; Pawtucket Home Guard, Capt. Jacob Dunnell. The regiment was received with great enthusiasm by our citizens.

August 6th, the Burnside Zouaves made an excursion to Smith's Palace, escorting Col. Ambrose E. Burnside from his residence to the steamer. They numbered about eighty, rank and file. Governor Sprague was also one of the guests of the day, and, in a brief address, congratulated the corps for the soldierly bearing of its members. It gave him great pleasure, he said, to see so many young men striving to perfect themselves in military science. There was a sad lack of that education which was demanded by the present crisis, and he trusted the country would never be found so lamentably deficient again. The people had come to realize that an efficient militia must be maintained. Our precious and dearest rights are in jeopardy; let us prepare to defend them.

August 7th. Lieut. John P. Shaw (a brother of James Shaw, Jr.,) left Providence for the front, with recruits for the Second Rhode Island Volunteers. This gallant officer lost his life in the battle of the Wilderness, May 12, 1864.

September 6th. Meetings were held this evening in four of the wards of the city, and in Cranston, to promote the organization of drill corps.

At the First Ward meeting patriotic addresses were made by the chairman, Alexander Duncan, Esq., Judge Thomas Durfee, Hon. Cæsar A. Updike, Hon. Benjamin F. Thurston, Noble W. De Munn, and others. The meeting adjourned to Monday evening, September 9th, when the military organization was effected and the drill commenced.

An interesting meeting was held the same evening in the Second Ward of citizens in favor of one or more companies for military drill. Stirring addresses were made by Senator Anthony, Samuel Currey, Hon. Thomas A. Jenckes, John F. Tobey, and others. The subject was referred to a committee to report on the 10th instant, when the organization was effected with Col. Stephen T. Olney for captain, and Sergeant Dunham, of the Infantry, for drill master, meetings to be held in Franklin Hall. In this company the venerable teacher, John Kingsbury, carried his musket as lightly as a boy, and was not alone in the patriotic example thus set.

A spirited meeting was also held in the Third Ward the same evening. Addresses were made by Speaker Cæsar A. Updike, Benjamin N. Lapham and Abraham Payne. A committee was appointed to procure hall, muskets, etc. The company organized on the 13th instant after addresses by Hon. Benjamin F. Thurston, Rev. Augustus Woodbury and Col. Nicholas Van Slyck.

Another meeting was held at this time in the Fifth Ward with Hon. Thomas A. Doyle, chairman. He stated that the object of the meeting was the formation of a new military organization in the ward, the previous one having failed through the refusal of the authorities to provide arms. The war spirit must be revived and kept up. The Rev. Mr. Clapp expressed his sympathy with the object of the meeting, and placed his name upon the rolls. "We have allowed ourselves to be taken unawares," he said, "but it is now the duty of every citizen to acquire that skill in the use of arms which we have forgotten by disuse." The venerable Deacon Greene also joined the company. Stephen H. Hall was again chosen captain.

In the Sixth Ward Company, Captain H. T. Grant resigned and First Lieut. James Shaw, Jr., was elected captain.

A meeting of the citizens of the Seventh Ward was very fully attended the same evening. Hon. Amos C. Barstow was chosen chairman. Stirring addresses were made by John Eddy, Rev. Mr. White, and Hon. Benjamin F. Thurston. It was voted to form a military company. At an adjourned meeting George B. Thomas was elected captain; Henry W. Gardner and Jeremiah M. Vose, lieutenants. Drill meetings, Monday and Friday evenings.

September 11th, the Home Battery was formed. About sixty men were drilled by Capt. William H. Parkhurst. First lieutenant, Samuel A. Pearce, Jr.; second lieutenant, J. Henry Wilbur; clerk, E. S. Cheney.

September 13th, the Washington Continentals were organized at the armory of the Providence Artillery, Captain, Westcott Handy.

September 16th. At the First Ward adjourned meeting a home guard company was organized, to meet Monday and Wednesday evenings for drill at the armory of the First Ward Light Guards.

September 19th, a meeting of the State Military Committee was held in Providence to devise some feasible mode of organizing drill corps in the various towns and cities of the State. Governor Sprague was chairman of the meeting. Able addresses were made by Colonels Henry Howard and N. Van Slyck, and by Rev. A. H. Clapp, urging the thorough organization of the entire population capable of bearing arms, and the cultivation of a proper military spirit. A committee of five was appointed, to report at a future meeting, as follows: His Excellency Governor Sprague, Colonels Olney Arnold, H. Howard, W. W. Browne, and Nicholas Van Slyck. An adjourned meeting was held on Saturday morning, 21st instant, at Franklin Hall, with Alexander Duncan chairman.

The committee of five made the following report which was adopted in full :

"The committee respectfully report the following recommendations :

"That it is desirable that the formation of volunteer associations or companies for military instruction be hastened in all the cities and towns of the State, and all able-bodied citizens, without distinction of age, or regardless of business engagements, urged to enroll themselves in some one of the companies.

"That men of wealth throughout the State contribute liberally toward defraying the expenses attending the organization and maintenance of these associations, and that men of influence should give every possible encouragement to the work.

"That the subject of a uniform be left entirely to each company to decide for itself, your committee earnestly recommending a cheap uniform.

"That said companies be enrolled, placed, and governed, and their officers appointed and commissioned, according to the provisions of sections 8, 9, and 10, of chapter 232, of the Revised Statutes.

"That a military committee be appointed, with power to fill vacancies, whose duties it shall be to take measures for the formation of volunteer drill companies throughout the State; to provide such regulations for them as they may deem suitable, and to exercise a general supervision over them. That said committee have power to appoint a secretary or clerk, and to select a corresponding member from each town of the State and from each ward in the City of Providence.

"That the following gentlemen constitute the said Military Central Committee: William Sprague, Providence; William T. Barton, Warren; George W. Hallett, Providence; Peleg W. Lippitt, Cumberland; William Goddard, Warwick; Joseph P. Balch, Providence; Henry Staples, Barrington; Walter S. Burges, Cranston; T. W. Wood, Newport; Horace Babcock, Westerly; Thomas A. Doyle, Providence; Henry Howard, Coventry; Olney Arnold, North Providence."

Rev. Frederick Denison, of Central Falls, spoke of the influence such organizations exerted. In Pawtucket and the adjoining villages the companies which had been formed had prepared many for the active regiments of the State, and deeply stirred the patriotic feelings of the entire community. He hoped the subject would be pressed till every village should have its drill corps, and every citizen capable of bearing arms should be practiced in their use. Bishop Clark said: "We need an immense reserve force. The entire physical force of the State should be trained to back up its moral force. Our own State has been exalted, very much so, throughout the land. Wherever you go you hear the praises of Rhode Island. Our honor and prestige must be maintained. Let us organize ourselves and hold our State in readiness for any emergency. If reverses come, if, unfortunately, our arms should be beaten back, let us have a reserve force to fall back upon."

September 24th, an important military meeting was held in the Fourth Ward in Unity Hall, for the purpose of organizing a drill corps. Hon. Elisha Dyer was elected chairman. Charles F. Phillips and George W. Prentice were chosen secretaries. The following resolution was adopted:

"WHEREAS, The gigantic efforts put forth by the misguided and rebellious South in its attempt to overthrow and destroy the just and beneficent Union of the United States, renders it imperative upon every citizen able to shoulder a musket to familiarize himself at once with the manual of arms, thus forming, as it were, a school of instruction and a power of reserve, it is, therefore,

"*Resolved*, That the citizens of the Fourth ward, animated with but one sentiment and one impulse in the perpetuation and unity of the States, and believing 'the gods help only those who help themselves,' do hereby resolve to aid, encourage and unite in the formation of the Fourth Ward Home Guards, thus assuring our sister wards that "the Fourth" gallantly and cheerfully closes up the column.

Hon. Nicholas Van Slyck, in an eloquent address, showing the advantage and utility of these home organizations, said: "If disaster should fall, as possibly it may, upon our army, and the enemy should pass the Potomac, then will these drill corps become the stay of the government and the hope of the nation." Hon. William W. Hoppin and Rev. Augustus Woodbury followed, both urging the importance of ward organization. Sixty-three names were enrolled. The entire third story of the Calender building was offered for a drill-room. Lieut. Charles F. Phillips wrote: "Ex-Gov. Elisha Dyer was elected captain, and at the following meeting more than a hundred men were in line, including two ex-governors, a prominent clergyman, besides merchants, bankers, and citizens, generally. Captain Dyer was a painstaking drill-master, fond of quoting Colonel Brown, of the Infantry, as supreme military authority, was exceedingly popular with his men, and the personification of the soldier and gentleman. Settees were provided for the ladies, who rallied in large numbers, regardless of the weather. After the severe drill of an hour and a half, the order to 'Break ranks' was obeyed with alacrity, and our caterer, 'Gil Rawson,' was made doubly happy by the grand rush for his hot coffee and the 'fixins,' of which there was always an abundance. Refreshments over, 'John Brown' and other patriotic songs were sung, the ladies heartily joining."

Thursday, September 26th, a meeting of the State Central Military Committee was held in Franklin Hall at 10.30 A. M., Wednesday, September 25th, Colonel Hallet in the chair. Representatives from sixteen towns reported 1,930 men, who have already attached themselves to the new volunteer organizations.

The following circular was adopted by the Committee:

The State Central Military Committee, who have in charge the organization of the volunteer drill corps in this State, have decided upon the following rules and orders:

Formation of Companies. It is particularly directed that every town and city in the State should immediately organize one or more military companies, of not less than 60 and not more than 100, rank and file, to be called, "*The National Guard of Rhode Island.*" In the smaller towns and villages the volunteers should, if practicable, unite to form together a full company.

Officers. Each company shall elect one captain and three lieutenants, who will be commissioned by the Governor, according to the provisions of sections 8, 9, and 10 of chapter 232 of the Revised Statutes; also, five sergeants and eight corporals, who will be appointed by the commanding officer. The commanding officer of each company will report to the Secretary of this Committee as soon as said company is organized, the names of his lieutenants, the number of men who hold themselves ready to parade at one day's notice, and the number of arms and equipments, if any, now in his possession.

The Committee particularly request that the names of no men be registered as members of the volunteers who intend to parade with any of the chartered companies.

Smaller bodies of men may be organized under the command of a first lieutenant.

The Drill. The drill of the companies will be strictly the United States infantry tactics for the musket, as promulgated by the Secretary of War in the United States Tactics, published May 1, 1861.

Uniforms. The uniform of the Volunteers shall consist of a blue army cap, dark blue tunic and light blue pants.

Arms and Equipments. As soon as the roll of the company is full, the Commandant will apply to the Secretary of this Committee for the necessary arms and equipments.

Object of the Organization. Every true patriot must readily perceive that it is of the utmost importance in the present crisis for Rhode Island to have, in addition to the force sent into the field, a "power of reserve."

This volunteer organization is the school of the citizen soldier. Men acquire, both as officers and privates, a knowledge of military drill and tactics. It generates a military spirit, at home and abroad, so that should the occasion call upon us to defend our own soil, or, as is more probable, should any of us wish to enlist with the noble band who have gone forth to MEET the foes of our country, we shall find ourselves ready.

We call upon every able-bodied man in Rhode Island who is not attached to any other military company, to become a member of this organization, and give it his personal presence and support.

Let it be manifest that the patriotism which was sealed by the blood of our fathers in the American Revolution, is alive to-day, and that WE stand ready to defend and support the Union, the Constitution, and the laws of our country.

WM. SPRAGUE,
President State Central Military Committee.

WM. E. HAMLIN,
    Secretary.

November 7th. Several of the companies of the National Guard of Providence paraded this afternoon on the Dexter Training Ground for battalion drill. The line was formed at 3.30 P. M. by Captain Dunham, acting adjutant, and Lieut. C. S. Sweet, acting sergeant-major. The following companies were present: Second Ward, Capt. Charles H. Dunham; Fourth Ward, Capt. Elisha Dyer; Fifth Ward, Capt. Stephen H. Hall; Sixth Ward, Capt. Hopkins B. Cady, and the Washington Continentals, Captain Westcott Handy. Acting Colonel James Shaw, Jr., assumed the command, receiving the customary honors as he took the position. The battalion was then exercised in various field movements and acquitted itself very creditably. At a little past five the line broke into column and moved from the parade down High and Westminster streets, under escort of the Horse Guards, Colonel Hallett. Colonel Shaw was much gratified at the success of the exhibition. He had long advocated the formation of battalions and the learning of battalion drill, and had made several trials with the Fifth and Sixth Ward companies. The *Journal* said, "The exhibition was, on the whole, very successful, and it will not be long before our people will possess enough of the military spirit and drill to gather, if necessary, a magnificent army of a million men. No effort should be spared to enlist in the State National Guard every able-bodied man. His Excellency the Governor enters warmly into the scheme, and has been untiring in his efforts to secure its accomplishment, until almost daily, throughout the State, fully seven thousand men have been under drill, and the name, 'The National Guard of Rhode Island,' has been adopted."

Another parade and drill of the Providence Guards occurred Thursday, November 21st. Five companies participated, with James Shaw, Jr., colonel; Charles H. Dunham, major; G. Frank Low, adjutant; and Charles J. Sweet, sergeant-major. It has been finally decided by the military authorities that there shall be a parade and review of the entire volunteer and militia forces of the State, on Saturday, November 30th.

December 2d. There was a grand parade and review of the reserve military forces of the State, on Saturday, November 30th.

The day was cold and stormy; still about two thousand men were in line. The First Brigade was commanded by Brig.-Gen. Charles T. Robbins, as follows: Providence Horse Guards, Home Battery Light Artillery; First Regiment under the command of Col. William W. Brown; Second Regiment under the command of Col. James Shaw, Jr., aided by the following officers: Lieut.-Col. Charles H. Merriman, Major Charles H. Dunham, Adjut. G Frank Low, Sergt.-Major Charles J. Sweet. The companies were: American Brass Band, eighteen pieces; Burnside Zouaves, Capt. H. Herbert Sheldon; First Ward National Guards, Capt. A. Crawford Greene; Second Ward, Lieut. Wm. S. Smith; Third Ward, Capt. Wm. M. Hale; Fourth Ward, Capt. Elisha Dyer; Fifth Ward, Capt. Stephen H. Hall; Sixth Ward, Capt. Hopkins B. Cady; Seventh Ward, Capt. Charles R. Dennis; Washington Continentals, Capt. Westcott Handy, and the Ellsworth Phalanx, Capt. Daniel W. Lyman (High School).

The Second Brigade was commanded by Brig. Gen. Wm. T. Barton, with Capt. Jacob Dunnell, aide-de-camp, and Major Christopher Duckworth brigade major and inspector, as follows: Third

Regiment, commanded by Col. Olney Arnold; Pawtucket Light Guard, Co. A, Capt. Robert McCloy; Pawtucket Light Guard, Co. B, Capt. Jesse Cudworth, Jr.; Woonsocket Guards, Captain Steere, 33 men; Pawtucket National Guard, Lieutenant Bliss; Woonsocket National Guards, Capt. C. L. Watson; Lonsdale National Guard, Capt. Geo. Kilburn ; Georgiaville National Guard, Capt. Edward Steere; Johnston National Guard, Capt. George Harris ; North Scituate National Guard, Capt. Moses F. Roberts; Slatersville National Guard, Capt. Isaac Place ; Slatersville Union Guard, Capt. Philip P. Hall; Slater Drill Corps, Pawtucket, Capt. Henry F. Smith; Cranston National Guard, Capt. Albert C. Howard.

Fourth Regiment, Col. Nicholas Van Slyck ; Kentish Artillery, Apponaug National Guards, Capt. Caleb Westcott ; Kentish Guards, Capt. E. H. Gardiner; Pettaquamscot Infantry, Capt. Jervis Perkins ; Narragansett Guards, Capt. L. H. Arnold; East Greenwich National Guards, Capt. George W. S. Allen ; Old Warwick National Guards, Capt. Christopher Wilcox.

The line was reviewed by the governor between twelve and one P. M., after which the division moved down Broadway, through the principal streets, to Exchange place, arriving about four P. M. The parade was then dismissed, and a collation was served in Howard and Phoenix Halls.

The exhibition was so satisfactory that His Excellency the governor issued an order returning his thanks to the Rhode Island National Guard for their patriotism and determination to uphold the rights of the people and the honor of the government. The document is as follows :

HEADQUARTERS COMDR.-IN-CHIEF OF MILITIA,
STATE OF RHODE ISLAND, &c., PROVIDENCE, Dec. 2, 1861.

To the National Guard:

The commander-in-chief congratulates the National Guard of Rhode Island on their successful review of Saturday, the 30th ult. He thanks the Military Committee and the officers and men comprising this organization for exhibiting to the State and to the country that Rhode Island has far more defenders of our sacred cause at home than she has yet sent into the field. This display of patriotism and zeal is encouraging and cheering to her brave sons now in the service, and a warning to foreign foes who would trifle with a people now making superhuman efforts to preserve the rights and sustain the honor of a free government. It also signifies to those who are entrusted with the direction of our national affairs that no cause will be permitted to intervene to prevent an energetic and determined prosecution of the contest to which the whole heart of this great people is devoted. Rhode Island was the first to offer the services of her citizens in defence of the government and the Union. She was first to organize her National Guard. She will be the last to lay down her arms, nor will she do so till secession and rebellion shall have been subdued; till foreign powers shall have learned to respect our rights; till those have been taught to become good and loyal citizens, who, for party purposes or personal gain, would stay the progress of the great work; till rebels and traitors shall flee the wrath of an outraged and indignant people.

WM. SPRAGUE.

December 23d. An adjourned meeting of the line officers was held at Governor Dyer's office on Saturday evening, 21st instant, for the purpose of forming a city regiment. The Burnside Zouaves desired to be attached to the regiment as skirmishers, and their request was granted. The regiment is to be called The First Regiment National Guard of Rhode Island.

The officers were elected as follows: Colonel, James Shaw, Jr.; Lieutenant-Colonel, Charles H. Merriman; Major, Charles H.

Dunham; Adjutant, George Frank Low; Quartermaster, Amos D. Smith; Assistant Quartermaster, William E. Hamlin; Commissary, William W. Hoppin; Assistant Commissary, Joseph P. Manton; Paymaster, William Viall; Assistant Paymaster, Thomas A. Doyle; Surgeon, A. H. Okie; Assistant Surgeon, William C. Beckwith; Chaplain, Thomas M. Clark; Sergeant-Major, Charles J. Sweet.

The companies then drew for positions, which resulted as follows: Company A, Fifth Ward; Company B, Fourth Ward; Company C, Seventh Ward; Company D, Second Ward; Company E, Sixth Ward; Washington Continentals; Companies F and G, First Ward; Company H, Burnside Zouaves.

Feb. 22, 1862. The birthday of Washington was celebrated in Providence in a manner and spirit befitting the day. The Infantry paraded with full ranks at ten o'clock A. M. At twelve, M., the bells were rung for an hour, and a salute was fired. A special service was also held at noon, in the First Baptist Church, His Excellency Governor Sprague and staff being present. Washington's farewell address was read by Lieut.-Gov. Samuel G. Arnold. Dr. Francis Wayland pronounced the benediction. At two o'clock P. M., the First Regiment Rhode Island National Guard assembled on Exchange place and were formed in regular line, as follows: Company H, Burnside Zouaves, Col. William W. Paine. During the formation of the line they deployed as skirmishers. Company A, Fifth Ward, Capt. Stephen H. Hall; Washington Continentals, Capt. C. Henry Alexander; Company F, First Ward Drill Corps, Capt. Henry A. Webb; Company C, Seventh Ward, Capt. H. W. Gardner; Company D, Second Ward,

William S. Smith, lieutenant commanding; Company G, First Ward Light Guard, Capt. A. Crawford Greene; Company E, Sixth Ward, Capt. Hopkins B. Cady; Company B, Fourth Ward, Capt. Elisha Dyer. The regiment was formed by Adjt. G. Frank Low, when Brig.-Gen. Charles T. Robbins assumed the command.

The officers of the regiment were as follows: Colonel, James Shaw, Jr.; Lieutenant-Colonel, Charles H. Merriman; Major, Charles H. Dunham; Adjutant, J. Frank Low; Sergeant-Major, Charles J. Sweet.

At 2.30 o'clock the line was reviewed by His Excellency Governor Sprague, who was accompanied by his aids, Colonels Sprague, Gardner, and Harris, Adjt.-Gen. Mauran, with Captain Hoppin, of his staff; Paymaster-General Knight, Captain Crandall, of the staff of the commanding general; Quartermaster Smith, of the Marine Artillery, and Lieutenant Buckley, of Battery C.

After the review, the line was thrown into column, and marched as per the programme laid down. The troops made an inspiring display. As the column passed the arsenal, the battery now recruiting was formed into line, and paid the honors of a salute, as did the Third Ward National Guard, drawn up on the sidewalk a short distance above. The regiment returned to Exchange place between five and six, and went through the formalities of dress parade, when the line was dismissed.

The Third Ward National Guard, Capt. William M. Hale, paraded at two o'clock. They wore a uniform, regulation cap, a dark blue tunic and dark pants. They were very spirited after deciding to parade. The uniform was voted on Tuesday evening, and the cloth was bought on Wednesday morning.

OBSEQUIES OF RHODE ISLAND OFFICERS.

> " Can storied urn or animated bust
> Back to its mansion call the fleeting breath?
> Can honor's voice provoke the silent dust,
> Or flattery soothe the dull, cold ear of death?"
>
> —*Gray's Elegy.*

March 31, 1862. The obsequies of Col. John S. Slocum, Maj. Sullivan Ballou, and Capt. Levi Tower, who fell at the Battle of Bull Run July 21, 1861, were publicly observed in Providence to-day. The line was formed under the command of Brigadier-General Robbins and staff in the following order: His Excellency the Governor, William Sprague; His Honor the Lieutenant-Governor, Samuel G. Arnold; aids and high military officers of the State and of United States Volunteers; Providence Horse Guards; American Brass Band; First Regiment Rhode Island National Guard; Col. James Shaw, Jr.; Lieut.-Col. Charles H. Merriman; Maj. Charles H. Dunham; Adjt. G. Frank Low; Company A, Fifth Ward, Capt. S. H. Hall; Company B, Fourth Ward, Captain Elisha Dyer; Company C, Seventh Ward, Capt. Henry W. Gardner; Company D, Second Ward, Lieut.-Commanding William S. Smith; Company E, Sixth Ward, Capt. H. B. Cady; Company F, First Ward, Capt. H. Webb; Company G, First Ward Light Guard, Capt. A. C. Greene; Company H, Burnside Zouaves, Capt. W. W. Paine; Battalion of Infantry, Col. Josiah Whitaker; Old Guard Providence Artillery, Capt. William Jackson; Sarsfield Guards, Captain Corcoran; Sowamsett Guards, Warren, Capt. Frank S. Brown; Barrington National

Guards, Capt. Henry Staples ; Portsmouth National Guards, Capt. Alonzo B. Tallman ; Pettaquamscot Light Infantry, Kingston, Capt. Elisha C. Clark ; Regiment of Infantry, the funeral escort of Col. John S. Slocum, under the command of Colonel Brown ; hearse and pall bearers ; caparisoned horse led by groom ; detail of officers from the Second Regiment, R. I. V. ; First Light Infantry, Company A, Capt. L. C. Warner ; First Light Infantry, Company B, Capt. C. R. Dennis ; University Cadets, Capt. G. T. Woodward ; Providence Artillery, Capt. J. R. Holman ; Ellsworth Phalanx (High School), Capt. D. W. Lyman ; National Cadets and Mechanics Rifles ; Third Ward National Guard, Capt. William M. Hale ; Pawtucket Home Guards, Lieut.-Commanding Albert Bliss ; Battalion of Infantry, the funeral escort of Maj. Sullivan Ballou, under command of Maj. Henry T. Sisson; hearse and pall-bearers; Maj. Albert S. Gallup and others ; Woonsocket Guards, Capt. Charles H. Watson ; Slatersville Drill Corps, Capt. Isaac Place ; Pawtucket Light Guard, Company B, Captain Cudworth ; Pawtucket Light Guard, Company C, Captain Smith ; one company of Infantry, the funeral escort of Capt. Levi Tower ; Pawtucket Light Guard, Company A. Capt. Robert McCloy ; hearse and pall-bearers.

Arriving at the cemetery at Swan Point, the funeral service was conducted by Bishop Clark, and, at its conclusion, three volleys were fired. The column was then reformed and proceeded to Dexter Training Ground, and passed in review before His Excellency the Governor, after which it marched down High and Westminster streets to Exchange place, where it was dismissed.

Memorial to Lieut. H. A. Prescott, Killed at Bull Run, July 21, 1861.

In March, 1862, when Governor Sprague went to Manassas, a special commission of three was sent by the Providence Light Infantry to look for the remains of Lieut. Henry A. Prescott, killed July 21, 1861, but their search for his grave was unsuccessful. A beautiful mural tablet has been erected to his memory in the chapel of Grace Church, with the following inscription:

In Memoriam.

LIEUTENANT HENRY A. PRESCOTT.
Born November 10th, 1823.
Killed in the Battle of Manassas Plain, Virginia,
July 21, 1861.
The Christian, the Patriot, the Good Soldier of
Jesus Christ.
In all his relations, by inflexible devotion to Truth,
and Duty, he illustrated his Faith.
At his Country's call, in defence of her Constitution
and Nationality, he laid down his life.

This Tablet is erected by the Teachers and Scholars of
Grace Church Sunday School, as an expression
of esteem for the worth and gratitude
for the example of their associate
and Constant Friend.

Mr. Prescott left a wife and five children, a mother and one sister to mourn their irreparable loss.

On the 12th day of April, 1867, the first Post of the Grand Army of the Republic in the State was organized under the name of Prescott Post No. 1, of the District of Providence, Department of Rhode Island. Lieutenant Prescott's army cap, with the bullet holes plainly visible, is sacredly preserved at the Post Headquarters. Four of the commanders of Prescott Post belonged to the Tenth Rhode Island Volunteers, viz.: James Shaw, Jr., commander, 1867; William Stone, 1871-72; William E. Taber, 1874; William A. Spicer, 1890.

THANKS TO THE RHODE ISLAND NATIONAL GUARD.

STATE OF RHODE ISLAND, &C.
ADJUTANT GENERAL'S OFFICE.
PROVIDENCE, April 7, 1862.

General Orders No. 23.

The Commander-in-Chief presents his thanks to Brig. Gen. Charles T. Robbins and staff for their signal efficiency in conducting the funeral ceremonies in honor of the martyred heroes of Rhode Island, the lamented Colonel Slocum, Major Ballou and Capt. Tower, who were killed in the battle of "Bull Run," July 21, 1861.

To the several military organizations composing the Second Brigade, for their full ranks and promptness.

To the First Regiment "National Guard," Colonel Shaw; Providence Light Battery, Old Guard Providence Artillery, Ellsworth Phalanx (Providence High School), University Cadets, Sarsfield Guards, Pettaquamscot Light Infantry, Barrington National Guards, Sowamsett Guards, Portsmouth Guards, Third Ward National Guard, and Slatersville Drill Corps for their voluntary attendance, with large numbers, adding so much to the efficiency and appearance of the column.

To the Providence Horse Guards, Colonel Hallett, for their escort.

The Burnside Zouaves added much to the impressiveness of the solemn occasion, guarding the remains while lying in state. It will ever be to them a proud satisfaction that in the early days of their history this sacred duty fell to their lot.

Thus Rhode Island honored those dead heroes as the sainted representatives of her living soldiers. While Rhode Island wept for the fatal past, her heart also beat proudly for the future. Her prayer is that a crushing retribution will speedily overwhelm the perpetrators of the gross indignities to her favorite sons, and that her own brave soldiers, and the soldiers of her sister States, will, with strong will and ready steel, quickly cancel the brutal outrages inflicted upon the lifeless bodies of these children of our common country.

By order of the Commander-in-Chief.

EDWARD C. MAURAN,
Adjutant-General.

April 18, 1862. The First Regiment Rhode Island National Guard, Colonel James Shaw, Jr., paraded this evening with full ranks. Everything passed off most satisfactorily.

April 19th. The Third Ward National Guards are now designated as the What Cheer Guards. They have been presented with an elegant silk standard by the ladies of the ward.

May 8th. Annual election of officers Company E, Sixth Ward, First Regiment Rhode Island National Guard: Captain, Hopkins B. Cady; Lieutenants, Ezra P. Bullock, C. F. Phillips, Stephen Thurber; Clerk, F. N. Seabury; Treasurer, C. F. Phillips; Corporals, Orsmus A. Taft, Frank Holden, C. Stone, Alfred Cady, and others; Drummer, Henry H. James; Armorers, Ira R. Wilbur, W. A. Greene.

May 17th. Annual election Company A, Fifth Ward, First Regiment Rhode Island National Guard: Captain, Wm. E. Taber, Jr., vice S. H. Hall, resigned; Lieutenants, Joseph L. Bennett, Jr., Leander C. Belcher; Sergeants, William A. James, A. R. Peck, John W. Briggs, W. C. Barker, Albert C. Winsor.

May 25th, Sunday. At midnight the urgent summons came for volunteers for the defence of the Capital, and from the First Regiment Rhode Island National Guard, bound together by no legal ties, subject to no military orders, simply banded together to learn the duties of the soldier, sprang to arms the Tenth Regiment Rhode Island Volunteers. Called together at 9 o'clock A. M. on the 26th, by 7 P. M. of the same day 613 men had placed their names upon the roll of service to their country.

The response of the town companies of the Rhode Island National Guard was equally prompt, and from them was organized the Ninth Regiment Rhode Island Volunteers, which left for Washington with the Tenth the day after the call. The companies were: The Lonsdale National Guard, Capt. John McKinley; Natick National Guard, Capt. John A. Bowen; the Pawtucket Battalion and Westerly National Guards.

The Tenth Regiment Rhode Island Volunteers, included the following city companies: First Ward Light Guards, Capt. A. Crawford Greene; First Ward Drill Corps, Capt. Benjamin W. Harris; Second Ward National Guard, Capt. Charles H. Dunham; What Cheer Guards, Third Ward, Capt. William M. Hale; Fourth Ward National Guard, Capt. Elisha Dyer; Fifth Ward National Guard, Capt. William E. Taber, Jr.; Sixth Ward National Guard, Capt. Hopkins B. Cady; Seventh Ward National Guard, Capt. Theodore Winn; Burnside Zouaves, Capt. Christopher Duckworth.

The first detachment of the Ninth and Tenth Regiments, Rhode Island Volunteers, left for Washington Tuesday afternoon, May 27th, and numbered upwards of one thousand men. It was quickly followed by the Tenth Light Battery, in three detachments. More volunteers for the Ninth and Tenth regiments from the National Guard were soon in the city awaiting marching orders, and the second detachment for those regiments started for Washington May 29th.

The history of the War for the Union presents no prouder example than we have recited, of prompt and patriotic response to the call of duty. Within thirty hours after the call, two regiments of infantry and a battery of artillery were organized, armed, and equipped. The novelty and excitement attending the first call for troops had largely subsided, and the days of liberal bounties had not yet come.

But men were needed at once. The order of the governor showed how pressing he deemed the emergency, and, as the news flashed along the wires, men leaped from their beds and hastened to the places of rendezvous. It was no night for sleep. Messengers on horses transmitted the alarm from hand to hand. City repeated it to town, and town to village, till the entire country was aroused. Well may the Rhode Island National Guard be proud of its record, for the emergency found it "ready and willing." Well was it for Rhode Island that she had in reserve such a noble organization to come forward when needed to the help of our armies in the field.

Let no one who saw it ever despair of the Republic.

That government of the people, by the people, for the people, shall not perish from the earth.

Abraham Lincoln

THE
NINTH AND TENTH R. I. VOLUNTEERS

AND THE

TENTH R. I. BATTERY.

The Capitol in 1862.

"Of all the true host that New England can boast,
Far down by the sea, unto highland.
No State is more true, or willing to do.
Than dear little Yankee Rhode Island;
Yes, you're loyal and true, little Rhody.
Then all honor to you, little Rhody,
Governor Sprague, was not very vague.
When he said, 'Shoulder arms, Little Rhody!'"

—*Old war song.*

ON the 25th of May, 1862, at midnight, a dispatch was received by Governor Sprague, announcing that the enemy in great force were marching on Washington, and calling for every available man to rally to its defence. Just an hour later the governor issued an order for two regiments of infantry, and a battery of artillery for immediate service. The response was prompt and the ranks quickly filled; marching orders were given, and the Ninth and Tenth Rhode Island Volunteers and the Tenth Rhode Island Battery promptly reported for duty at the Capital.

In order to understand the military situation in Virginia, at this time it will be necessary to go back a little.

The whole campaign of 1861, beginning with Bull Run, had been discouraging, and the winter passed away without further active service except picket duty. But in March, 1862, the Confederates having been defeated at Winchester, and, having fallen back from Manassas to a new line of defence on the Rappahannock, the Army of the Potomac was in motion. It was conveyed by water from Alexandria to Fortress Monroe, and marched up the Peninsula to attack the rebel capital. Although resisted at Yorktown and Williamsburg, it pressed steadily forward, till on the 21st of May it was within a few miles of Richmond. Meanwhile, McClellan had sent repeated calls for reinforcements from McDowell's corps of 40,000 men, which had been withheld for the defence of Washington, and, on the 17th of May, President Lincoln telegraphed, "At your urgent call for reinforcements McDowell is sent forward, but is not in any event to uncover Washington."

Unfortunately for the delay, a disturbing element now appeared, which not only prevented the junction of McDowell with McClellan, but totally disarranged all the well-laid Union plans in Virginia. Early in May, Stonewall Jackson (whose daring activity was worth an army to the Confederates) left his position before Richmond with a force of twenty thousand men, and made one of his brilliant raids up the Valley of the Shenandoah. Falling like a hammer on General Banks's little army at Winchester, on the 24th, he sent it whirling before him across the Potomac, and threatened the city of Washington. Great was the alarm and consternation.

McDowell was ordered back when within a day's march of McClellan. The President took military possession of the railroads, and, on the 25th, Secretary Stanton issued orders calling upon the militia of the loyal States to defend the Capital.

The following is the despatch sent to the Governor of Rhode Island:

WASHINGTON, May 25, 1862.

To the Governor of Rhode Island:

Intelligence from various quarters leaves no doubt that the enemy in great force are advancing on Washington. You will please organize and forward immediately all the militia and volunteer forces in your State.

Signed,   EDWIN M. STANTON,
Secretary of War.

Later a second despatch was received from Washington by Governor Sprague:

Send all the troops forward that you can immediately. Banks is completely routed. Enemy are in large force advancing upon Harper's Ferry.

Signed,   EDWIN M. STANTON,
Secretary of War.

Just an hour later the Governor issued the following order:

PROVIDENCE, May 25, 1862.

Citizens of the State capable of bearing arms will at once report themselves to the nearest military organization. The commandants of the chartered and volunteer military companies, will at once organize their companies and the men so reporting, into companies of eighty-three men, rank and file, and report to their headquarters, where they will be armed, equipped and moved

William Sprague

under the direction of the Commander-in-chief, to Washington, to protect the National Capital from the advance of the rebels, who are now rapidly approaching.

Gen. Robbins is directed to organize and command the first regiment, and will order his brigade under arms, and form it into a regiment.

The second regiment will be under command of Capt. Bliss, of the United States Army.

The Providence Marine Corps of Artillery will be placed under the command of Lieut.-Col. E. C. Gallup, as Captain, and he is directed to organize the same.

Col. Shaw is ordered to assemble the National Guard for organization.

Rhode Island troops will move through Baltimore, and if their progress is impeded by the rebel mob of that city they will mete out to it the punishment which it has long merited.

Our regiments will move to Washington to defend the Capital in common with thousands of our patriotic countrymen who will rush to arms to ward off the danger which is imminent.

WM. SPRAGUE,
Governor.

Aug. Hoppin,
Ass't Adjt. General.

The alarm thus indicated aroused every loyal heart, and the excitement was almost as tumultuous as when Sumter was fired on a year before. The response was equally prompt and worthy of the State, and demonstrated that our citizens are fully impressed with the patriotic duties of American citizenship, and ready to discharge them in time of peril. Within an incredibly short space of time, the Ninth and Tenth Regiments of Volunteers, and the Tenth Light Battery were organized and started for Washington.

The Ninth Regiment

R. I. VOLUNTEERS.

Picket Duty near Tennallytown.

THE Ninth Regiment Rhode Island Volunteers was organized from the volunteer companies of the State National Guard, together with the chartered and other companies, not including the Providence National Guard, first reporting for duty under the following special order:

ADJUTANT-GENERAL'S OFFICE,
PROVIDENCE, R. I., May 23, 1862.

Commandants of the several military companies of the State will immediately assemble their respective commands at their usual places of rendezvous, and report one company minimum standard from each organization, to the office of the Adjutant-General, for three months' service in Washington.

By order of the Commander-in-Chief.

Signed,   E. C. MAURAN,
   Adjutant-General.

This special call for troops was made to meet a threatened attack upon the National Capital.

During the same month of May, 1862, the rebel Gen. Thomas J. Jackson, familiarly known as "Stonewall," with a large body of men, made a sudden raid upon the Valley of the Shenandoah, routed the weakened army of General Banks, at Winchester, and threatened the safety of Washington. In view of actual and possible needs, the Secretary of War sent, on the 25th of May, a telegram to the Governor of Rhode Island, calling for the immediate forwarding to the National Capital, of all the available troops in the State, to serve in the defences for a period of three months. This telegram was received by Governor Sprague at midnight, and before sunrise measures had been taken to comply with the call. The spirit of the people was well represented by this prompt action of the Executive. The excitement and enthusiasm was as intense as when the integrity of the nation was first threatened, and affected alike all classes. The Rhode Island National Guard, then for some time organized, furnished an ample reserve from which to draw the State's proportion of the new levy. Volunteers came pouring in with great rapidity, and in two days the Lonsdale National Guard, the Natick National Guard, the Westerly National Guard, and Pawtucket Battalion (two full companies), Company A, Pawtucket Light Guard, and Company H, which was composed of the Slater Drill Corps and the Cudworth Zouaves, and companies from Newport and Woonsocket, were reported for duty, and left Providence May 27th, for Washington, as the Ninth Regiment Rhode Island Volunteers. The second detachment of the Ninth and Tenth Regiments, under command of Col. Zenas R. Bliss, of the Tenth, followed May 29th, thus in four days completing their organization, and commencing their journey to the field of duty.

The Ninth Regiment was organized by Col. Charles T. Robbins, who accompanied it to Washington. It was subsequently placed under the command of Col. John T. Pitman, whose commission bore date July 3, 1862. Colonel Pitman had previously served as captain of Company G, First Rhode Island Detached Militia, in 1861. He was appointed major of the Ninth, May 26, 1862; lieutenant-colonel, June 9, 1862, and colonel, July 3, 1862, and was mustered out Sept. 1, 1862. He afterwards served as lieutenant-colonel of the Eleventh Rhode Island Volunteers, Oct. 1, 1862, and was mustered out of service, July 13, 1863.

Col. John T. Pitman.

The Ninth Regiment left Providence Tuesday afternoon, May 27th, by rail for New York, amidst cheers and shouts and farewell waving of handkerchiefs. But the sad parting was apparently soon forgotten, for the boys shouted, and sang, and laughed at each other's jokes the greater part of the way. There was little sleep on the way that night. Some tried to rest as best they could in the crowded steamer, but this was well nigh impossible. About breakfast time the regiment arrived in New York where "rations" were served. After some delay the line of travel was resumed for Philadelphia, crowds cheering the volunteers at all the stopping places. It was late in the afternoon when the long train rolled into the passenger station of the Quaker City, and the men, tired and hungry, landed at the foot of Washington Square. A splendid reception was now tendered them with an invitation to a banquet at the rooms of the Cooper Volunteer

Refreshment Association, on Otsego street. This welcome news was received with a shout. The hospitable invitation was accepted with alacrity, and with a profusion of thanks that came from the innermost recesses of their drooping hearts, the companies fell into line, one of the men saying, "Hard tack may taste good sometimes, but it must be when a feller's real hungry an' ain't got nothin' else to eat. I reckon some soft bread, and cake, and coffee, will taste better to us just now." The progress of the Ninth to the "Cooper Shop" was a perfect ovation. "We were welcomed all the way," wrote one of the men, "like conquering heroes returning from victory, rather than a weary band of raw recruits, moving to the assistance of our comrades at the Capital. On our arrival we were liberally supplied with towels, water and soap, and after washing our hands and faces we felt greatly refreshed. Then we filed into the long dining-room and partook of an excellent collation, consisting of cold chicken and ham sandwiches, hot coffee, and other delicacies; and didn't it all go good, served by the hands of the ladies of Philadelphia, who did everything in their power to make our stay pleasant and make us feel at home. We filled not only our stomachs but our haversacks also, and after conveying our grateful acknowledgments, for what seemed hardly less than a royal banquet and reception, some of us started out to get a view of the city. It was about this time that one of the captains of the Ninth met with an interesting experience. He had gone on ahead, a little way up the street, when pausing for a few moments, deeply absorbed in tender memories of home—a trifle homesick he afterwards admitted,—he heard the voice of a child behind him to which, at first, he gave no heed, till it appeared to come nearer, 'Soldier!' Turning he beheld a charming little girl looking up into his face, and holding out a pretty flower, saying, 'Soldier, this is for you!' The captain gratefully accepted the sweet remembrance with many good wishes for the child, and returned to his company greatly comforted by this little interview. To one who has never left kindred and friends, perhaps never to return, this little incident

The Captain Surprised.

may appear trivial, but to those on their way to the enemy's country, to face the stern realities of war, experiences like this told plainer than words the depth of that loyalty in the young as well as the old, which did much to cheer the heart of the soldier, and made an impression on his memory more lasting than the stirring words of the patriotic orator. Soon the order came to 'fall in' for the march to the Baltimore depot, and amidst mutual cheering and shouting the column moved off. After quite a long march came the welcome order, 'All aboard for Baltimore!' It was after dark when the eager men packed themselves into the cars. The engines whistled and puffed, the bells rang, the people hurrahed and waved hats and handkerchiefs, and the boys of the Ninth put their heads out of the windows and yelled, as the train moved off at last, with

Washington only a hundred and forty miles away. The regiment arrived at Baltimore on the morning of the 29th, pretty well fagged out, and the boys thought on the whole they had had a pretty rough night of it. There was no such reception as at Philadelphia. No opposition was made to the march of the regiment across the city to the Washington depot, as had been anticipated. But none of the men, women or children, came out to welcome them. No, the people maintained a perfect silence as the column moved on to the rooms of the Union Relief Association, 120 Eutaw Street, where a free collation had been provided; some of the men also feasted on strawberries at fifteen cents per quart, nice ones, too.

"At two o'clock in the afternoon," wrote one of the men, "we left the Monumental City, with Washington only forty miles away. On the route we passed Annapolis Junction, rendered famous in song and story by the march of the First Rhode Island Regiment a year before, when ''twas only nine miles to the junction.' There was a good deal on the way to interest us, Perryville, Havre de Grace, and other places, but we were just beginning to tire of the long ride, standing up, sitting down, and lying around, when the great unfinished dome of the capitol loomed up into view, above the hills, and we knew that we were nearing our destination." As the men alighted from the train at five o'clock P. M., they found themselves surrounded by many reminders of the war. During a long delay here, doubtless caused in waiting for orders, some of the men stole away into the city, and reported soldiers everywhere, and the streets full of wagons loaded with army supplies of all kinds. Everything was bustle and confusion such as the eyes of these new soldiers had never looked upon before. The regiment remained that night in Washington at the barracks, near the depot, and subsisted on the "army rations" dealt out to them, but they had neither supper nor breakfast the next morning worthy of the name. How be it, there was no immediate danger of starvation, after the supply which they had stored away during their stay in Philadelphia and Baltimore, at the Union refreshment saloons.

Marching orders soon arrived, and on the morning of the 30th the regiment took its line of march up Pennsylvania avenue, making a halt near the White House. One of the men wrote home : "We were halted for a few minutes near the President's house— and I thought I would jot down a few lines,—but the thread of my narrative was rudely severed by the order 'Fall in!' and we resumed our march under a scorching sun, through dust ankle-deep, and of a degree of fineness and penetration which beggars description. On we marched out of Washington, and through Georgetown, and towards night reached our present quarters near Tennallytown. Just as we arrived here after our six-mile tramp we were favored with a drenching rain, which converted the dust upon our persons and garments into a very fine paste, and has made us ornamental as well as useful members of society. Just after dark we pitched our tents and 'turned in' upon the ground, somewhat wet, but upon the whole very comfortable. Tennallytown appears to be a collection of two blacksmith shops, a hotel, a small church, a post-office, and a toll-gate about three miles beyond Georgetown. High street in Georgetown leads directly to it." The Ninth Encampment was located just beyond the toll-gate, in a beautiful grove of oaks, which had been occupied for some time previous by Pennsylvania troops, and it was laid out with rows of white Sibley tents in straight lines, with streets of

Gen. Samuel P. Sturgis.

equal width between. By General Orders Number One, it was named "Camp Frieze," in honor of the Quartermaster General of Rhode Island. Officers' quarters, in square tents, were at the head of the camp, nicely shaded by great oaks. Afterward the streets of the camp were finely graded, with their names printed on neat signs. Many of the tents were named also. One was called the "Miller House," corner of Rhode Island and Boston avenues, and next door was the "Foster House," then the "Pawtucket Hotel." On the 6th of June the regiment was sworn into the service of the United States. It formed a part of the brigade of General Sturgis, who had been recently called to Washington to assist General Wadsworth, the military governor, and who was given command of the fortifications around the city.

Several interesting official orders have been preserved:

GENERAL STURGIS'S ORDERS.

HEADQUARTERS COLLEGE VILLA,
TENNALLYTOWN, D. C., June 4, 1862.

General Orders No. 9.

I. The commanders of camps will allow none of the men in their respective commands to pass beyond the lines of their camps without a special permit from said commanders.

II. The attention of commanding officers is called to Article 41 of the rules and articles of war which reads as follows:

"All non-commissioned officers and soldiers who shall be found one mile from the camp, without leave, in writing, from their commanding officer, shall suffer such punishment as shall be inflicted upon them by the sentence of a court martial."

By order of
Brigadier-General STURGIS,
HENRY R. MIGHELS,
Capt. and A. A. G.

HEADQUARTERS COLLEGE VILLA,
TENNALLYTOWN, D. C., June 1, 1862.

COLONEL ROBBINS,
Com'dg 9th and 10th R. I. Reg'ts.

SIR: You will please detail pickets for to-night, as on previous nights, and henceforth until further orders.

I have received no consolidated morning reports from your command for the last two mornings. Please have one made out for to-day and on each morning hereafter.

By imperative orders from Headquarters, Washington, I am obliged to transmit at once, monthly returns of the strength of the Brigade. In view of this, you will please have prepared, to-day, if possible, a monthly return for the month of May, of the strength of your entire command.

By order of
Brigadier-General STURGIS,
HENRY R. MIGHELS,
Capt. and A. A. G.

HEADQUARTERS COLLEGE VILLA,
TENNALLYTOWN, D. C., June 6, 1862.

General Orders No. 1.

1st. The commanding officer of each Regiment, Battery, Battalion or Detachment assigned to the command of Brig.-Gen. S. P. Sturgis will make consolidated morning reports daily to the commanding General, at Headquarters, College Villa, Tennallytown, D. C.

2d. The Adjutant of each command assigned as above, shall report in person to the Commanding General, every day at eleven o'clock A. M.

By order of
Brigadier-General STURGIS,
HENRY R. MIGHELS,
Capt. and A. A. G.

Col. C. T. ROBBINS,
Com'dg 9th and 10th R. I. Regiments.

HEADQUARTERS COLLEGE VILLA,
TENNALLYTOWN, D. C., June 6, 1862.

Col. CHAS. T. ROBBINS,
9th Rhode Island Reg't.

SIR: For to-night's picket duty you will please detail ten men of your command, said men to be accompanied by a non-commissioned officer.

This arrangement to be observed until further orders.

By order of
Brigadier-General STURGIS,
HENRY R. MIGHELS,
Capt. and A. A. G.

HEADQUARTERS STURGIS'S BRIGADE,
WASHINGTON, June 8, 1862.

General Orders No. 12.

I. The headquarters of the general commanding Sturgis's Brigade, are now and will be until further orders in building northeast corner of Nineteenth and I streets, Washington City.

II. Official communications will be addressed as heretofore, to Henry R Mighels, Capt. and A. A. G., College Villa, Tennallytown, D. C.

By order of
Brigadier-General STURGIS,
HENRY R. MIGHELS,
Capt. and A. A. G.

RHODE ISLAND VOLUNTEERS.   77

WAR DEPARTMENT,
Washington City, D. C., June 24, 1862.

ORDERED, That all applications for passes and permits for persons or property within the lines of the United States forces shall hereafter be made to Brigadier-General Wadsworth, Military Governor of the District of Columbia, and be subject to such terms and conditions as he may prescribe.

Signed,   EDWIN M. STANTON,
Secretary of War.

HEADQUARTERS 9TH AND 10TH REGIMENTS,
R. I. VOLUNTEERS,
TENNALLYTOWN, D. C., June 9th, 1862.

General Orders No. 1.

1. In compliment to Brig. General Lyman B. Frieze, Quartermaster-Gen. of the State of Rhode Island, this camp will hereafter be known as Camp Frieze.

2. The strictest discipline and good order will be observed, and all derelictions from duty, or failure to comply with these orders, will be promptly reported and summarily punished.

3. It is indispensable to health that the strictest neatness and cleanliness should prevail; no nuisance therefore of any description in or about the quarters will be tolerated, and all slovenly and disorderly habits will be corrected.

4. The camp grounds and quarters will be thoroughly policed each morning immediately after reveille, when in pleasant weather the bed sacks and blankets should be aired and exposed for half an hour to the sun. The bed-sacks must then be put in order and the blankets neatly folded. Articles of clothing must not be left in disorder about the tents, but all furniture, clothing and equipments, must be arranged in their proper places ready for inspection.

5. A daily detail of two men will be made by each mess to serve meals and to keep the dishes and table furniture clean and in good order. All mess utensils, wash-basins, &c., must be neatly and orderly arranged when not in use. A barrel in which clean water must be kept, will be furnished to each mess, and also a barrel in which all slops or refuse must be thrown. No water or litter of any description must be thrown or permitted to remain about the quarters.

6. At all meal hours a commissioned officer will superintend the issue of food to the detail from the messes of their respective companies.

7. A daily police guard will be detailed from each regiment for general police duties, the officers of which will see that all slop barrels are removed and their contents emptied at suitable places to be designated. All company streets and grounds will be kept in order by the companies to which they belong.

8. There will be until further orders the following calls sounded each day:

    1. *Reveille* at $4\frac{1}{2}$ o'clock A. M.

    2. *Police call* immediately after first roll call.

    3. *Breakfast call* at $6\frac{1}{2}$ A. M.

    4. *Sick call* at 7 A. M., when the sick will report themselves to the first sergeants of their respective companies, who will take them to the surgeons for examination.

    5. Adjutant's call at $8\frac{3}{4}$ A. M., when the guard will assemble on the parade. Guard mounting at 9 A. M., after which the officers of the day will report to headquarters for orders.

    6. Orderly call at 12 M. when the first sergeants of each company will report to the Adjutant for orders, and will receive from him a detail for guard, police and picket duty for the following day.

    7. *Roast beef* will be sounded at 1 P. M.

    8. *Supper call* at $6\frac{1}{2}$ P. M.

    9. *Retreat* at sunset when companies will be formed on their company parades under arms.

    10. *Tattoo* at 9 P. M.

    11. *Taps* at $9\frac{1}{2}$ P. M. when all lights must be extinguished and all noise in quarters cease.

9. There will be each day until further orders the following roll calls:

    The First at Reveille,

    The Second when Roast beef is sounded,

    The Third at Retreat,

    The Fourth at Tattoo.

10. The Routine for the day will be until further orders:

    1. Squad drills from $5\frac{1}{2}$ to $6\frac{1}{2}$ A. M., under the direction of a sergeant and superintended by the company officers.

2. Peas on a trencher at 6¼ A. M.
3. Company drill from 10 to 11½ A. M.
4. Roast Beef at 1 P. M.
5. Company drill from 3 to 5 P. M.
6. Supper at 6¼ P. M.

11. The morning reports of companies signed by the captains and first sergeants must be handed to the Adjutant before 8 o'clock A. M., who will consolidate them within the next hour for the information of the General commanding the brigade to which these regiments are attached, and make his report at headquarters.

12. On Sunday squad and company drills only will be omitted. At 9 o'clock each company's quarters will be inspected by a field officer attended by the captain, and all uncleanliness or want of attention to the requirements in which the quarters are to be kept, will be reported to the commanding officer.

13. Divine Service will be held every Sunday at 11 A. M. upon grounds to be designated, and each officer and soldier not on duty or on the sick report, is expected to be present neatly dressed in uniform without arms.

14. The body-belt will be worn on all occasions when the officers or men are out of camp, and no article of dress other than the regular uniform prescribed for these regiments will be permitted to be worn at any time.

15. No salutes will be given between Retreat and Reveille. After Guard Mounting, the officer of the guard will see that the muskets of the old guard are discharged, and no pieces will be loaded in camp, unless by special order, and any soldier disturbing the camp by discharging his musket or pistol without orders, will be immediately reported to headquarters for punishment. Muskets when loaded will be carried at the half-cock.

16. No horses and wagons except the water-carts, and carts for the removal of slop barrels, will be allowed to pass through the company streets or between the company officers' and Field officers' quarters, and no horses will be permitted to stand in rear of the line of tents occupied by the Field and Staff.

By order,

CHARLES T. ROBBINS,

Acting Colonel 9th & 10th R. I. V. Is.

General Orders Number One, just recited, lays out the programme of work for each day : Reveille is sounded at 4.30 A. M., when the roll is called and the quarters put in order. One of the boys thus described it : " Reveille at 4.30 A. M. is the 'cock-crow' of the gallant Ninth. A single bugle call is heard, when instantly the proper officer, rouses the drum-corps ; they then beat the reveille, the sound rolling in from every direction, far and near; the first sergeants are running down the company streets, parting the tent-openings, and shouting inside, 'Turn out here for roll-call!' The men turn out, in every imaginable state of dress and undress, answer to their names in the roll-call, in every tone and compass of which the human voice is capable, a perfect babel, and are assigned to their duties for the day. The whole noisy breeze is past in five minutes, and the day's work begins. But let us not overlook the poor little drummer boy in this noise of reveille, as he stands at his tent door, half awake, half asleep, 'mit nottings on sgarsly,' unkempt, shivering or half frozen, peddling around his rattling 'r-r-rap-a-tap-tap.' At half-past five we have 'squad drill' until half-past six, then ' peas on a trencher,' which means breakfast. At ten o'clock, company drill until half-past eleven. At one o'clock, 'roast beef,' which means dinner. At three o'clock, drill, until five o'clock. Supper at half-past six, and at sunset, roll-call for retreat. At nine o'clock P. M , 'tattoo and roll-call,' and at 9.30, ' taps,' which means all lights in camp must be extinguished and all noise must cease. This is the regular routine, but we have to take our turn for guard duty and for camp police. I was recently one of a detail of thirty men for police duty. Our business was not very pleasant, chiefly cleaning up the streets of the camp and carting off the dirt and waste. As soon as breakfast was over the orderly directed each man to provide himself with a small bundle of sticks or brush, three or four feet long, which was bound together, for 'police duty,' which meant cleaning up the camp, not a particularly pleasant occupation on a dry and dusty day, 'not much like policemen's duty,' one of the boys said.

Police Duty.

The weather is very hot, the mercury registering one hundred degrees in the shade. Tell Captain Hale that we are practicing 'double quick' every day so that we may not be too far behind when that foot-race comes off. When Richmond falls, as fall it must, we hope they will send us home to repose upon our laurels. Until then we must be men of war.

"Last night I was drawn in a crowd of fifty for picket duty and it promised to be no very delightful duty either, on a dark, rainy night. Soon we were ordered into line, armed and equipped with plenty of ball cartridges, and trudged out two or three miles into the country. Knowing that shooting pickets was a favorite amusement with the prowling secesh in the vicinity, we found the employment quite exciting, and as I filled the dignified position of corporal of the guard, I managed to keep my eyes open and the

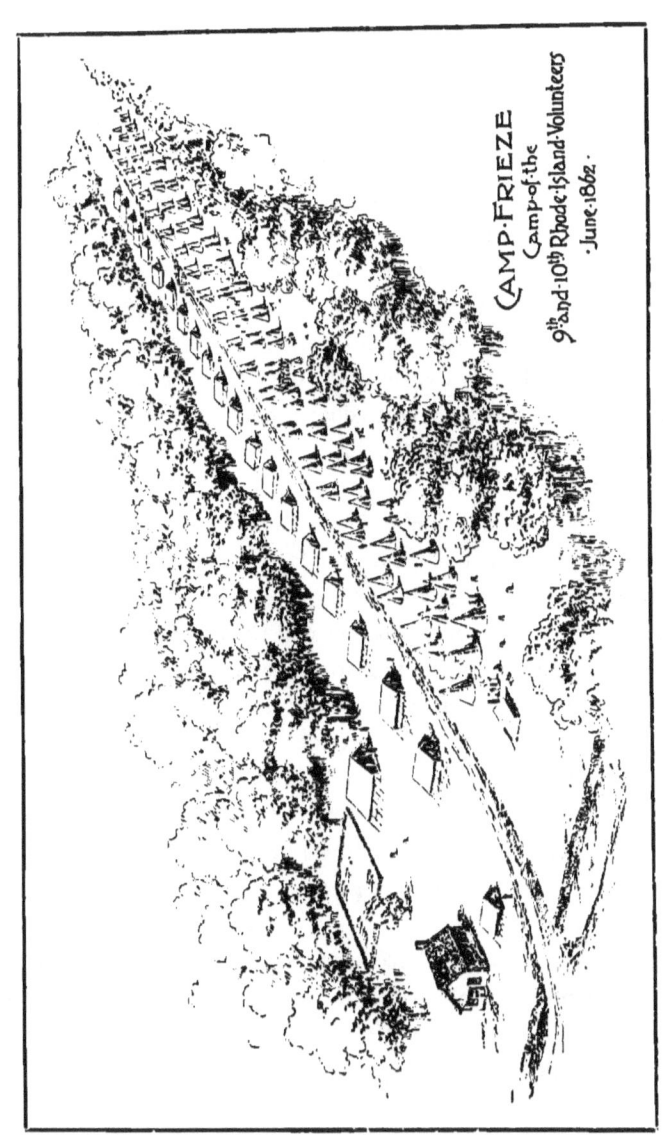

CAMP FRIEZE, TENNALLYTOWN, D. C.

Union safe through the night, and at daylight we splashed through the mud back to camp again, pretty well drenched, besides being tired and sleepy. As soon as dismissed we rolled into the straw as we were, and slept until ten this morning. We then turned out, and some of us bathed in a mud-puddle. I then breakfasted on hard-bread and cheese, and now I am ready for anything.

"June 18th. We have at last got our full equipments and clothing, and, among other things, our pantaloons, for, dreadful to relate, we have all had to wear our old ones that we brought from home, so that most of us might adopt the language of the military tactics, 'to the rear open order.' Some of them are misfits, and much too large for the boys. They remind us of the school boy's trousers, which didn't signify whether he was going to school or coming home. On Sundays we assemble at eleven o'clock for church, and again at six o'clock P. M., for dress parade.

"The men are allowed to go, now and then, to Chain Bridge, on the Potomac, for bathing. The other day a party of us went, and enjoyed it very much. It is a beautiful region, but completely studded with camps and forts. After getting back to camp it occurred to me as I kicked off my heavy army 'whangs,' as our shoes are called, that a nice, easy pair of slippers would be agreeable. Another towel, also, would be acceptable when you send the box. Even cake would not go amiss, as the boys of the mess will gladly share it with me.

"June 19th. *Bread.* I have been to Washington to-day with an order for to-morrow's bread for the regiment. Brought out 900 loaves, baked in the basement of the capitol. They bake about 21,000 loaves per day."

Eating Rations.

The "rations" were rather hard to get used to, but the men of the Ninth soon learned that a soldier's life is no holiday, and his real wants necessarily simple and few, so that there was really little cause for complaint. It was all in getting used to it.

The regular army "ration," as established by the government, for each soldier, was composed as follows: Twelve ounces of pork and bacon, or twelve ounces of salt or fresh beef; twenty-two ounces of soft bread or flour, or one pound of hard bread (hard-tack), or twenty ounces of corn meal; and to every one hundred men, fifteen pounds of beans or peas, ten pounds of rice, or hominy, eight pounds of roasted coffee, or twenty-four ounces of tea, fifteen pounds of sugar, four quarts of vinegar, twenty ounces of candles, four pounds of soap, four pounds of salt, four ounces of pepper, thirty pounds of potatoes and one quart of molasses. This was the "ration" the first year of the war. But to meet the wants of fellows with big appetites, Congress passed an act, increasing the allowance of several of the items, notably; potatoes, of which each man was to have one pound three times a week, "when practicable." But as the war wore on, most of the less important items disappeared, and during the last year it was mostly hard-tack, beans and coffee, with a little sugar and salt.

"The haversack was an indispensable part of our outfit. It consisted of a black canvass bag with a strap attached to the opposite side to adjust it to the neck or the shoulder. To use the language of an old soldier, "Your haversack's to carry your grub in! Hold on to your haversack through thick and thin! It'll be the best friend you'll find in the army!" When we left Providence our haversacks had neat white cotton linings, but after they had been in use a few weeks as receptacles for chunks of fat meat, damp sugar tied up in a rag, broken crackers and bread, with a lump of cheese or two, they took on the color of a printing-office towel. We were told that they were water-proof, but practically they were quite the reverse. Very likely you would have gone hungry a good while before eating anything out of them. Not so with the boys of the Ninth.

"The 'Camp-Kettle' was a good and useful article of furniture, made of heavy black sheet-iron, very tall, and of the same diameter from top to bottom. All were of the same height, but there were three or four sizes of them, so that they could be conveniently 'nested' for transportation. They were chiefly used for making coffee and bean soup, and sometimes for laundry purposes

"The 'Canteen' was another important feature of our outfit. It was a simple article made of tin and covered with cloth, shaped like the earth, except that it was a good deal more 'flattened at the poles,' and with a cloth strap running around it at the equator, by which it was suspended over one shoulder and carried against the opposite hip. It would hold about three pints. Its chief duty was for the transportation of water, although it was found equally adapted to carry some other things. It came handy to the forager for milk, cider or molasses. In very rare instances it was also used for liquids of a more vigorous and searching character.

The Industrious Woodtick.
This portrait is many times larger than he really was, but not half as big as he often felt.

"The greatest, or at least the most troublesome enemies we have to encounter here are the wood-ticks. As I never knew until I came here what they were, I will take it for granted that you don't, and will inform you in the words of the poet:

'De-fire-fly hab de golden wings,
De lightnin' bug de flame,
De wood-tick he hab no wing at all,
But he get dar all de same!'

They infest the trees, bushes, grass, and apparently everything else out of doors. We are seldom conscious of their presence, but the chief end and object of their existence seems to be to make their way by slow degrees under our skin, where, embedded in the flesh, they soon become very disagreeable. When they make up their mind to have a taste of Yankee blood, they find easy access to the body through the openings of the uniform. I have found several of them already, but only one that had made any progress through the skin, and he was discovered and executed before any harm was done. They generally put their work in at night, and neither slumber nor sleep. This country appears to abound in such creeping things, very much to my disgust. I am told the only sure way to exterminate them is to boil your clothing."

The wood-ticks and gray-backs were the great pests of the Union army from '61 to '65. One of the great problems of the war was how to get rid of them. They attacked all the soldiers, from the major-generals down to the privates.

WASHINGTON AND ITS DEFENCES.

In 1861 every considerable eminence in the vicinity of the National Capital was crowned with a fort or redoubt well mounted. Early in 1862, the second of the war, the number of these works was fifty-two, whose names and locations are indicated on the accompanying map.

This system of works was so complete, that at no time afterward, during the war, did the Confederates ever seriously attempt to assail them.

The month of June was spent in thorough attention to drill, and in the performance of picket duty. The regiment was expected to be ready for "inspection" every Sunday morning.

After getting thus comfortably settled down at Camp Frieze, the members of the Ninth were surprised to receive an order from Colonel Pitman to be ready to march at short notice. The news spread rapidly through the neighborhood, and our friends began to compliment us, supposing that we were likely to be sent towards "the front," but that seemed hardly probable unless McClellan should suffer an overwhelming defeat and the enemy make an advance on Washington, in force. June 28th, the regiment was called at early dawn, broke up its camp, hurriedly partook of its morning meal of salt-junk, hard-tack and coffee, and started at sunrise for Washington. It was a beautiful morning, and the men started off in fine spirits, with a long train of sixty army wagons, loaded with tents and other camp equipage. A march of seven miles brought them to Long Bridge, a little before eight o'clock, with but two halts of five minutes each, in a tramp of seven miles. The contrabands in fantastic dress and head-gear swarmed about the men pressing them to buy their pies, gingerbread and hoe-cake. Said one of the men: "The sun's rays beat down fiercely on the perspiring volunteers of the Ninth Rhode Island as we went marching over Long Bridge and planted our 'whangs' squarely upon Virginia sacred soil, which appeared to rise indignant in our faces, completely enveloping us in a very fine dust, which stuck to us like wax, and entered our eyes, mouths and noses, adding greatly to the discomforts of the long march. It was a very hot day, if not the hottest we ever experienced, but we keep tramping on in the cloud of dust with but two halts, the latter of about one hour, to consult about our route of march. Then we started again, and at length reached Alexandria, said to be seven miles from Long Bridge. We then made a detour of two or three miles around the outskirts of the city, through marshy fields and rough roads until at length the drum gave

A Hot Day for the Ninth Rhode Island.

the welcome signal for the final halt, and the weary and dusty men dropped by the roadside all pretty well used up,—and glad enough to 'call it a day's work,' and find needed rest. One of the privates of Company K, William Henry Harrison Swan, escaped the long march, as follows: The day before we left Camp Frieze found him suffering with a severe and protracted attack of side-ache, and on recommendation of the 'orderly sergeant' he went to the doctor with a request for some mustard, for an external application. He was also warned to get a supply of the article for seasoning the 'orderly's' salt-horse or beef. He succeeded in getting a satisfactory amount of mustard, but ignorantly made a direct application in full strength to his lame side. In a short time he was moving around lively in great distress, and when we left for Fairfax his side was badly blistered and swollen. He was deposited in one of the wagons, and thus rode to Fairfax. He afterwards claimed to be the best 'mustered' recruit in the Ninth. After narrating the incident to Sergt. Charles P. Gay, of the Tenth, a few days ago, he added, 'singularly enough, I have never had the side-ache since, and never was "mustered out "' After the march, hard-tack and coffee were served, and I tell you it went good. As the first encampment was named 'Camp Frieze' the second was appropriately termed 'Camp Scorch,' or 'Camp Misery.' Not a tree is in sight, everything has been removed to clear the way before the guns of the forts. In the vicinity are Forts Ward, Worth, Lyon and Blenker; the camp being upon an elevated site, we have a fine view of Washington and the Potomac. Fairfax Seminary is near by."

The regiment was assigned to the Second Brigade, Reserve Army Corps, south of the Potomac, commanded by Col. Zenas R. Bliss, of the Tenth Rhode Island Volunteers, Acting Brigadier-General. The brigade consisted of Battery L, Second New York; Battery C, First New York; Sixteenth Indiana Battery, Ninth and Tenth Rhode Island Volunteers, Thirty-Second Massachusetts Volunteers, Second Excelsior Battery, and the Twelfth Pennsylvania Cavalry. The Tenth Rhode Island Battery, Captain Gallup, was stationed about a mile from camp, near Cloud's Mills. This forward movement of the forces around Washington was made to support the advance of General McDowell's Corps towards Richmond, to co-operate with the Army of the Potomac, under General McClellan, in the reduction of the confederate capital. But on June 26th, after the indecisive battle of Gaines's Mills, McClellan commenced his retreat to the James River. The campaign against

Richmond had ended in failure, June 30th, and the Army of the Potomac had retired to a new base of operations at Harrison's Landing. McDowell's army was ordered back to Fredericksburg, and the Ninth and Tenth Rhode Island Volunteers with other organizations were ordered back to the neighborhood of the forts surrounding Washington. The Ninth Regiment returned by water to Washington by the way of Alexandria.

The Marshall House.

It was an ancient and dilapidated looking place, trying to live on its old reputation in slave-holding days. "We marched," says a correspondent, "by the historic Marshall House where the youthful commander, Colonel Ellsworth, had been shot in 1861. Alexandria had been in quiet possession of the National troops since May of that year, but there were many violent secessionists there who would not submit. Among them was a man named Jackson, the proprietor of the Marshall House. The Confederate flag had been flying over his premises for many days, and had been plainly visible from the President's house in Washington. It was still there when Colonel Ellsworth went in person, with a few of his men, to

Col. Elmer E. Ellsworth.

take it down. When descending an upper staircase with the flag, which he had lowered, he was shot by Jackson, who was waiting for him in a dark passage with a double-barreled gun loaded with buck-shot. Ellsworth fell dead, and his murderer met the same fate an instant afterwards at the hands of Francis E. Brownell, who with six others had accompanied his commander to the roof of the house. He shot Jackson through the heart with a bullet, and pierced his body several times with his sabre-bayonet. Ellsworth's body was borne in sadness to Washington, where funeral services were held in the East Room of the White House, with President Lincoln as chief mourner." Ellsworth was a very young and attractive officer, and greatly beloved for his bravery and patriotism. His death produced great excitement throughout the country. It was one of the first that had occurred in consequence of the National troubles.

"Leaving Alexandria the Ninth Regiment embarked on board 'the steamer *Hero*, for Washington.' After a splendid run of about an hour we landed near the Arsenal, and then marched a short distance till we came to a fine piece of turfed ground, where we rested about two hours, while the colonel departed for orders. Resuming our march we passed near the east front of the Capitol, by the Navy Yard, across the east branch of the Potomac, through a little place called Union Town, up and over some of the longest and steepest hills, until covered with dust, we halted at a fork in the roads, where the regiment was divided; Captain McCloy's company, with three others passed on to the right, and the remaining ones, moved straight on, and soon reached their destination. The regiment is now distributed among ten or a dozen forts, extending around Washington, on the east side, and relieved the Ninety-ninth Pennsylvania Volunteers who joined the army of General McClellan on the Peninsula. One of the forts, Wagner, mounts four thirty-two-pounders, which goes to show that our men are to learn to be artillerymen. Fort Wagner is finely situated, on an eminence overlooking the city and the Potomac, and commands an extensive view. There is an abundance of water, shade, and pure air. There is also a great supply of nothing to eat, as all we have is what was left of the rations we brought from Camp Misery, in our haversacks, yesterday morning.

"The distribution of the companies is as follows: Company A, Capt. Robert McCloy, at Fort Greble; Company F, Capt. John M. Taylor, Fort Carroll; Company D, Capt. John McKinley, Fort Snyder; Company I, Capt. Samuel Pierce, Fort Stanton; Company C, Capt. John A. Bowen, Fort Ricketts; Company H, Capt. Henry F. Jenks, Fort Wagner; Company E, Capt. Isaac Place, and Company K, Capt. James R. Holden, Fort Baker (regimental headquarters); Company G, Capt. Charles L. Watson, Fort Dupont; Company B, Capt. Henry C. Card, Fort Meigs; Company L, Capt. Benjamin L. Slocum, Fort Davis.

"We have neither tents, blankets, overcoats, or clothing, except what we marched in yesterday; all are in the wagons, which have not as yet reached camp. But most of us had foraged plenty

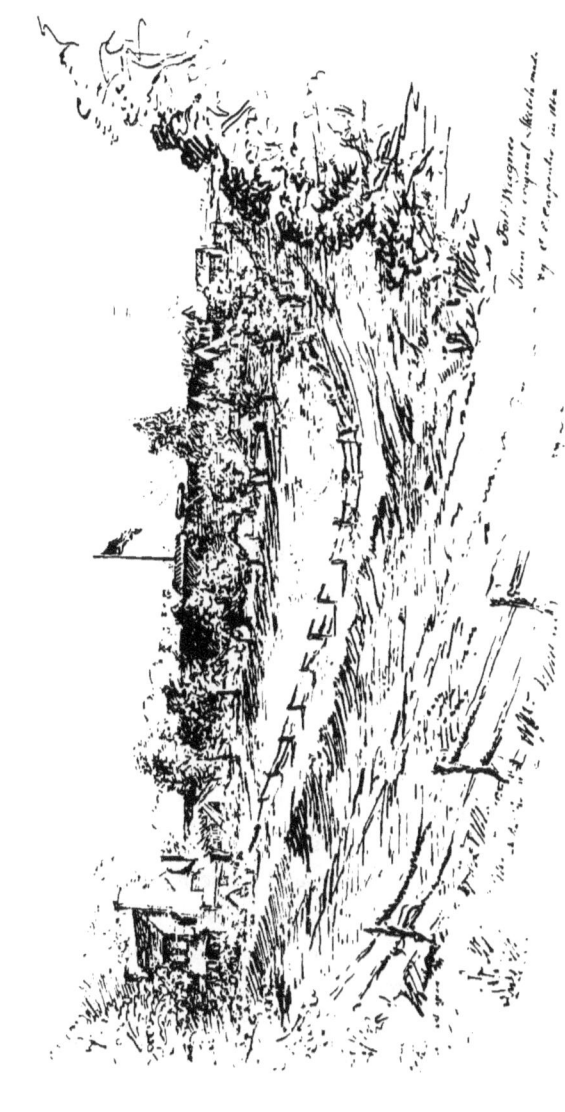

FORT WAGNER AND THE RICHARDSON HOUSE.

of cherries and blackberries, and some of the boys had found little difficulty in deluding some cows into the belief that they were their own calves, so that we became quite reconciled to the non-appearance of our baggage wagons. Soon Captain Jenks announced that he had made arrangements for hot coffee, and the use of the African Methodist Episcopal Church near by, for our company to lodge in. So we shouldered our muskets, and marched into the church, a small brick edifice, about the form and size of a New England country school-house. It was nearly new, and quite neat and clean, and we slept none the worse for its being a negro church. Some of the men were disappointed because they found no cushions on the seats, for myself I gladly stretched myself upon one of them near the pulpit, with my cartridge-box for a pillow and slept the sleep of the weary, while the boys were making the house ring with their vocal music, singing army songs mixed with hymns and psalms; yet I think I never slept more soundly.

"July 4th. To-day, at nine o'clock A. M., I commenced my duties as sergeant of the guard. The guard is divided into three 'reliefs,' each 'relief' being on duty two hours and four hours off duty. The officer of the guard, instead of pacing a beat, remains in the fort ready to attend to any call.

"July 9th. Yesterday I proposed to our mess that we have a blackberry pudding, they agreed at once, and by request I went to the store and bought five pounds of flour, some butter and sugar, and while I was gone the boys went out and picked three quarts of berries, and we soon had our pudding boiling in three bags. It was very fine, some of the boys pronouncing it almost as good as 'mother made at home.'

Our Washerwoman.

"Our washerwoman is a curious, good-natured old darkey, who is generally found at home among her pigs, chickens and "chilluns." She lives in a very modest sort of a cabin, keeps her cow, sells some butter, and like most of the "cullud folks" around here appears to get on very well. The contrabands are friendly, freely lend us any of their household utensils, and welcome us to their social gatherings. You should hear their singing. I can give you no adequate idea of their sweet rendering of the old plantation melodies and gospel choruses. Some of the boys have come to the conclusion that they are "the best society of the place." To-day is washing day, and "auntie" has come for our clothes which she does up brown at the rate of fifty to seventy-five cents per dozen. All well—with prospect of a scorching day, as usual. Temperature way up among the nineties.

"Quartermaster George Lewis Cooke (promoted to major, July 3d), is a busy man. Although surrounded with stores, he can hardly find time to eat his own meals, and this morning, I noticed him, bright and early, at the commissary store-house in the general post-office building at Washington, as busy as a bee in loading up his teams. It is said that he can provide everything for our comfort, from a tent pin to a twenty-inch collar."

A correspondent of the *Evening Press*, wrote July 24th: "Judging from the weather tables spread before your readers

FORT WAGNER.—Bird's Eye View.

Maj. George Lewis Cooke.

so regularly in your columns, you have had hot days at home, but here, we of the Ninth have sweltered through the blazing hours of days and weeks together, on the bare summit of a shadeless hill, our only comfort being to look down upon smoky Washington and say 'Sorry for the Senators.' Our post, the regimental headquarters, is named in honor of the brave Senator Baker, who made the name heroic at Ball's Bluff; but we get familiar with heroism—we soldiers—and have taken the liberty of calling our earth-works 'the Bakery.' According to our 'Cooke,' however, we shall all be 'done' in about thirty days more. An admirable 'Cooke,' a very 'model cook,' have we; but I cannot speak of his praises without including our other field officers. We *pit* our colonel against 'any other man'; and to say of our lieutenant-colonel that he is 'every inch a soldier,' is to give him only about *seventy-six* inches of justice. Lieutenant-Colonel Powell is a faithful and accomplished officer and has won the respect of all. The three officers are sleeplessly vigilant. Many's the night on which they gird on sword and pistol, mount their chargers, and spur away through the woods. . . Weary and worn, wet with the night dews, they return during the small hours. May the consciousness of having done their duty faithfully, at their own risk, without calling upon anyone to aid them, be their sufficient reward."

Another correspondent describes what he saw at Fort Wagner, the quarters of Company H. He says: "Col. J. A. Haskin—an officer who left his arm at Chepultepec, but who has never left anywhere a certain cheerful manliness which secures the admiration of all who meet him—has charge of the defences north of the Potomac. He often visits our forts, and the other day, just after battalion drill, he asked to see a specimen of our proficiency in handling the 32-pounders. Either because Fort Wagner was close at hand, or because of

Lieut.-Col. John H. Powel.

a dim suspicion in the minds of Colonel Pitman and Lieutenant-Colonel Powell that Company H would as fairly represent the artilleryism of the regiment as any other men, the little fortress commanded by Capt. Henry F. Jenks was chosen as the scene of operations. Two or three hours of field drill, under the sun, hadn't quite taken all the starch out of the Pawtucketers, and they were ready.

"I could the better describe artillery practice were I sure whether the '*cascable*' should first be removed from the muzzle, or the 'tompion' secured to the breech; but ignorant as I am of the nomenclature of big guns and the details of loading and firing them, I could appreciate the fact that the 'babes' of Company H were lively, rather, and that between 'From Battery' and 'Fire,' the intervals were busy and brief.

"It is a mistake to suppose that '32-pounders' weigh only thirty-two pounds; they are in fact much heavier. Several of them will weigh a good deal. On a warm day the metal becomes penetrated with heat, and reflects caloric upon all who approach

A short corporal of Company H has assured me that it is conducive to perspiration to stand long near these guns. He thinks, I suppose, that the *shorter* you stand by them the better. Speaking of size, I may remark that very few of the members of Company H are eminent for personal altitude; indeed, on account of their juvenility of stature and appearance, they are sometimes called 'the babies' by the bearded men of other companies. It may be said, however, by your correspondent, that if infants can handle the thirty-two pounders as they do, what a racket, with handspikes and rammers, there must be, when adults take hold.

"Out of tender compassion, of course, for these 'babes in arms,' the *men* of the Ninth allowed the *boys* of Company H to take the prize from them all, at our recent 'target-shoot.' General orders were, a week before, that each company should keep accurate account of its target practice for the week, and send the record of its five best shots to headquarters for a regimental trial of skill. A prize of five dollars was made up by the field-officers, to give a little more interest to the trial, but the chief incitement was *honor* rather than *gold*. Last Saturday morning the squads of five came in, each man clasping his polished Enfield, while the expectation of V–ictory gleamed upon his sunburnt brow. Target at two hundred yards; three rounds to each man; result, Company H ahead of all others. Then came the trial to decide who of the five of H should get the five of dollars. Out of their fifteen shots at this last, eleven hit the target, and Sergt. Ambrose P. Rice made the closest shooting and won the 'Five.'" Alas! that this gallant soldier, who afterwards re-entered the service, should have perished of starvation in the Andersonville prison pen!

"It is noticeable that there has been less talk about 'weaning the babies' of Company H, since these '*enfants terribles*' have won at the target match for which, and at which, the whole regiment did its best. Captain Jenks takes some pride, also, in the general drill and behavior of the little ones committed to his charge. He will not admit, and few others will affirm, that they can be surpassed in the manual of arms. And it is to the credit of any company to stand comparatively well with them in the Ninth Rhode Island Volunteers. We shall not be unwilling to compare ourselves with our predecessors or our contemporaries, on Dexter Training Ground, or anywhere else, when we get back to the martial city of Providence. In comparative anatomy, philology, entomology and cookery, we may be surpassed by the 'inimitable' punsters of the 'Tenth Rhode Island,' but in drill, dear friends, we venture, humbly, to claim that you can't sustain a spermaceti to us."

"July 30th. General orders were read to-day, to the effect that our term of service will expire August 26th, and that permission is granted to any member of the Ninth Regiment to re-enlist in the new Seventh Rhode Island Regiment, now being organized, and who can thereupon be mustered out of the Ninth and into the Seventh."

Another correspondent says : "Yesterday, I paid a visit to a few of the forts on the east of the city, garrisoned by our gallant boys of the Ninth Rhode Island, and had the pleasure of witnessing a battalion drill. Although these drills are in great disrepute with the men these hot midsummer days, yet they are undoubtedly the basis of their military proficiency. The accuracy of their drill, and general excellence in battalion movements, call forth the warmest commendations of all who are so fortunate as to witness them, and should afford ample compensation to the men of the Ninth, for the physical hardships they have endured in acquiring their present military status."

"The different companies of the regiment are provided with the large Sibley tents, and if the number of tents were only increased,

The Sibley Tent.   The "A" Tent.   The Shelter Tent.

they would be very comfortable; but to have nineteen or twenty men sleeping in one tent in this warm weather seems rather close packing." But the Sibley tent soon had to "go." The armies of the Union were growing rapidly, and the shrinkage of tents began. "In the years 1861 and 1862 most of the troops on taking the field were furnished with the Sibley tent. It was quite a spacious pavilion, large enough almost for a good size circus side show. When pitched it was a perfect cone in shape, the apex being fully twelve feet from the ground. The foot of the centre-pole was held in position by an iron frame, called a tri-pod, the three legs of which straddled out like those of a daddy-long-legs. This straddling attachment seems to have been invented expressly for the soldiers to stumble over when moving about at night. It served its purpose admirably. Five or six and sometimes eight Sibley tents were supplied to a company, and the men were packed like sardines in a box, from fifteen to twenty in each tent. At night they lay with their feet mixed up around the centre-pole, their heads fringing the outer line. Each man's knapsack marked the particular section of ground that belonged to him. When the messes were very full the men slept like a great circular row of spoons, and if one wanted to turn over to give the bones on the other side a chance, he would yell out the order to 'flop' and all would go over together, thus reversing the spoon along the whole line. But the Sibley tents proved to be cumbrous things to handle, and enormously bulky. A regiment with sixty of them and all other baggage in proportion, required a train of wagons sufficient to transport a menagerie. So the Sibley tent had to 'go.' New and larger calls for troops were made, and it became a grave question whether there were in the country enough mules available to haul Sibleys for a million men. The second year of the war the shrinkage began. After the Sibley came the A or Wedge tent—the shape of which is, perhaps indicated clearly enough by its name—and the "Bell" tent, much like it, except that it swelled out at each end, increasing its capacity. Five or six men could be comfortably domiciled in the A tent, and from eight to ten in the Bell. A year or so later the quartermaster gave the thumb-screw another turn and squeezed out the unique shelter tent, which was as near the point of none at all as it was possible to reach. To each man was given a piece of stout cotton cloth, about six feet long and four feet wide; along one edge half of them had a row of buttons, and the other half had buttonholes to correspond. It took two—one of each kind—to make a shelter tent, in which two men were to live and move, and have their being. The shelter-tent was three feet high to the ridge, and the 'spread' at the bottom was about four feet. It was soon dubbed the 'pup' tent, and henceforward to the close of the war, the 'pup' tent became the only protection of our armies from the sun and storm." Lieut.-Col. Hinman's "Corporal Klegg."

The hot summer of 1862 was passed away in the forts manned by the Ninth Rhode Island Volunteers, in regular drills and customary fortification duties, preparing those who afterwards re-enlisted for greater efficiency. Fort life thus proved an excellent school for military order and improvement. The separation of the companies necessarily prevented much regimental intercourse and the monotony of spare hours was broken by such sports as were warranted within the limits of a fortification, and by frequent correspondence with home.

Sergt. H. H. Richardson, of Company H, wrote home:

"Some of us were in Washington yesterday, and I managed to dispatch my business quite early, so that I had no need to hurry back to camp. I sent the team back and devoted the remainder of the day to visiting the Smithsonian Institute, and the halls of Congress. I have become somewhat familiar with the intricate passages about the Capitol so that I can find what I want without difficulty. I find it quite interesting to visit the House and the Senate, and listen to the debates, especially in the Senate, where Vice-President Hamlin is the presiding officer, and where I can hear many of our most noted men, whose names have long been familiar to us. The House of Representatives is the much larger and the popular body. The speaker is Mr. Grow, of Pennsylvania."

Vice-President Hamlin, statesman and governor of Maine, served as United States Senator from that state for several terms, until 1861, when he resigned, having been elected vice-president on the ticket with Abraham Lincoln. He presided over the Senate from March 4, 1861, till March 3, 1865. When elected vice-president with Mr. Lincoln in 1861, he accepted an invitation to visit the latter at Chicago, and, calling on the President-elect, found him in a room alone. Mr. Lincoln arose, and coming toward his guest, said abruptly: "Have we ever been introduced to each other, Mr. Hamlin?" "No sir, I think not," was the reply. "That also is my impression," continued Mr. Lincoln, "but I remember distinctly while I was in Congress to have heard you make a speech in the Senate. I was very much struck with that speech, Senator—particularly struck with it—and for the reason that it was filled, chock up, with the very best kind of anti-slavery doctrine." "Well now," replied Hamlin, laughing, "that is very singular, for my own and first recollection of yourself is of having heard you make a speech in the

'House,' a speech that was so full of good humor and sharp points that I, together with others of your auditors were convulsed with laughter." The acquaintance thus cordially begun, ripened into a close friendship, and it is affirmed that during all the years of trial, war and bloodshed that followed, Abraham Lincoln continued to repose the utmost confidence in his friend and official associate, Hannibal Hamlin.

Galusha A. Grow, statesman, was a native of Connecticut, and had rendered important service in Congress previous to the war for the Union, and helped secure the election of Nathaniel P. Banks as speaker of the House, and the election of Abraham Lincoln as President of the United States, in 1860. At the convening of the first, or extra session of the Thirty-seventh Congress, on July 4, 1861, Mr. Grow was elected speaker of the House of Representatives, and held the position until March 4, 1863, when, on retiring, he received a unanimous vote of thanks, the first vote of the kind given to any speaker in many years.

"I don't see anything in the papers about a scarcity of specie at the North. It is worth ten per cent. premium in Washington. It is now four o'clock, and the order will soon be given for 'Dress Parade,' so I must stop and give my 'whangs' a little polish, and equip myself in all the paraphernalia of war."

"July 23d. An order has just been issued by our general-in-chief, Pope, forbidding all officers or soldiers leaving their camp on any account, without an order from his headquarters. This shuts us up pretty close, and had it been in force when we went on our night expeditions to Washington, we should very likely have been taken prisoners by the provost guard.

"If we remain here very long we shall have to fall back upon General Pope's late general order, July 18, that the troops in the army under his command (and we are) shall draw their subsistence from the region in which they may be quartered. There is no doubt but that we might do that to our hearts' content without robbing a single *Union man*. Twice since we have been here a body of cavalry have moved past our camp scouting, and both times, after being away several days, have brought in several prisoners. Day before yesterday they went by with ten or twelve prisoners, among them one wearing a captain's uniform. He was taken within five or six miles of here.

[A Recent Picture.]

"A court-martial is now in session in the Ninth regiment. Lieut. Francello G. Jillson, of Company G, is the judge-advocate. The court sits Wednesday and Saturday of each week, provided there is any business before it. Several cases have been disposed of for fighting, stealing and sleeping on guard. My duties are similar to those of a sheriff in the civil courts, viz.: To bring in the prisoners for trial and return them to the guard-house and to see that witnesses are in attendance. A few days ago, while the court was in session a most terrific whirlwind came up, bringing with it such dense clouds of dust as to completely conceal from view objects not ten feet distant.

Colonel Pitman at Battalion Drill.

That august body, the court, was scattered, and with the judge left for parts unknown, leaving only your valiant sergeant and six guards, with five prisoners in charge. The tent itself now violently threatened to disperse and follow the court, but by the united efforts of sergeant, guards and prisoners, who all lent a hand, one at each tent-pin, the court-house was saved from demolition. When the lowering elements finally subsided and peace was restored, it was no small task to remove the dust which had accumulated on the premises. Upon the reassembling of the court its members appeared metamorphosed from a group of spruce, blue-uniformed Federal officers into a sorry looking set of fellows, wearing a garb of sackcloth and ashes.

"We are now practising daily on our heavy guns. In the morning and every afternoon we have battalion drill at headquarters, under the immediate orders of Colonel Pitman. We drill in battalion movements three or four hours at a time. The more distant companies are conveyed to and from the field in our army wagons, but we, being quite near, march. Some of the officers appeared at first to be sadly ignorant of military phrases, and the movements executed were something startling." Said one of the boys, "it reminded me of the officer whose last command had been a pair of draft horses on his Pennsylvania farm. Coming with his company to a pit in the road, he electrified them with the order to 'Gee around that hole.' But any little errors of this sort were quickly corrected, and by one officer particularly, with the order, 'as you were, men, my mistake.' We are now making commendable progress in battalion movements, and expect to astonish our friends at home when we return."

A. D. Nickerson, Eleventh Rhode Island Volunteers, says, in his "War Experiences:" "It is not within the province of a private soldier—more especially a 'raw recruit'—to criticise his superiors, and consequently I will not attempt it, notwithstanding this is the 'piping time of peace,' and all fear of the guard-house has forever vanished. I will say, however, that all of the officers named had their peculiarities, but that our lieutenant-colonel was *peculiarly* peculiar; and yet I believe him to have been every inch a soldier—at any rate, there was no such word as fear in his dictionary. He was in command when the regiment came the nearest to being in an engagement, and I fancy I see him now, mounted on his horse and riding at the head of the column, wearing a moth-eaten blouse and an exceedingly dilapidated straw hat, with a very black 'T. D.' clay pipe stuck in his mouth, the bowl downwards. He looked more like the 'cowboy' of modern times than the pictures of military heroes which I used to see in my school-books when I was a boy. This was our lieutenant-colonel—John Talbot Pitman. He had good 'staying qualities.' He never threw up his commission, nor did he die. He remained with us to the last, and rose considerably in the estimation of the men after his appearance at the head of the regiment at the time I have just mentioned. Men everywhere—especially soldiers—admire pluck. Our lieutenant-colonel had pluck, even though his heart seemed somewhat lacking in tenderness. He never winked at any breach of discipline on the part of an officer or a private while he was in command of the regiment. If at times he appeared to have too little consideration for his men, he never failed to exact the fullest measure of consideration for them from all others."

"July 27th. The routine of camp-life has been interrupted by another long march. The forts which the regiment occupy are all new, and had never been furnished with flags, until a few days ago, when one was sent to each fort. Suitable flag-staffs having been erected on Friday last, the staff officers with the companies at headquarters started in the morning fully equipped with twenty rounds of blank cartridges for the fort at the right of the line, receiving as they went along the companies at the several forts, similarly armed and equipped. Upon reaching the most distant fort (manned by Company A, Captain McCloy). Their flag was run up and saluted by the battalion with two volleys of musketry and three cheers for the flag. Captain McCloy's company then fell into line with us and the march was continued to the other extremity of the line, eight or ten miles distant, raising and saluting the flag at each fort in passing until headquarters, Fort Baker, was reached. Here there were two flags, one for the fort, and the other for the colonel's quarters. These were saluted with three volleys of musketry and twenty-one guns from the fort. A rest was then taken for dinner, after which the march was resumed towards the forts at the left, the flag of each of which was raised and saluted as those on the right had been, after which all marched back to their quarters again. The whole march probably exceeded sixteen miles, and as the day was hot, the men were not sorry to 'call it a day' and find themselves back again, and relieved of their heavy equipments. The view from some of the forts was magnificent, that from Fort Greble (Captain McCloy), being particularly fine. Fort Greble is located upon the heights exactly opposite Alexandria, and commands a fine view of the Potomac, both shores, and for many miles each way, including camps and forts innumerable, with the cities of Washington, Alexandria and Georgetown in full view. On my last visit to Washington I found the flags displayed at half mast, and the public buildings closed and draped in respect to the memory of Ex-President Martin Van Buren."

"*Box from home.* One of the best things in the box you so kindly sent us was the cake. There is no danger of its being slighted, as the boys always want to enjoy the boxes together. The only regret I feel about it is that I cannot eat my cake and still have it. When I opened the package, a quarrel immediately followed, the 'corporal' disputing the possession of the cake with me. I suspect nothing but my superior rank saved it. Finally the matter was compromised by my giving him a good piece of it, whereupon he left me in peaceable possession of the remainder."

Foraging. One of the men wrote home to his mother that his bright new bayonet had been stained with Southern blood, and the old lady shuddered at the awful thought. " But," he added, " it wasn't a man I killed, only just a pig."

Foraging.

"Our team has just come in, loaded with bed-sacks, so that we must buy or steal (or else in camp language, 'forage'), some straw to put in them or go without. Some of the boys have recently managed to 'find' some new potatoes, cabbages, cucumbers and other good things, so that the straw will probably soon be found. We are also enjoying some ripe pears which were raised *out of* our garden.

"We are nearing the end of our three months' service in the Ninth regiment. In that period we have seen quite a variety of soldier life, although we have made but few movements. We have held an exposed position in a chain of forts of the eastern defences of Washington, but have encountered no raiding Early or Jackson, so that the results achieved are not conspicuous, but we have stood at the post of duty assigned us, thus relieving older troops for more active service, and we feel that without our history the record of the war for the Union would be incomplete.

"I notice that the Tenth regiment has written more letters to the papers than our regiment. As the two organizations have not met since we parted at Cloud's Mills, Va., we can have no idea what progress they may have made in the art of war, and doubtless each regiment will be prepared to criticize the other pretty sharply when we meet at home. As they are composed of city companies, and rather 'aristocratic' withal, it will perhaps be becoming to *us* while the crowd is admiring *them*."

The duties of chaplain were satisfactorily performed by Rev. Mr. Root, of Lonsdale, R. I. As postmaster of the regiment, also, and in various other ways, he found daily opportunity to render acceptable and appreciated services to the men.

Chaplain N. W. T. Root.

Religious services were maintained through the summer, which were well attended by officers and men.

The bugle sounded the call for public worship, and the men seated themselves upon the ground or stood in groups to hear the preaching of the Gospel, and sing the old, familiar hymns. The chaplain, in his best uniform, stood and prayed fervently for the Divine guidance and protection, while the men listened with heads reverently bowed. After the sermon the chaplain would give out some familiar hymn in our red-covered hymn books.

One of the regiment wrote home, "Last Sabbath Chaplain Root preached a very practical sermon on 'profanity.' After the sermon, the Warren boys agreed among their several messes, that whenever one of them uttered a profane word he should be immediately compelled to go and fetch a pail of water for the cook's galley. As the distance to the camp is about half a mile, it will be readily seen that this was no light task thus voluntarily imposed upon themselves. To their honor, be it said, that they fully kept their agreement (so far as heard from), and I commend their example as worthy of imitation."

"August 3d. We have lost one of our comrades by death. He was a young man belonging in the south part of the State, a member of Company K. His death is supposed to be the result of injuries received from a fall while wrestling at Tennallytown. His remains have been sent home in a metallic burial case, at the expense of the general government. I was frequently at the hospital during his sickness, and should say that he received every care and attention possible. Both our doctors, Morton and King, spared no time or pains to relieve him.

"During the three months' campaign of the Ninth, the health of the regiment was generally good, and but three deaths occurred during its term of service: Hollis Taber, Jr., Company C, died Aug. 13, 1862, in hospital; Sylvester B. Arnold, Company K, died Aug. 2. 1862, in hospital; Joseph H. Simonds, Company I, died September, 1862, in Warren, R. I."

August 24th. The following order was received by the regiment:

HEADQUARTERS DEFENCES OF WASHINGTON.
General Orders No. 2.   WASHINGTON, August 23. 1862.
  [Extract 1.]

In pursuance of orders from the War Department:

1st. All regiments of three months volunteers within this command, will be mustered out of service at the points where they organized respectively. They will be placed *en route* for the rendezvous so as to arrive there one or two days before the expiration of their time.

By order of
Brigadier-General BARNARD,
(Signed)   J. B. SMITH,
A. A. G.

The regiment in accordance with the above order broke up its camps at the forts, Monday morning, August 25th, and took up its line of march for Washington. It left for home in the afternoon and proceeded by rail to New York, with the customary delays at Baltimore and Philadelphia. At New York the regiment was delayed a day and a half for transportation. It was finally conveyed to Fall River by steamer *Metropolis*, and from there was transferred to steamer *Bay State*, and arrived at Providence on the morning of the 29th. Company L, Captain Slocum, was left at Newport. After disembarking the "Ninth" was received by the "Tenth Regiment," and escorted to Exchange place, and dismissed. With one exception the companies belonged to other towns, and left the city in the earliest trains for their respective homes. Companies A and H, of Pawtucket, were handsomely received there, and a bountiful collation provided. A similar reception was given to Company I, in Warren, and a speech of welcome made by Asa M. Gammell, Esq. A few days after, the regiment assembled in Providence, was paid off, and mustered out.

The history of the Ninth Regiment is necessarily brief and uneventful. It is not identified with brilliant deeds, such as attract the gaze and call forth expressions of wonder or admiration. It cannot point to hard fought battles, and exhibit a long list of casualties as evidence of its prowess. But if destitute of these features, impartial history will nevertheless give it a deserved recognition as a reserved power. Important but not dazzling duties were assigned it, and these duties were quietly and faithfully performed. In every respect it was a credit to the State, and worthy of being held in honorable remembrance.

THE SOLDIER'S RETURN.

Tune—*Marching Along.*

BY CAPT. JOHN MCKINLEY, CO. D, 9TH R. I. VOLS.

FROM far distant fort and from white tented plain,
How gladly we come to our old homes again;
Though stained not as heroes in battle's red gore,
We've all done our duty, and none can do more.

To father and mother what joy it imparts
To meet the loved son they have mourned in their hearts;
Where sad looks have lingered, a smile seems to reign,
And friends, weary sighing, are cheerful again.

The lone-hearted maiden and fond loving wife,
That longed for their loved one's return from the strife,
With sister and brother have happy become,
To see the brave soldier return to his home.

Though weary with wandering, 'tis pleasure sincere,
Dear friends, kind neighbors, and kindred, to hear,
In sweet tones of welcome, your voices arise,
As you meet us and greet us with love's beaming eyes.

RHODE ISLAND VOLUNTEERS.

Farewell for a while, now, the fort and the field,
We return to the comforts our firesides can yield,
And gladly forget our brief, weary sojourn
Where friends meet to welcome the soldier's return.

May God speed the time when the battle's loud roar
Shall no longer be heard on Columbia's shore;
When " peace and good will " all our people shall learn,
And no longer prevent the soldier's return.

Chorus:

Homeward we come, proudly homeward we come,
And sweet is the welcome of kind friends at home.
How warmly love's feeling in each heart will burn
When friends fondly welcome the soldier's return.

NINTH R. I. VOLUNTEERS.

FIELD AND STAFF.

Colonel—JOHN T. PITMAN.
Lieutenant-Colonels—JOHN T. PITMAN, JOHN HARE POWEL.
Majors—JOHN T. PITMAN, JOHN HARE POWEL, GEORGE LEWIS COOKE.
Surgeon—LLOYD MORTON.
Assistant-Surgeon—HENRY KING.
Chaplain—N. W. TAYLOR ROOT.
Adjutant—HENRY C. BROWN.
Quartermasters—GEORGE LEWIS COOKE, WILLIAM MCCREADY, JR.
Sergeant-Major—ROBERT FESSENDEN.
Quartermaster-Sergeant—ALFRED O. TILDEN.
Hospital Steward—HENRY E. TYLER.
Commissary-Sergeant—HORACE G. MILLER.

COMPANY OFFICERS.

COMPANY A.

Capt. ROBERT MCCLOY,   1st Lt. ALBERT W. TOMPKINS,
2d Lt. HENRY C. BROWN.

COMPANY B.

Capt. HENRY C. CARD,   1st Lt. J. CLARKE BARBER,
2d Lt. JAMES MCDONALD.

COMPANY C.
Capt. John A. Bowen,   1st Lt. George A. Spink,
2d Lt. William H. Potter.

COMPANY D.
Capt. John McKinley,   1st Lt. John Pollard,
2d Lt. William McCready, Jr.

COMPANY E.
Capt. Isaac Place,   1st Lt. Philip D. Hall,
2d Lt. Nathan Benton.

COMPANY F.
Capt. John M. Taylor,   1st Lt. Randall Holden,
2d Lt. Richard W. Howard.

COMPANY G.
Capt. Charles S. Watson,   1st Lt. Francello G. Jillson,
2d Lt. Henry J. Whitaker.

COMPANY H.
Capt. Henry F. Jenks,   1st Lt. Frank Allen,
2d Lt. George A. Bucklin.

COMPANY I.
Capt. Samuel Pearce,
1st Lt. George Lewis Cooke,   2d Lt. William H. Surgens,
1st Lt. William H. Surgens,   2d Lt. Horace G. Barrus.

COMPANY K.
Capt. James R. Holden,   1st Lt. William H. Gardner,
2d Lt. George H. Burnham.

COMPANY L.
Capt. John Hare Powel,   1st Lt. William R. Landers,
Capt. Benjamin L. Slocum,   2d Lt. William H. King.

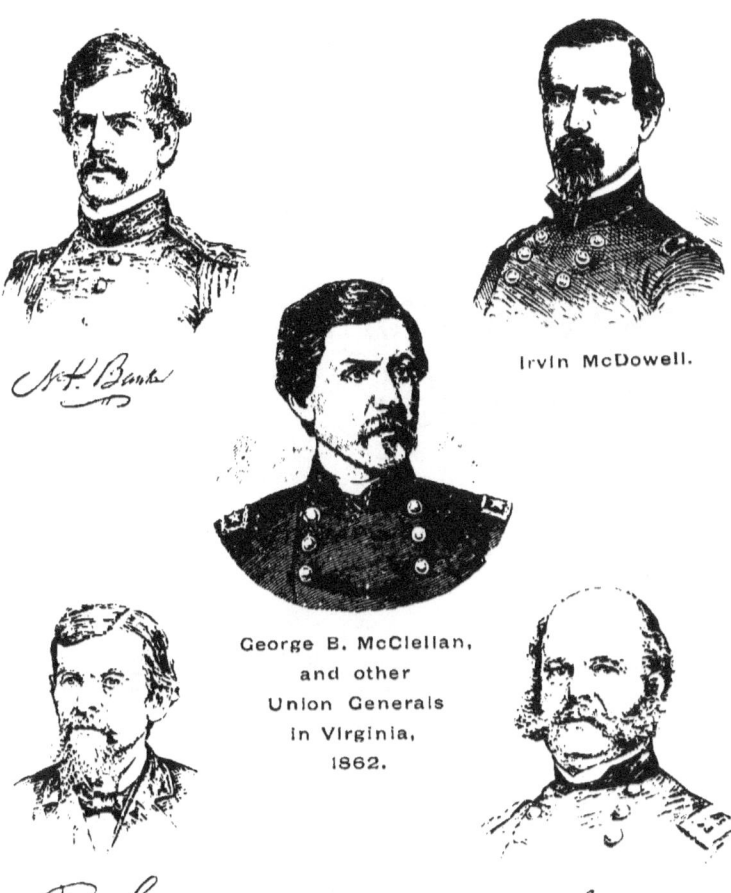

George B. McClellan, and other Union Generals in Virginia, 1862.

The Tenth Regiment

R. I. VOLUNTEERS.

The White House.

THE Tenth Regiment Rhode Island Volunteers was principally recruited from an organization of the citizens of Providence, banded together for State defence, and known as the First Regiment Rhode Island National Guards. On the 23d of May, 1862, the following special order was issued from the Adjutant General's office of the State, viz.:

Commandants of the several military companies of the State, will immediately assemble their respective commands, at their usual place of rendezvous, and report one company, minimum standard from each organization, to the office of the Adjutant-General, for three months' service in Washington.

Signed,   E. C. MAURAN,
Adjutant-General.

A meeting of the officers of the several companies comprising the "First Regiment Rhode Island National Guards," was immediately held, and the following resolution was unanimously passed:

RESOLVED, That Col. James Shaw, Jr., is hereby requested to offer to His Excellency the Governor, the services of the organization known as the 'First Regiment Rhode Island National Guards,' as now officered and organized, in response to the call for service made by him as above.

Signed, ELISHA DYER,
Commanding Co. B, being Fourth Ward Drill Corps,
Chairman.

A reply was promptly received from the Governor, accepting the services of the regiment according to the terms of the resolution.

"On the night of the 25th," says Colonel Shaw (in his official report to Governor Sprague the following October), "the despatch announcing the defeat of General Banks was received, and at one o'clock on the 26th, I received from you an order to immediately organize the National Guards. I at once ordered the several companies to meet at their respective armories at 9 o'clock, A. M., and at seven P. M., of the same day, had the honor to report to you six hundred and thirteen men ready for duty. As I had seen no service in the field, and there was a prospect of immediate active service, I preferred to waive the right to command the regiment, according to the terms on which you had accepted it, and requested your Excellency to appoint some one who had received a military education as its commander. I was further directed by you to send in a list of company officers, and was informed that the quartermaster would be at my service at daylight the following morning.

"At 2.15 P. M., the next day, by my order, the regiment was paraded on Exchange place, armed, clothed and equipped,—in less than thirty hours from the time it was first ordered to meet."

General Orders No. 29, Adjutant-General's Office, Providence, May 26, 1862, announced that the National Guards of Providence will be organized as the Tenth Rhode Island Volunteers; Capt. Zenas R. Bliss, United States Army, Colonel; James Shaw, Jr., Lieutenant-Colonel.

Colonel Bliss being obliged to remain at home for a day or two, on account of his father's death, the following order was issued, viz. :

Col. Z. R. Bliss.

Special Orders,   STATE OF RHODE ISLAND, ETC.,
No. 29.   ADJUTANT-GENERAL'S OFFICE.
     PROVIDENCE, May 26, 1862.

Lieutenant-Colonel Shaw is hereby ordered to have the baggage belonging to his regiment at the Stonington Railroad Freight Depot, at 11 A. M., on Tuesday, the 27th instant.

You will also order your companies to report punctually at the Stonington Depot, at 3 o'clock, P. M., same date.

By order of the Commander-in-Chief,

AUG. HOPPIN,
Assistant Adjutant-General.

"We left Providence," wrote a member of the regiment, "Tuesday afternoon, and were received everywhere on the route with great enthusiasm." The impression seemed to prevail that Washington was safe now that the "Tenth" was on its way. Certainly no regiment ever left the State more promptly in response to the Governor's call, and no regiment hastened to the rescue of the capital under a more solemn sense of duty.

Lieut.-Col. James Shaw, Jr.

Some of the best citizens of Providence were members of this regiment from almost every rank and profession. There was the merchant, the lawyer and the banker; the mechanic and tradesman, with the clerk from behind his counter. There were the students, from the college and high school, led by that grand man, Capt. Elisha Dyer, formerly governor of the State, whose former position gave increased value to the service now rendered. It was the general desire and expectation that Col. James Shaw, Jr., should be the colonel of the regiment, but he chose to be content with deserving the position, and declining the honor in favor of a worthy officer who had seen service.

"The regiment assembled on Exchange place," wrote Lieut. Charles F. Phillips, of Company B, "on Tuesday afternoon, May 27th, at three o'clock, and about five o'clock it filed into the cars. During the interim, while standing in line, we were all pretty well drenched by a heavy shower of rain, besides being bent well nigh double by the unaccustomed weight of our equipments. Some one pointed out a stranger, of fine soldierly physique, and face well bronzed by service with the regulars in Texas, as our future colonel, and an efficient commander he afterwards proved, but as we were then in *blissful* ignorance of his merits, we were hardly disposed to look upon him with favor at first." Colonel Bliss was detained at home on account of his father's death, and Lieutenant-Colonel Shaw assumed command of the regiment, and directed its movement to Washington.

The commander of Company A, was Capt. William E. Taber, a young and efficient officer, who had seen service with the First Rhode Island Regiment. At the head of Company B, marched Capt. Elisha Dyer, one of the war governors of Rhode Island. The men are few who at his age and with his responsibilities, would have surrendered the comforts of home for the arduous duties of the camp.

Capt. Elisha Dyer.

Within eight hours time from the opening of the armory, he paraded his company of a hundred and twenty-five men up Broadway and down Westminster street. The other captains were: Jeremiah Vose, Company C; William S. Smith, Company D; Hopkins B. Cady, Company E; Benjamin W. Harris, Company F; A. Crawford Greene, Company G; Christopher Duckworth, Company H; William M. Hale, Company I; G. Frank Low, Company K (Second Lieutenant First Regiment). Most of the officers of the "Tenth" were citizens of Providence, well known to the men, and good order and discipline prevailed.

Resuming, Lieutenant Phillips wrote: "As soon as the regiment had passed into the cars, guards were stationed with strict orders to allow no one to enter or leave the train. Soon a stout, well built man, with eyes and hair as black as the raven, and a countenance indicating a generous disposition, attempted to enter one of the cars. The guard disputed his entrance at the point of the bayonet. 'I am the Governor's aide,' he said with considerable vigor. 'And my orders are imperative,' as firmly insisted the guard. Here was a quandary. Captain Dyer's sergeant was attending to business closely, but after further parleying, the necessary order came, and Col. Byron Sprague of his excellency's staff was allowed to pass in. A few moments later the final commands were given, the conductor gave the signal for departure, and the long train moved out of the depot amid loud cheering by the assembled crowd and a general waving of hats and handkerchiefs."

To such a regiment might be fitly applied the words of Abraham Lincoln when, in a message to Congress, he said: "There are regiments in the national service which could fill with dignity and honor, every important place in the central administration of the national government."

Lieut. Winthrop DeWolf, of Company D, wrote: "The first realizing sense of the rough work we had undertaken, I think, came over us at Groton, when for the first time we underwent 'rations.' At the gangway leading to the boat stood the commissary and his assistants with a barrel before them. Our unsuspecting recruits marched up in single file with open haversacks, when instead of the neat package of sandwiches and sponge cake which most of them expected to be deposited therein, the aforesaid assistant disappeared for an instant, head and shoulders into the barrel, then rising suddenly crammed into the opening a greasy mass, which might be meat or bone, as it happened. The old soldiers (First Regiment men are old soldiers now), looked doubtfully at it from the corners of their eyes, the younger members received it with enthusiasm, as the first trial of patriotism, and retained it till far out in the Sound, when a certain unsteady motion taking possession of the steamer, they might be observed stealing to the guards and quietly dropping it overboard. The floor of the saloon was now assigned the men for sleeping quarters. From New York we took the Amboy boat, and arrived at Philadelphia about five P. M., of Wednesday. A capital supper was awaiting us at the rooms of the Cooper Volunteer Relief Asso-

Cooper Volunteer Refreshment Building.

ciation, and, not to be forgotten, plenty of water and towels. This association has fed since the war commenced more than 200,000 hungry, way-worn men. Overhead are the hospital rooms. Two of our men being sick were taken thither, and treated with every possible attention. If blessings were shingles, these association rooms would be new roofed every week; yet I am told its charities are supported by the poor, and not the rich of that great city; that the subscriptions to it are mostly of one and two dollars; that market-women and small store-keepers and countrymen strain to the utmost their scant resources to spread that hospitable table."

The city of Philadelphia lay in the channel of the great stream of Union volunteers from New England, New York and New Jersey, that commenced flowing abundantly early in May, 1861. These soldiers crossing New Jersey and the Delaware river at Camden, were landed at the foot of Washington avenue, where wearied and hungry, they often vainly sought for sufficient refreshments in the bakeries and groceries in the neighborhood before entering the cars for Baltimore. One morning the wife of a mechanic living near, commiserating the situation of some soldiers who had just arrived, went out with her coffee pot and a cup, and distributed its contents among them. That generous hint was the germ of a wonderful system of relief for the passing soldiers which was immediately developed in that city. Some benevolent women of the vicinity, imitating their patriotic sister, formed themselves into a committee for the regular distribution of coffee to the soldiers on their arrival. Gentlemen of the neighborhood also interested themselves in procuring other supplies, and, for a few days, they were dispensed under the shade of trees, in front of the cooper shop of William M. Cooper, on Otsego street near Washington avenue. Then the shop itself, generously offered for the purpose by Mr. Cooper, was used for the refreshment of the soldiers, and very soon whole regiments were fed there, at tables supplied by the contributions of the citizens of Philadelphia, and were waited on by their wives and daughters. The first regiment supplied was Colonel Blenker's (German) Rifles, more than a thousand strong, who breakfasted there on the 27th of May, 1861. A hospital was also established for sick and wounded soldiers. The "Cooper Shop" not proving spacious enough, other places of refreshment were afterwards opened. This benevolent work was continued all through the period of the War of the Rebellion; and to the immortal honor of Mr. Cooper and the citizens of Philadelphia, it must be recorded that they liberally supplied these saloons with ample materials to give a bountiful meal during the four years of war to almost 1,200,000 Union soldiers. Over 600,000 were fed at the "Cooper Shop" at an expense of ten to fifteen cents per meal. It caused the loss of Mr. Cooper's business, and reduced the family to severe straits. To the women especially, who devoted themselves to the service of preparing the meals, and waiting upon this vast host of the defenders of the Union, belong the choicest blessings of their country. At all hours of the day and night, these self-sacrificing heroines—to whom a little signal gun, employed for the purpose, announced the approach of a regiment or a company of troops,—would repair to the saloon, and with the greatest cheerfulness dispense the generous bounty of the citizens of Philadelphia. This noble work continued till August, 1865, when peace had been restored, and the flag of the republic was waving unmolested over every acre of its domain. Without disparagement to other cities (for all did noble work), it may with propriety be said, that in labors of genuine benevolence and generous giving for the comfort of the soldiers of the great Union army, the citizens of Philadelphia stand peerless.

Resuming, Lieutenant DeWolf wrote: "The night's ride to Baltimore was ludicrously uncomfortable, but with the sunrise we left the cars and marched through the debatable land unmolested. Cartridges had been previously served to one or two companies, but no disloyal word or act gave excuse for their employment. The southern sympathizers had disappeared from the streets and the 'stars and stripes' were flying from the public buildings. All the forenoon we lazed about the railroad station, while some officers were dispatched to Washington to report our arrival.

"They received at first the startling order to join the advance near Richmond at once, but when the locating officer came to understand that we were 'emergency' men, ordered to the defence of Washington, we were permitted to pursue our journey to the capital. To this end we were furnished with a few passenger cars and fourteen or fifteen freight and cattle cars, into which we tumbled after the manner of our cloven footed predecessors, whose aroma, bovine, porcine and equine, yet lingered lovingly about the spot. The sun was intensely hot, with no wind. In our car some air was obtained by bringing a pair of 'whangs' (army shoes, a trifle broader than they are long), to bear upon the boards at either ends, but the next car to us being completely iron-clad, roof and sides, reduced its inmates to a semi-fluid state. One man declared that the water 'sizzled' in his canteen, while the eggs bought in Baltimore were found to be handsomely baked upon his arrival at Washington.

"But at length we did arrive. Before us stood invitingly a row of wooden barracks, seemingly filled already to their utmost capacity with soldiers. Into these we filed and deposited our accoutrements. The floor that night presented a curious appearance. A conglomerate pavement of sleeping men, reclining every way, dovetailed, criss-crossed, head and heels, pillowed on knapsacks and cartridge boxes, heaving with the restless tides of slumber, from which arose the gleaming stacks of muskets, festooned with haversacks and canteens. So completely was the floor covered that the unfortunate guard, *quorum parva pars fui*, coming heavy-eyed from their posts, sought in vain for a vacant spot, and were finally compelled to spread their blankets upon the ground outside. A little after midnight, a man sprang to his feet in a distant corner of the room shouting, 'The enemy are upon us! Seize your arms, boys!'

"Instantly five hundred men awoke and commenced scrambling for their arms and equipments. A scene of more perfect confusion can hardly be imagined.

"One dim lantern shed an uncertain light over the room. Now and then a stack of muskets came down with a crash to help matters. Few were wide awake enough to reason about the grounds of the alarm, and the officers' shouts went for nothing in the hurley-burley. When quiet had been a little restored, it was discovered that the man who started the alarm had been suffering from nightmare. He could not be persuaded in the morning of the excitement he had created."

A few years later the author found himself uncomfortably locked up in a stateroom with a Baltimore man who had a similar attack on board a steamer on Lake Champlain: "I was on my way home from Montreal and arrived late one evening at Burlington, Vt., where I took the night boat for Whitehall. It was crowded with passengers, and every stateroom was engaged. As I sat watching the crowd and looking about for a convenient camping spot on the floor, I recalled the night in 1862 when the 'Tenth Rhode Island boys' crowded the decks of the steamer *Plymouth Rock*, on the way to the capital. Then, as now, the staterooms were all *taken*, but we cheerfully camped down 'on deck' with our knapsacks for pillows, and after receiving our first rations, we dropped off to sleep, dreaming of the comforts of home and of the thin assurances made us, when we put our names down, that nothing but *the best* was good enough for us, and that the best government upon the face of the earth would take care that we were supplied with every good thing.

"While musing thus, a mild-appearing individual approached me and said, 'I'm sorry that you are unable to obtain a stateroom. I am traveling alone to my home in Baltimore, and you are welcome to the upper berth of my room if you'll accept it.'

"If I had been on my way home with the boys of the 'Tenth' at the end of our campaign, I might have replied, thank you, my friend, but we've got used to it, and prefer to sleep on the floor, but reflecting that I was several years older than I was then, and much heavier than when I was much lighter, I gladly accepted the kind offer of a soft bed from the Baltimore gentleman, and retired early, the suggestion occurring to me, at the last moment, as I was composing myself to rest, that perhaps it was a trifle risky being locked up for the night in a small stateroom with an entire stranger.

"Soon all was quiet on the steamer. The lights burned low in the saloon, and all were apparently asleep, when suddenly, about the hour of midnight, I was aroused from my slumbers by a terrific yell from the Baltimore gentleman in the lower berth. A moment later he was on his feet, shouting 'Murder! thieves! robbers!' and tearing about like a madman." Mrs. Partington said: "Some people are more courageous than others, and some ain't! But for my part," she added, "I think it requires a good deal of courage to wake up in the middle of the night and find a strange man standing horizontally by your bedside!" "As soon as I could speak I called out, what's the matter with you? but received no soothing reply, and the startling conviction forced itself upon me that I was locked up with a lunatic. Suddenly, in his frenzy, the Baltimore man turned and started for the stateroom window. Here was my opportunity. With a bound I leaped from the upper berth to the floor, unlocked the door and rushed out into the saloon with the Baltimore man in hot pursuit. A crowd had already gathered, and he was quickly secured. Anxious faces, some in night-caps, might be seen peering out of their stateroom doors. Meanwhile the cause of the alarm attempted to explain that it was only one of his periodical spells of nightmare, although he guessed it must have been an unusually bad spell; no one need be alarmed on his account, as he was entirely harmless at such times. With this assurance quiet was at length restored."

Thursday night, May 29th, the Tenth Regiment slept in the barracks in Washington. "Early the next morning," wrote James F. Field, of Company B, "we packed our knapsacks, and at eleven o'clock started on the march, halting for some time at the Capitol for orders. The day was excessively warm, and as we moved on, the dust was so thick that we could scarcely see the left of the line from our position on the right. I was much disappointed in the general appearance of the city, as we saw it from Pennsylvania avenue, the main thoroughfare. The public buildings were all on a grand scale, such as the Capitol, White House, Patent Office (where the First Rhode Island Regiment was stationed a year ago), the Post-Office Building, and the Postmaster-General's residence, but the private residences were not so attractive. When we reached the White House, we loaded our knapsacks, at the suggestion of Governor Sprague, into the baggage wagons of the Sixty-third Indiana Regiment, which were following us, which proved a great relief. We were further allowed to carry 'arms at will' and take our own 'step.' Thus we marched on, through Georgetown and beyond, six miles or more, till we came to the village of Tennallytown near our present camp."

"After the hot, two hours' march," resumed Lieutenant Phillips, "the regiment halted, the right resting near the village hotel. Suddenly the black clouds which had been gathering, were rent with vivid flashes of lightning, and poured down their fierce vials of wrath upon us, the invaders of 'Maryland, my Maryland,' till we were soaked through and through. The officers had gone into the hotel to pay their respects to Gen. Samuel P. Sturgis, to whose brigade we had been assigned.

"The rain poured; some of the men broke ranks, and tried shelter under the veranda. General Robbins stalked across the street with measured dignity, and, whilst the rain formed rivulets down his back exclaimed: 'For God's sake, sergeant, keep the men in line, this is General Sturgis's headquarters!'

The men had great respect for General Sturgis, knowing that he was a regular, the second in command to General Lyon, at Wilson's Creek, and with his raw troops from Kansas had fought with great valor. Not a man was hazardous enough to leave the line after this. Corbin, on the extreme right, one of the tall men, slim and straight, and too thin it was declared for even a shadow, as well as others of 'old Brown,' amused themselves

A Wet Day in Camp.

by emptying the water out of their shoes. In the meantime Lieutenant-Colonel Shaw had seized a building at the junction of the roads, in spite of protests and threats, and prepared a hasty cup of coffee for the command. Upon the orders of General Robbins, Company B was ordered to pass in single file by the open windows, receive a cup of coffee, and go into the woods upon the left and unload the wagons. It was a heavy task, but soon accomplished. The camp fixings, including the knapsacks, were sorted and distributed to company quarters. As there was neither saw, hammer, or chisel, we had to break open the cases with uplifted boulders, and with jackknives only we whittled, fitted and wedged the handles of the picks in their places. As the darkness settled down, the conical peaks of the Sibley tents popped up like mushrooms, and considering that very few of the men had ever helped pitch a tent or ever stood under one, the work was marvellous. A member of Company B was commanded to take a detail and pitch the general's headquarters near the burying ground fence. This was a wall tent, soaked with water, and nearly as large as the meeting-house near by. The soil composed of gravel and boulders, was almost impenetrable to the pick, but the work was accomplished, dark as it was, to the satisfaction of all concerned. Upon returning to quarters, we were unable to find knapsack, blanket or haversack. Every inch of the tent was occupied by men drenched to the skin; some were counting the blisters upon their hands, and others trying to improvise a cup of coffee. Poor McGlaulin was doing his best to build a fire from the green wood chopped after we came into camp. The sergeant sought refuge in the windowless church, and slept upon the wet floor without pillow or blanket. At length, the morning dawned, and the sun, as if to welcome us, touched up the walls of our canvas city with golden hues, while the birds, never happier, warbled their morning songs from the tree-tops above us. Some of the first orders were to open the quartermaster's stores and mount guard. The camp was further laid out by measure, and rightly named Camp Frieze, in honor of the Quartermaster-General of Rhode Island. It occupies the northwesterly slope of the hill, on which the village of Tennallytown clings with feeble grasp. The regular routine of military drill now began, and was strictly enforced from that day."

CAMP FRIEZE, TENTH RHODE ISLAND VOLUNTEERS, JUNE, 1862.

THE TENTH REGIMENT

HEADQUARTERS, COLLEGE VILLA,
General Orders, No. 1.   TENNALLYTOWN, D. C., May 31, 1862.

1st. The commanding officers of each regiment, battery, battalion or detachment assigned to the command of Brigadier-General Sturgis, will make consolidated morning reports daily to the commanding general at headquarters, College Villa, Tennallytown, D. C.

2d. The adjutant of each command, assigned as above, will report in person to the commanding general, every day at 11 o'clock A. M.

By order of Brigadier-General STURGIS.

HENRY R. MIGHELS,
Captain and A. A. G.

HEADQUARTERS, TENTH R. I. VOLUNTEERS,
Circular: June 3, 1862.

For the present water will be obtained from the spring for the use of the camp. It has been freely tested by companies encamped here previously, and is reported perfectly good.

ZENAS R. BLISS,
Colonel Commanding.

HEADQUARTERS, TENTH R. I. VOLUNTEERS,
Circular: June 3, 1862.

Divine service will be held at six o'clock this evening, at which the officers, non-commissioned officers and privates, are invited to be present. Such of the men of the several companies who desire to attend will assemble at a quarter before six upon their respective company parades, and be conducted under the charge of a non-commissioned officer to the grove in front of the camp.

ZENAS R. BLISS,
B. F. THURSTON,   *Colonel Commanding.*
Lieutenant and Adjutant.

HEADQUARTERS, COLLEGE VILLA,
COL. ZENAS R. BLISS,   June 6, 1862.
Commanding Tenth R. I. Vols.

SIR: You will please detail ten men of your command for picket duty tonight, said ten men to be accompanied by a non-commissioned officer.

This arrangement to be observed until further orders.

By order of Brigadier-General STURGIS.

HENRY R. MIGHELS,
Captain and A. A. G.

Meanwhile the alarm for the safety of the capital had slowly subsided. Stonewall Jackson, after accomplishing his mission of alarming Washington, and saving Richmond, by preventing the junction of McDowell and McClellan, rapidly retreated down the Valley, burning the bridges after him, and successfully eluded the combined pursuit of Fremont, Banks, and McDowell, with 60,000 men.

Taking advantage of the confusion which had been created, the Confederate army defending Richmond under Gen. Joseph E. Johnston, made a furious and successful attack upon the left wing of General McClellan's army, May 31st, at Fair Oaks, but the day following, June 1st, it turned into disaster and rout, which sent them back to Richmond in a panic. General Johnston was severely wounded, and General Lee assumed the chief command.

After Fair Oaks there was a pause of several weeks in active operations in front of Richmond. Rain storms of great severity, and Virginia mud, rendered further advance almost impossible. All was quiet also on the Potomac, among the troops around the capital, and the regular routine of camp-life continued at Camp Frieze, with its daily drills and details for guard and picket duty.

May 29th, a second detachment for the regiment was sent forward under command of Colonel Bliss, and arrived at camp on Saturday evening, June 1st. The regiment was assigned to the brigade of General Sturgis, and was mustered into the service of the United States, by Adjutant-General Thomas, June 9th.

Capt. William M. Hale, Company I, wrote: "Camp Frieze, Tennallytown, D. C., June 3d. The country is safe again. The gallant Tenth is on the tented field, or rather a side hill covered with beautiful oaks, so that perhaps it can hardly be called a field. At any rate here we are in Tennallytown, and if you know where that is, your knowledge of geography is more extensive than mine was a week ago, for I must confess that in the whole course of my travels, the name of this ancient borough had never before greeted my ears. And in fact I find that even the residents here are uncertain as to the precise locality. The postmaster says it is in 'the District.' The oldest inhabitants say it is in Maryland, and the younger inhabitants don't care a copper where it is.

"As to the personnel of the town, little requires to be said. A few barns and hungry looking houses straggle along a lean and hungry looking street. A tavern and blacksmith's shop confront each other, and are flanked by the post-office. In the rear of the latter and at the entrance of our camp, stands the village church, never, from appearances, a very notable structure, but now, alas! sadly dilapidated, and converted to other uses than originally intended. I am not honored with the acquaintance of the worthy parson who formerly ministered to the wants of the little flock that gathered within its walls, but I can vouch that his ministrations were not more acceptable to them than are those of his successor, our worthy quartermaster, to the more numerous flock over whom he is called to preside.

"Do you know what a ration is? If not, Private Stiness, of Company I (since promoted to corporal), can tell you, for I saw him receive one. It consisted of four bones, gross weight two and a quarter pounds, and some meat, gross weight the same, minus the two. The bones formerly constituted what are technically called the 'chuck ribs' of some quadruped, genus, species and sex unknown. The corporal has carried those bones in his haversack ever since. He says he started with the intention of leaving his 'bones' on the battlefield if necessary, and he is looking for a field that he thinks capable of holding them. He is the feature of the company, stands five feet eleven, in army socks, and girths a little less, and is known among the comrades as the 'little giant.' His first pair of army drawers reached to his chin. This he considers very economical, as it saves the necessity of shirts, and enables him to cut up those useful articles into pocket handkerchiefs. When he shoulders arms, he looks like a pumpkin with a bean-pole attachment, and, at charge bayonets, a private is detailed to hold up the muzzle, in which position they resemble a miniature battering ram with the point sharpened."

H. T. Chase, of Company D, wrote June 3d: "They gave us rations of salt meat and pork in Washington which would almost motion to us when to come to dinner. We have eaten so much salt pork of late that we are inclined to speak in grunts, prick up our ears, and perform other animal demonstrations." Another man said he had some hard-tack that was marked "B. C." "Still I find no fault," wrote Chase. "These things have now changed for the better. I am well and good natured, but I never had so tough an experience in the same time in my life. This afternoon I saw a man sitting on a stump getting his hair cut. So I took my turn and went through the same operation. Charge, five cents. The barber belongs to one of the companies. He said he left a wife and two little children at home, but would not let his wife bring the children down to the cars, 'For,' said he, as the *tears started*, 'I could not stand it.' Saw a southern woman to-day give her little girl a penny. On my asking her what she would do with it, the mother replied, 'Oh, she will get *shet* of it!'"

Lieutenant DeWolf, of Company D, June 3d, wrote: "The elevation of our camp is considerable, for it appears to be down hill for three miles in every direction, the air is deliciously pure, water good and plentiful. To the north and west a line of gray mist marks the valley of the Potomac, whose rapid stream is confined at present to its summer bed, a deep, rocky channel of 150 feet, on the east side of which a bottom 500 yards, strewn with huge boulders, marks the width of the winter torrents. The point nearest to us is Chain Bridge, three miles distant, whose approaches are strictly guarded. Just above, in the eddies of the rapids, your correspondent, with a couple of friends, dove and splashed and dabbled, the other day, attaining to that beatific condition so rare with a soldier, perfect cleanliness.

"It was Sunday. Shadows from the dense Virginia forests overhung the stream. We had no Sabbath services, no chaplain then, but if the duty of godliness met no outward recognition, the very next injunction of the apostle was most scrupulously observed.

"A few words will tell how we got here. One night in the Washington barracks satisfied us all. We fell in with alacrity to march anywhere. The day was warm, so that the order to pile knapsacks and overcoats into the wagons was a great relief. On passing through the city, many friends from Providence waved their hats from sidewalk and windows, while those of us who were here last year recognized more than one familiar face among the Washingtonians. Governor Sprague accompanied us, and Messrs. Anthony, Browne and Sheffield of our Congressional delegation, have been constant in their attentions to our regiments. As we passed along the question was heard on every side, 'What regiments are those?'

"'Ninth and Tenth Rhode Island?'

"'When were you enlisted?'

"'Monday morning, and started Tuesday afternoon,' — of course we could not help adding — '800 more are on the way.'

"'Good Lord!' ejaculated one by-stander, 'how many men have you got in Rhode Island? I thought you was played out long ago.'

"The Secretary of War is reported to have said that at the rate the 'emergency men' were coming in, he should soon have 500,000, and he believed 100,000 of them would be from Rhode Island.

"The march of six miles to this place, commencing with dust and ending with mud and a hard rain, was rather severe upon a few of the men; but the next morning found them as well as ever.

"Company D were fortunate enough to obtain dry quarters in a house. The next day was occupied in laying out the camp and pitching the tents. The Tenth Regiment occupies the side next the road, the Ninth west of them, and the battery just north of the latter. The men are provided with tents of the Sibley pattern, intended for fifteen each, but made to hold twenty-two the first night. The men sleep in a circle, heads outward, and at night, when every man is in his place, the resemblance of the group to a huge wheel, with the pile of muddy feet in the centre for a hub, every man a spoke, and the continuous line of knapsacks around the outside for the felloe, is decidedly striking. The officers have wall tents facing the streets upon which their several companies reside.

"But, oh, the first guard mounting and posting of sentinels! In after time you shall hear our youthful sergeants and corporals telling their grandchildren, with a quiet laugh, of their blunders and perplexities on that rainy, dismal night. But at length the guards are posted. My beat is along a narrow lane skirting a little churchyard. The edifice itself, shabby and windowless, is filled with commissary stores. Its rafters echo anything but the voice of prayer. Up and down I pace in the dreary rain, shielding the lock of my musket as well as I can in my rubber capote. A figure approaches, dimly visible in the shadows.

"'Halt! Who goes there?'

"'A friend, with the countersign.'

"'Advance, friend, and give the countersign.'

"The talisman is whispered at the point of my bayonet, and the figure passes on. Now and then I hear a challenge at some distant point. The reply is not satisfactory, and the call is passed from guard to guard.

"'Corporal of the guard—post 17!'

"The sleepy officer stumbles through the mud to post 17, and the case is soon settled.

"In the silence I resume my beat. Over the low paling, in a grass grown corner of the enclosure, half a dozen headstones, yellow and streaked with rain, are visible. Round about the resting place where

'The rude forefathers of the hamlet sleep,'

has been heard the bustle of great camps, the tread of armies for more than a year, yet they slumber on. Their march is over. They have passed beyond the camps of life, and long ago heard the challenge of the other world sentinels. Had they the countersign?

"As I pace my lonely round, I hear a bustle in the guard tent. "'Third relief, turn out. Turn out!'

"Presently they come, the challenge is exchanged. I am off duty for four hours, and fling myself to sleep upon the wet straw of the guard-tent, wedged in among twenty-two men, reeking with rain and perspiration, and do sleep soundly,—so good night."

Corp. George T. Baker, of Company B, says: "The members of the Tenth Rhode Island were indeed in a sorry plight the first night in camp. They were without shelter in a dreary rainstorm, and darkness came on before the tents arrived in camp, when all hands, although wet and tired, went to work with a will, putting them up. Company E, Capt. Hopkins B. Cady, were detailed for picket duty about a mile in advance of our position. At a late hour, after the camp was still, Capt. Elisha Dyer, of Company B, made a visit to each tent to inquire after the welfare of his men. Stopping at the High School headquarters, he asked, 'Can I do anything for you, men?' 'Nothing, thank you, captain,' was the courteous reply, when some joker bent on mischief, added, 'We wouldn't mind having a candle, captain!' This proved too much for even the gravity of the captain, and he exclaimed, 'God bless you, men, do you think you're in a hotel?'"

Capt. A. Crawford Greene, Company G, wrote, June 5th: "Our regiments have had no time to perfect themselves in drill, neither have we received our necessary quartermaster stores. We are sadly in need of clothing, as many of our men wore the poorest garments they had, expecting to exchange them for the government uniform. The rations served have also been short of the allowance, but on the whole we are getting along well, and the mass of the men are contented. The health of the regiment is good, and with our present rations we may safely say that it will continue. (At present they consist of salt junk, bread, and coffee without milk.) The story of the poisoning of one of the men of Company G, in Baltimore, is entirely incorrect. We did not know but that we might have some trouble in that city, and distributed ten rounds of ball-cartridges, but we had no occasion to use them; on the contrary we were served with a good collation by the Baltimore Union Soldiers' Relief Association. One of the pickets of the New York Sixty-ninth Regiment, which is encamped near us, was shot while on duty, Friday evening last. The scoundrel who committed the deed was arrested and sent to Washington on Saturday. He was a desperate looking fellow, and made his boast that he had shot six Union soldiers before. May he meet the retribution he so justly deserves.

"The tented fields loom up on almost every side. Quite a large number of forts also surround us. The almost hourly belching forth of their numerous weapons of destruction give ample assurance that they are well manned and ready for action,

The sharp crack of the picket's rifle enlivens the monotony of camp-life. We shall now commence the regular routine of drill, which will keep us fully employed. At present a large number of the secessionists have left the neighborhood, and retreated to a safer locality further down in Dixie. The houses are generally left in charge of one or two slaves. The country is very rich and fertile, but owing to the cold dry spring vegetation is rather backward. The stock of grass is very heavy, the farmers tell us the yield being larger by far than last year. Quartermaster Cook is occupying the meeting-house of the town for our stores, to the disappointment of those who have been in the habit of appropriating it for religious purposes. We learn, however, that it is to be cleared out and that our beloved chaplain, Rev. Mr. Clapp, is to occupy it for religious services on the coming Sabbath. So far as our knowledge extends, there are a large number of Christian people in our regiments, and by the services held here nightly, we think they are determined to improve the opportunity for showing it, and when we return home we hope to be better men than when we came out."

James F. Field, wrote Sunday, June 1st: "Friday night, the 30th, was our first in camp after the march from Washington. It was dark and rainy, and I slept on the ground in an old building, which looked as though it had been formerly a school-house or a church. The next day, Saturday, we had the job of pulling down our tents and putting them up again. The company tents are now in parallel rows, all facing one way with the officers' tents at the head of the rows. Just as our work was about completed a battery of ten guns came thundering along from Washington, bound for Harper's Ferry (threatened by Stonewall Jackson). It is about forty-five miles southwest of here. They reported that they left the second detachment of the Ninth and Tenth Regiments at the White House, and that they would be here in about an hour. This caused quite a thrill of joy in the camp. As soon as we were relieved, quite a number of us started up the road to meet them. Soon the line appeared in sight, and as they came up I was surprised to find several acquaintances, among them five from the High School. It had just commenced raining, and we welcomed them with a great deal of pleasure into our own tent, while we put up others for them. One of the second detachment (William A. Spicer), joined our 'mess,' which was very agreeable to him and to us. He brought with him two or three papers, and one-half of Thursday's *Evening Press* which were eagerly read.

"June 6th. Dr. George D. Wilcox has been appointed surgeon, and Dr. Albert G. Sprague, assistant-surgeon. Rev. A. H. Clapp, of the Beneficent Church, our chaplain, is settled down in camp and is to be also the postmaster of the regiment. It is said that there are seven or eight thousand troops around here. Among them are the Sixty-third Indiana, the Fifty-ninth New York and Seventy-first New York, the Eleventh and Seventeenth Regulars, the Ninth Rhode Island Volunteers, the Tenth Rhode Island Battery, and a Pennsylvania regiment. A few rods from here is Fort Pennsylvania, mounting a dozen heavy guns. It is manned by a portion of the Fifty-ninth New York Volunteers. There are several other large forts and batteries near by which guard the approaches to the capital from the upper Potomac.

"June 8th. Our duties for each day are as follows: We are obliged to get up and form in line at half past four in the morning for 'reveille' or roll-call. After that each 'mess' has a 'squad drill' for an hour, and then breakfast at half past six. Drill from ten to half past eleven. Dinner at one o'clock, preceded by another roll-call. From three to five 'company drill,' roll call at six, and supper at 6.30. Another roll-call at nine, 'tattoo' and 'taps' at 9.30, when all lights must be out, and all noise cease.

"Yesterday I was on guard from nine o'clock A. M., until nine o'clock this morning. My beat was in front of the colonel's, adjutant's, and quartermaster's tents of the Ninth Regiment Rhode Island Volunteers (the Ninth and Tenth are in the same camp). In the day time I did not have much to do, simply preventing persons not belonging to the tents from going into them. At night, by mistake, the countersign was given to me, which should not have been done as it is only intended for the outside guards. I had orders not to let any one pass between the tents across my beat, or in or out of the tent without the countersign. Some of the officers were not provided with the password as they had never been obliged to use it. Scarcely had I passed a few times, back and forth, when the quartermaster approached his tent. I stopped him, saying, 'Halt!' 'Who comes there?' He answered 'the quartermaster.' 'Advance quartermaster, and give the countersign!' He said that he was the quartermaster, but had not the countersign. I called for the corporal of the guard, who allowed him go to his tent. I also halted the colonel, who gave me the countersign. To-day I ought to have slept, but I took the time for writing letters home."

Home correspondence was now commenced with an alacrity which nearly "snowed under" the village post-office. Corp. C. F. Pabodie, of Company H, wrote a few days later: "We have our letters directed to us at Washington now, instead of at Tennallytown as at first. It appears that the village postmaster had been in the habit of receiving only one or two letters per day, previous to our arrival, and when he begun to get upwards of a thousand, he didn't know 'what on 'airth to do with them.' They say he has been in the hospital ever since.

"A detachment of the Seventeenth Regulars are now encamped near us. They are illy provided with camp utensils, knapsacks, overcoats, etc., and it is reported, help themselves to anything they can lay their hands on. I lost my overcoat while helping to pitch tents, but have held on to my knapsack. We get used to the fatigue here. My knapsack keeps growing lighter every day. We have had not much else but rain since we have been here. When it is pleasant it is quite warm.

"Monday, June 2d, we (Company H), were informed that we were detailed for guard duty for the next twenty-four hours. At 9.30 A. M., we were marched out and went through the ceremony of guard mounting and taking our position at the guard tent. Guard mounting is done in the following way: The new guard being drawn up in double line, are divided into three portions generally. The first detachment are kept in line, the rest are allowed to hang around the guard tent until wanted. The first detachment then marches off under charge of the corporal, who puts the men in the places occupied by the old guard, who fall in behind. Thus they go round the lines. There are many minutæ required by the tactics which would take too long to describe. The corporal of the guard, after posting his men, has to remain at the guard tent till they are relieved, for whenever any disturbance happens in the lines, the guard, if he cannot decide nor quiet it himself, calls out the number of his post and calls for the corporal of the guard, who must proceed to the post and see what is the matter.

"During the day, the guards are on two hours and off four hours. When there are enough the same arrangement is carried out again at night. But there were not enough of us, as the guard has to be doubled at night, so our men were on two hours and off two hours, the three detachments we had during the day, being divided into two. During the day the guard had orders to allow no one to pass in or out except commissioned officers, men with passes, men for water, and civilians. At night a countersign was given them, and no one was allowed to pass except with that countersign. The orders were to pass all men to the guard house, who attempted to come in without the word. Towards morning I had just started away from the guard house accompanying the men who were to relieve my guard then on duty, when the cry was passed along the lines for the corporal of the guard, post 16. I hurried to the post designated, which was down at the extremity of the camp in a swamp, and found the affair as follows: Number 15, was a small, very stupid Irishman, who had got off his beat into number 16's beat, and, being challenged, had forgotten the countersign. Number 16 held him at the point of the bayonet, and threatened to run him through if he stirred. When I reached them, number 15 was shaking with fear, and when I inquired what was the matter, could hardly ejaculate that he had forgotten the countersign. This round was the hardest one I made during the night. It was so dark I could not see the length of my musket ahead, except when it lightened, and could only find the old guard by calling out so they could hear us and challenge us. Once I ran against a stump about three feet high, and tumbled over, musket and all. We were glad to be relieved at ten the next morning. The day after being on guard we were relieved from all duty, so we had the whole day to rest in."

"Chain Bridge," wrote Lieut. C. F. Phillips, "barricaded and guarded by a German regiment, is about two miles to the left of our camp. The position of the Tenth Rhode Island Battery, recently arrived, is at the foot of the slope of our camp. They have for neighbors an artillery company of the regular army. Our guard tent is for the most part orderly except in one instance, when the man with iron jaws persisted in chewing up several tent pins into fragments, which had been improvised as a 'gag' to keep him quiet.

"Picket duty. The first detail from Company B for picket duty was made two or three nights ago, in the midst of a furious thunder storm. The squad was accompanied by Captain Dyer, and marched perhaps two miles down the Fredericktown road, and halted in front of a wheelwright shop. Captain Dyer went to the adjoining house for the key of the shop and knocked. Instantly the lights inside were extinguished, but as the knocking grew louder a head appeared at an upper window. 'What do you want?' 'The key of your wagon shop and a light.' 'Well, you won't get them,' and down went the window with a bang. 'Take forcible possession of the shop,' shouted Captain Dyer, and the key and light were instantly forthcoming, just in time to save the door, and the men, wet to the skin, found a shelter. The wheelwright shop from that hour became the headquarters of the picket guard, and the picket line was established about half a mile beyond."

An amusing capture was made during the night by Captain Dyer's men, which is thus described in the author's personal narrative:

"Last night a fellow was brought in from our picket line who had stayed out too late, courting one of the fair F. F. V.'s. He was decked out in light vest and pants, and came galloping along on horseback, when Fiske, one of our mess, jumped into the middle of the road, with bayonet at the charge, and yelled, 'Who goes there?' The rider jumped back in his stirrups and pulled up, badly frightened, exclaiming, 'It's m-m-me!' 'Advance *me* and give the countersign!' 'Twas no go, he had to give it up. 'Then you're my prisoner,' says Fiske, and he had to go into camp with us for the rest of the night, and was turned over to the officer of the guard. Colonel Robbins told one of the guard 'to keep his eye on that fellow who had been out to see his gal!' 'Twas pretty rough, I'll admit, but I guess he'll keep better hours in future."

Cleaning Up

Bathing and swimming at Chain Bridge, on the Potomac, and in Rock Creek, near by, were luxuries which we greatly enjoyed during our month's stay at Camp Frieze, and they did much, no doubt, towards promoting the health of the regiment.

"On the first Sunday afternoon, the chaplain not having yet arrived, a company of us obtained permission for a tramp to Rock Creek. We kept well together, as the neighborhood was considered unfriendly. We took our canteens along, which served a novel and useful purpose. The banks were lined with soldiers enjoying the cleansing and reviving influences of the water."

"Last Saturday," wrote James F. Field, "nine of us crossed the Potomac into Virginia. We obtained a pass from Captain Dyer, endorsed by Colonel Bliss, which allowed us to go over the river into Virginia, if we behaved ourselves, which we did accordingly. The principal road to the Potomac was so narrow in some places as to allow but one carriage to pass along. What they do when two carriages meet I do not know. We tramped about five miles in going, not knowing exactly the way, but in returning to camp we traveled only two miles. We went across the

Potomac on Chain Bridge, which is made of wood, with seven heavy stone abutments. It was formerly held by chains, which probably gave it the name of Chain Bridge. There was a guard of artillery stationed on this side of the bridge to prevent any one from going across without a pass. Commanding the bridge and on a level with it was an earthen breastwork, pierced for three guns, which could sweep the bridge if necessary. On a high bluff right above this is another earthwork, with three or four heavy guns, which command the opposite shore. Near the centre of the bridge are two large, heavy gates, which completely divide the bridge. The gates are plated with iron, with slits for skirmishers and pickets to fire through, which were dented in several places by bullet and rifle-balls fired by secession pickets. The river at that time was only about forty or fifty feet wide, it being the dry season. It is of a muddy color, about the same as the color of the soil. We walked about a quarter of a mile into Virginia, and bathed ourselves thoroughly in a stream which flowed into the Potomac. Close to the bank were the remains of some bowers or huts, which, probably, the secession pickets had made for their quarters, as there were remains of fire-places near them. The day was the warmest that we have yet had, the thermometer being at camp that noon, 104°. On our way back we stopped at 'Fort Gaines.' It mounted four 32-pound barbette guns. It is garrisoned by a company of the Fifty-ninth New York Volunteers. The earthwork was about ten or twelve feet thick, with a ditch about as wide and six or eight feet deep, on the outside of which were large trees, laid lengthwise, to hinder infantry from going through them to the fort."

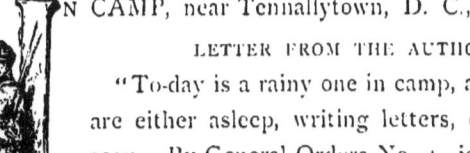
IN CAMP, near Tennallytown, D. C., June 10th.

LETTER FROM THE AUTHOR.

"To-day is a rainy one in camp, and the boys are either asleep, writing letters, or taking it easy. By General Orders No. 1, issued yesterday, our camp will hereafter be known as Camp Frieze, and the strictest discipline and good order will be observed. According to the order there will be eleven calls sounded each day, as follows: Reveille, at 4.30 o'clock A. M.; Police call, Breakfast, 6.30 A. M.; Sick call at 7 A. M.; Adjutant's call at 8.45 A. M.; Guard-mounting at 9 A. M.; Orderly call at 12 M.; Roast Beef, Dinner, at 1 P. M.; Supper, 6.30 P. M.; Retreat at sunset (when the companies form under arms); Tattoo at 9 P. M.; Taps 9.30 P. M. There are four roll calls each day, and as many drills. Divine service will be held every Sunday at 11 A. M. (For full order, see pages 77, 78 and 79.)

Our tents are arranged in parallel rows, with streets or avenues between. Company A, Captain Taber, has Atwood avenue, named in honor of Mrs. Alice Atwood, who made and presented the men with a hundred pin-cushions, filled with pins. Company B, Captain Dyer, has Dyer avenue; Company C, Captain Vose, Broadway; Company D, Captain Dunham, Benefit street, and so on. The college boys of Brown, in the tent adjoining ours, call their quarters 'Hope College.' Per order of the High School boys I have printed the sign 'Whang Hotel,' on a board, and hung it up over our tent opening. 'Whang' is a broad 'slang' expression for our broader army shoes, seventeen pairs of which lie mixed up round the centre-pole every night. The names of the proprietors are as follows: Sergt. Charles L. Stafford, Corporals William P. Vaughan, George T. Baker, John B. Kelly, Nathan H. Baker, and high privates Edwin B. Fiske, John A. Reynolds, Frank Frost, James F. Field, F. F. Tingley, Charles B. Greene, Charles T. Greene, Horace K. Blanchard, George H. Sparhawk, William A. Spicer, David Hunt, and Jesse M. Bush. William Grant and Ira Wilbur are in Company E, Captain Cady.

"Many of the tents in the other companies have pet names, such as 'Uncle Tom's Cabin,' 'Hawkins's Happy Family,' 'Blue Point House,' 'Mess of Cabbage, Company F,' 'Chateau de Salt Junk,' and 'The Rhubarb Mess' of Company G. So you see there is considerable 'spice' mixed with army life. There is indeed some 'fun,' although a great deal more of the reverse character. Every morning we have to be up and in the ranks at half past four, which you must know is hard for some of us. So also are the military drills in the hot sun morning and afternoon, We sleep on the hard ground with only a thin layer of straw and a rubber blanket to keep off the dampness. Yet we sleep well, with our knapsacks under our heads, and one blanket apiece for a covering.

"Fiske, of our 'mess,' told Captain Dyer that it was pretty 'tough' for him to come down to such hard fare, as for two or three weeks before enlisting he'd been out 'visiting' among 'his folks,' and never had such high living in his life. Another said that he was going to write home, that he'd never object any more to 'corned beef and cabbage' once a week.

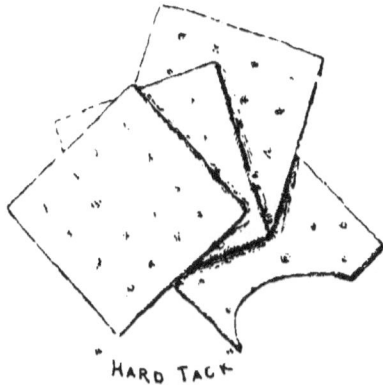

"Our rations have thus far consisted of salt meat and pork, 'hard tack' or hard crackers, and black, strong coffee. They have been of such a uniformly bad quality since we arrived in Washington, that some of us have been out to a neighboring farmhouse, to get a good square meal for twenty-five cents! And didn't it go good? One trouble is that there is no variety to our bill of fare, it is the same old horse day after day." As I now look back upon the situation, it reminds me of the story of a boarder in a small country tavern, who came down into the dining-room one morning, and casting a sweeping glance over the table, jammed down into his chair, and muttered under his breath, "Liver again, of course. We've had liver every morning for two weeks." "What's the matter," asked the landlady, "aren't you feeling well this morning?" "No, ma'am," he replied, shortly, "I am suffering with liver complaint."

But thanks to the efficiency of our new quartermaster, James H. Armington, our rations greatly improved after this time. He was second lieutenant of Company D, and by General Orders No. 11, June 7th, was promoted to first lieutenant Company C, and detailed as quartermaster. He proceeded to Washington, and pressed our claims upon the Commissary Department with such persistency that he was ordered to report under arrest.

The return of the genial quartermaster to camp, and his report at headquarters, with the order of arrest signed by General Wadsworth, caused a considerable sensation. Colonel Bliss laughed heartily, and thought it was a good joke on Armington, but sustained him by issuing General Orders No. 15, relieving him from arrest. He proved a very capable and faithful quartermaster, and our 'rations' steadily improved, but at the best

"Ther warn't overly much pie et, endurin' 'the army.'"

Captain Duckworth, of Company H, furnishes the following for publication:

BROOKLYN, N. Y., July 12, 1887.

MAJ. CHRISTOPHER DUCKWORTH,
Pawtucket, R. I.

MY DEAR MAJOR: My friend Stiness has this day forwarded me the copy of General Orders No. 15, issued at headquarters of the Tenth Rhode Island Volunteers, June 16, 1862. Permit me to thank you, not only for the preservation of this old document, but for your kindness in sending it to me.

How much it reminds me of the particular instance which caused the ordering of my arrest; and of the good fellow, and brave soldier, who was with me on the occasion, Adjt. John F. Tobey, and who has now "passed to his rest." Full well, too, do I remember the martinet who ordered me to "report under arrest," and the hearty laugh with which his explanation for ordering me under arrest was received, when he was waited upon by Colonel Bliss and Adjutant Tobey. I remember also, that this same officer was to have been nominated by Hon. John P. Hale, for a brigadier-general, but that after he (Hale) had visited our camp, in company with Governor Anthony, the said officer was *not* nominated, and did not receive that honor, while his brother officers who were associated with him were nominated and confirmed as brigadier-generals.

I should be very much pleased to meet you, and I hope that whenever you visit your brother here, you will not forget to call on me. With kind regards I am

Very truly yours,
JAMES H. ARMINGTON.

THE TENTH REGIMENT

Army Cap.

"Yesterday we were mustered into the service of the United States by Adjt.-Gen. Lorenzo Thomas, United States Army. There was no 'special service at Washington' in the agreement. The general said there was but one oath for a Union soldier to take, and that was the unconditional one, to serve in any place where he was ordered We all concluded therefore to 'take it straight.' After the oath, which we repeated slowly after General Thomas, he called out, 'Now, three cheers for your flag, men!' which were heartily given." Much importance is attached by professional soldiers to this outward demonstration of respect for our country's flag, and certainly every Union soldier and sailor will respond to the sentiment

> "Off with your cap as the flag goes by!
> And let the heart have its say.
> You're man enough for a tear in your eye,
> That you will not wipe away."

"Adjutant-General Thomas had a very difficult place to fill. Secretary of War, Simon Cameron, relied on him greatly in the management of military affairs, so suddenly and so vastly brought into the most prominent of all functions of the government. It was at that time thought important that as much *éclat* as possible should be given to the arrival of the volunteer regiments which came to re-enforce the army, and the adjutant-general was called upon to make addresses, present flags, and attend to the mustering exercises, etc., at the various camps around the capital." (See portrait, page 139.)

HEADQUARTERS TENTH REGIMENT R. I. VOLS.,
CAMP NEAR TENNALLYTOWN, D. C., June 7, 1862.

Special Orders No. 1.

The Tenth Battery of Rhode Island Light Artillery, commanded by Capt. Edwin C. Gallup, is hereby attached to this regiment, and will be designated as Company "L."

By order of

ZENAS R. BLISS,

BENJAMIN F. THURSTON,   *Colonel Commanding.*
   Lieutenant and Adjutant.

NOTE. Maj. Charles H. Merriman, Capt. Charles H. Dunham, Company D, and Adjt. Benjamin F. Thurston, went out with the regiment, and served with it until June 9th, but resigned and returned home before the officers' commissions were issued.

The blanks in the regimental staff were filled, and the officers mustered in as follows, June 9, 1862:

ZENAS R. BLISS, Colonel;
JAMES SHAW, JR., Lieutenant-Colonel;
JACOB BABBITT, Major;
GEORGE D. WILCOX, Surgeon;
ALBERT G. SPRAGUE, Assistant-Surgeon;
A. HUNTINGTON CLAPP, Chaplain;
JOHN F. TOBEY, Adjutant;
JAMES H. ARMINGTON, Quartermaster;
EDWARD K. GLEZEN, Sergeant-Major;
LYSANDER FLAGG, Quartermaster-Sergeant;
JAMES O. SWAN, Commissary-Sergeant;
CHARLES G. KING, Hospital Steward.

HEADQUARTERS, CAMP FRIEZE,
June 10, 1862.

Captains of companies will furnish this office requisitions for such clothing as is necessary for the men, also requisition for arms for each member of the company, and such equipments as are required, in addition to those on hand, to complete the equipment of the men.

By order of

ZENAS R. BLISS,

JOHN F. TOBEY,   *Colonel Commanding.*
   Lieutenant and Adjutant.

Dressed Up.

Our uniforms were a bad fit. They did not take our measure and make them to order. The government appeared to cut out clothes not according to the shape of the boy, but to what he was expected to grow to. Then our altitude ranged from four feet six to six feet four. Private Maguire said he was four foot ten or ten foot four, he *dis*remembered which. "We have received our blue overcoats, but mine is a very loose fit. We had to take them just as they came, but can 'swap' with some other fellow. Beside the overcoat, each of us received a woolen blanket, a rubber blanket, some coarse shirts and drawers, two pairs socks or 'foot-gear,' cap, one pair 'pontoons' or army shoes, one knapsack, one haversack, and one blue blouse. Many of us are disappointed in the non-arrival of the promised invoice of government trousers from Washington. The old ones we brought from home are getting pretty dilapidated. The wear and tear of camp-life, with the rain, and slippery mud which so quickly follows here, have done their work, and its getting a little unpleasant and embarrassing to appear in line." "To realize what this southern mud is," wrote one of the privates, "spread several inches of tar all over your back-yard, and then try to walk through it; and when you have succeeded in getting it well baked on to your 'pontoons' try to make them presentable for dress parade." "If you decide to send anything, don't forget to put in some blacking and a brush, for we haven't half enough to go round."

"June 10th. I was handed your letter while washing the mess-pans and cups. Two are detailed for this duty each day. How do we like the job? Well, we don't like it. I never realized before how much easier it is to *eat* a good dinner than to 'pick up' and wash the dishes afterwards. One of the boys says when he enlists again he's going to have it all put down in black and white, just what he's got to do, and helping the cook wash the dishes and cleaning up the camp won't be in it.

"We have little real cause for complaint. We have good officers, well-known to you all at home, who treat the men with the kindest consideration. Captain Dyer is a model commander, and our company has the right of the line, he being the senior captain. He gave us quite a lively exercise the other morning, in military movements. One of the hardest things for us is to get up early enough in the morning. Reveille is sounded at half past four, when we form in line for roll-call, generally in a very drowsy-headed condition. The captain thought he'd wake us up and warm us up too. So he started us off on the 'double-quick,' a very pretty movement when well executed by a wide awake, well disciplined company on a level road, but our boys made a very pretty mess of it, half asleep, on a down-hill and dusty road. We hadn't gone far when unfortunate number one lost the step, stumbled and fell. 'Left! left! left!' shouted Captain Dyer sharply, stamping his left foot on the ground, to give force to the word, 'Get the step there, men!' But 'getting the step' was an easier thing for the tongue to say than for some awkward feet to do. Graceful John Reynolds, of our mess, now lost the step, and, while attempting to leap over the back of his file leader, was rolled over and over into the ditch by the wayside. Then number three followed, displaying his broad 'whangs,' alias army shoes, to the rising sun, and so the fun went on, till order was at length restored, and we returned to camp as wide-awake and smiling a company as you can find in 'Rhode Island and Providence Plantations.'

"It was John Reynolds's night for guard duty, and the boys determined to 'put up a job on him,' and you should have seen the merchandise piled up in his allotted place in the tent. When he came in at a late hour, he went stumbling over the pile of rubbish, and got very angry at first, but knowing the crowd, he concluded 'the easiest way's to take it as it comes.' He not only took the pile of rubbish as it came, but proceeded to throw it in every direction, regardless of where it hit, until he had cleared out his quarters. In vain arose the general protest—he satisfied his revengeful feelings—and composed himself to rest with calm satisfaction. It was fortunate there were no broken heads."

Company K: "The boys have done well, thus far, in not getting caught 'napping' on picket duty. You remember Samuel Mitchell. He and Jesse Eddy, Zephaniah Brown, and Carlo Mauran belong to Company K. Lieutenant-Colonel Shaw tried to pass Sam the other night without the countersign. He said he must pass as he was making the rounds of the camp. But Sam replied, 'No, sir, you can't pass that on me,' and called the corporal of the guard. Colonel Bliss and Captain Dyer have also happened round on the picket line, and have tried, on some pretence or other, to get the boys to let them examine their muskets. No guns have been captured yet, however.

"June 12th. Last night was my first experience 'on picket.' The night was dark, the moon being off 'on an eclipse.' Our squad marched down a lonesome-looking road, about a mile and a half toward Fredericktown, and attempted to force an entrance into an old school-house by the roadside, but the barred shutters resisted all our efforts. We never felt so sorry for a school lock-out before! We marched further on, and took the best quarters we could get, in a wheelwright shop, opening to the road. I was on 'the relief,' and had just got fairly into an uncomfortable snooze, when we were all suddenly startled by an alarm, and ordered by the sergeant to buckle on equipments, right shoulder arms, and double-quick down the road for the picket line—all the work of perhaps two or three minutes. Were we wide awake? Oh, yes, some, if not some scared! But the trouble was soon explained. Some drunken soldiers from a neighboring regiment were attempting to pass our line without the countersign. Order was soon restored, and we were glad to march back to quarters, with all the arms and legs we brought out. It was about four o'clock in the morning when I found myself posted as sentinel. I paced my beat regularly, back and forth, *nothing* escaping my keen vision. Suddenly there came the sound of approaching wheels; when, with bayonet at the charge, and, summoning all my voice to command, I called a 'Halt!' and the driver instantly halted! He proved to be a fishmonger on his early way to Georgetown. He strongly protested,—and his fish also *strongly* protested, against being interfered with—but we marched fish and fisherman to the sergeant of the guard, as orders were to let nobody pass without the countersign.

"June 14th. There is nothing that gives such delight as boxes from home. When a box arrives at camp, the eatable portion of the contents, if sent to any of our boys, is considered the common property of the mess. When my box was opened, therefore, the boys all gathered round me, and, as each package was taken out, they set up a terrible yelling and howling, whether they knew what was in it or not. You can guess the peanuts disappeared in double-quick time, and, when I came to the lemons, there was 'tremendous applause and cheering in the galleries!' We not only had lots of fun over the box, but it was worth almost its weight in gold, for it contained everything we wanted. The combined knife, fork and spoon which can be folded up and carried in the pocket or haversack, will be very useful, and will allow my fingers to take a rest, as no army knives and forks have yet been issued. The towels, also, are just what I needed, as I've been trying to make that same poor, single towel go for more than a fortnight! You ought to have seen me skinning my fingers trying to wash it! But relief has come at last, and the contrabands now come round regularly for any washing on hand. So I 'put mine out,' to the tune of six cents a piece for shirts, and so on. I shall like the woolen shirts very much. I was getting to be truly 'a shiftless concern.' I never ate any ham which tasted so good as that in the box; and we should have had small pieces if the whole seventeen had staid to dinner, as some of us are 'great feeders.' We are very much like the boys at the Thanksgiving dinner who kept on eating as long as the supply lasted. So it was agreed that as quite a squad was going to the Potomac for a swim, those who remained at camp should have the ham; and I tell you we enjoyed it, to the last hitch! The mustard you sent flavored it in good shape, and will also help season the 'salt horse,' as you wrote.

"I am going to dig a hole right under my knapsack, and drop the box in, with the top a little above the ground. This, with my blue army overcoat, will make a good pillow at night. It will not make things damp in the box, because the soil, where the rain does not reach it, is very dry and hard."

Some home messages and directions which came with the box: "We didn't want to put in too much so as to make your knapsack too heavy. The lemons and oranges are in, as many as could be. The sugar we thought would be handy for lemonade. The sardines and peanuts will be acceptable, I guess, as well as the sugar ham. That is 'mustard' in the two bottles. We thought it would go well with the ham, and would season up the 'salt horse.' We put in the woolen shirts, beside two calico ones. The little roll of old cloth and glove fingers mother thought would be useful, if your *toes* were sore after marching. The box of salve you can use the same as tallow. 'Old Morse's' Dockroot is to keep your stomach in good trim, but you are not to use it unless you really need it. It might have the same effect upon you that Brandreth's pills had upon the old lady. We should want more than your cap to come home with the regiment. The necktie and collars are also in. The fancy pillow is filled with feathers from the old black hen. Mother covered it with dark cloth so that it would not appear soiled so soon. The padlock, which is *non est* in this box shall be *e pluribus unum* in the second. The pocket inkstand is right down in one corner. The paper,

Letters from Home.

envelopes, pencils, pens, and jack-knife, all went into the portfolio. There was no room for the shoe-brush, although we got in a box of blacking. We had an idea of putting in some cream-cakes with the oranges, but were afraid they would get flattened and *sour*. In regard to the tea mother says, if you chew a little while marching, you won't be half so thirsty." This reminds the author of a story of the virtues of pennyroyal tea, one of the old-time remedies. A good old lady, in telling her experience, said she had seen a great deal of trouble through life, but, she continued, 'I have triumphed over it all with my three Ps, 'Prayer, Patience, and Pennyroyal!'"

In approving of the presence of ladies at our recent reunions, General Rogers said: "The anxiety, the suffering, and the suspense, endured by the mothers and sisters of the soldiers, during the war, can never be fitly measured. Theirs was the service which furrowed the brow and whitened the hair."

June 14th. A letter to the writer says: "It was college exhibition (class-day), Thursday, and the orator was a student named Addeman, who went out in your regiment. He got a leave of absence to come on and deliver his oration, and then went back the same night. His subject was 'The Alliance of Scholarship and Patriotism.' The audience cheered him like fun, I can tell you, but he looked kind o' gray, as though he was smelling 'salt-horse,' in the distance!"

Two more home letters are added for the special entertainment of our youthful readers :

"Providence, June 4th. I meant last night to be up this morning, at half past four, and write this letter, to show you that I could be as smart as some other folks ! I woke up and double-quicked it out to the clock, when behold, to my astonishment, the hands were in the neighborhood of six !

"I guess by this time you'll like to hear how we are all flourishing in Providence, and I shouldn't wonder either if you'd like to be here yourself, on the identical old lounge sleeping off the effects of 'salt-horse' and those beautiful soft crackers ! I guess slippers would feel better than 'whangs.' I suppose you are as tough now as a pitch knot, can eat anything or nothing, probably just as it happens ; but I mind that your stomach now and then requires a meal at a neighboring farm-house. How glorious it must be to sleep sixteen in a bed, with now and then the variety of standing out in a thunder-storm to shoot secesh. There was a letter in the *Press* the other night about your regiment, and it said the men were very much disappointed because there was no fighting to do. Now don't you have any such 'gassy' talk as that. They may take you at your word and send you right on to Richmond ! Do you know of anybody in your regiment that was poisoned in Baltimore ? There was such a rumor in last Saturday evening's *Press*. It didn't give any name, and was enough to frighten anybody to death. I think it was a story started by the New York *Tribune* to sell the papers. I guess if you hadn't got away that night, you wouldn't have got to the war at all. We are thinking you are sick, or out on picket duty or something, the whole time. The fact is, we have learned a lesson in intellectual philosophy, viz.: People are fools to let green boys go to the war! You are a green boy! Therefore we were fools to let you go! By the way, I haven't seen any of that bounty money I was to have for being on your side!

"We are very glad to hear you are having such 'a gay old time,' but you mustn't try to make it out any better than it really is. Your friend Sam Mitchell said the same thing in his first letter, in his second he didn't say anything about it, and in his third he sent home three sheets of blank paper. His father didn't know what had come over Sam. It now appears that he wrote his letter one evening, in his tent, and had just finished it when lights were ordered to be put out. In the dark he sent home the three sheets of blank paper by mistake, and kept all the cream of the correspondence to himself! Write as often as you can. Enclosed you will find some postage stamps.

"Your friends went trouting together yesterday and brought home some nice ones. We had one for breakfast thirteen or fourteen inches long. It tasted about right I can tell you; but you will pardon me for writing about the delicacies that grace our table. Still, Mary, the cook, wants me to ask you if you've had any waffles since you went away? I told her the nearest to them you had written about was having some Virginia hoe-cake. You have enough to eat, now, don't you? Our cherries are ripening fast. The peaches will be ready for eating about the time of your return. Your fowls are all in good health, and the chickens increasing in stature. The rooster and other friends send love. So good-bye, from the folks at home."

The following selection will conclude "letters from home:"

"Providence, June 6th. Would you like to know what all the girls are up to, while all the boys, 'beaux,' I mean, are gone off to the war? Well here we are, trying to make the best of it, but it is real 'Old Maidendom,' for it seems as if almost everybody that we knew has gone. When we go anywhere now, in the evening, we must get back the best way we can, three or four together perhaps. Isn't it too bad? I did not have even time to bid you good-bye, you went off in such a hurry. I started for the depot to see you off, and arrived only to find, not you, but a crowd of people, and an empty depot. You must have had a delightful journey from your description. Such nice accommodations on the floor; such delicate rations of sandwiches and sponge-cake!

"I should like to be out to your camp, if only for just a few minutes, to see how you are living, and how nicely you keep your tent that you live in. Please write me all about your soldier-life if you can find time. Tell me how you get along housekeeping; who makes the fires, cooks the breakfast, and fries the hot cakes in the morning. Auntie says you must try to take good care of yourself, and be careful and keep out of danger!"

June 16th, Lieutenant DeWolf wrote: "Our commissariat, has now become pretty well regulated, and we have rations of pork, bacon, salt beef, fresh beef, loaf-bread, hard bread, beans, rice, coffee, tea, sugar, vinegar, and salt, with the accessories of soap and candles. Gradually such conveniences as cups, plates, knives forks and spoons are being supplied. Our government pantaloons have also arrived, and we are no longer obliged to take the backward march at the approach of visitors."

Puss in Army Shoes.

Henry T. Chace, of Company D, declares that his "'ferry-boats,' alias 'whangs,' alias 'scows,' alias 'tan-yards,' alias 'army shoes,' alias 'pontoons,' are great institutions: Easy to march in, easy to drill in, and large enough to sleep in. They are so broad-soled, that I have taken one off, and, putting a piece of brown paper on it, have improvised a satisfactory writing-desk."

Thirty years later an old soldier said to his wife, "Mrs. Sage, I should like to know whose 'ferry-boats' those are that I stumbled over in the hall?" "Ferry-boats, indeed, sir! Those are my shoes. Very polite of you to call them ferry-boats!" "I didn't say 'ferry-boats,' Mrs. Sage; you misunderstood me—'fairy boots'—I said, my dear."

"It is pleasant to-day, and the boys feel accordingly jolly. The morning has been improved by most of the mess in cleaning our guns and in writing home. I have been out with Mason sweeping Benefit street in front of our quarters. Price and I are now at the foot of a tree, sitting on the ground, just above the Athenæum tent. Terms for board in this tent $3.00 per year, commanding officers no charge. Three of the tents are emptied of their contents, and the proprietors are busy 'cleaning house!' Some of the tents have spruce trees located near the doors, with short branches and bark off, which serve as clothes-horses, and blankets, coats, and towels, are out for an airing.

"Samuel Dorrance is sitting on a pile of knapsacks, overcoats, and blankets, putting a letter 'D' on his cap. Mr. Vose, who used to keep a shoe store near father's, is now captain of the seventh ward company, called 'Company C.'"

"Wednesday, June 4th. At about six, this evening, nearly three hundred of the regiment gathered together upon the rising ground between the streets of Companies B and I., and formed in hollow square to our chaplain, Rev. Mr. Clapp, for an introductory Divine service. It commenced with singing the familiar hymn, 'All hail the power of Jesus' name,' and was followed by the reading of the twenty-seventh psalm, remarks and prayer by the chaplain. During the meeting, which was an interesting one, we had a slight shower. We are now waiting for rations. These have improved. When they are served we form in line and march to the foot of the street, and receive them in turn. This morning we had meat, bread, and coffee, with a dish of cold beans, which was good enough as long as it lasted, but there wasn't enough to go round. I didn't hanker after either the beans or the strong black coffee. So, with others, I took a sharp stick for a fork, and holding several slices of bread before the fire, 'dry toast for three,' soon crowned our efforts. We have found out that 'fingers were made before forks,' and that knives, plates, and napkins, cups, and saucers, are all modern innovations. When I return home you will fail to elicit a single growl from me, whether the meat is cooked too much or too little. Camp-life is thus doing us good in making us willing and obliging.

"Raining again to-night, and the company streets are slippery and disagreeable, but we must take our turn for guard duty.

Senator N. W. Aldrich.

Fred Armington and John Cady from our 'mess,' N. W. Aldrich, Aborn, and Newcomb, all of Company D, with thirty five from other companies, are off to-night on picket duty, under command of Lieut. Stephen Thurber, of Company E. It promises to be a dark and rainy night. Aldrich, the youthful volunteer, marching with his comrades to the post of duty, worthy to command and ready to obey, is a fitting type of the private soldier in the War for the Union. Content to serve in an humble position in times of trial and danger, he was soon called by his native state as her chosen representative at the capital, which his youthful footsteps had hastened to defend. He has long continued, as senior senator, to dignify and adorn the high position of official trust committed to his charge. At one of our regimental reunions Senator Aldrich spoke highly of the officers of the regiment and of his own company, saying to them he owed some of the first and best lessons of his life. He learned by his service with them that in every sphere of life one can show the greatest amount of heroism by performing the duties assigned to him in a quiet and unobstrusive manner. The privates of the Tenth Rhode Island Regiment learned in their brief campaign a lesson which should last them through life— that heroism is not in brilliant achievement, but in an unselfish devotion to duty, and the performance of every trust committed to them in a manner which shall receive the respect of men and the commendation of God.

Resuming, Chace, of Company D, says: "We 'turned in' at nine o'clock, but did not get to sleep until ten, listening to the good singing in another tent. We have some fine voices, George Briggs, Levi Burdon, Albert Ham, Ned Glezen, and W. C. Benedict of the Ninth." "The Sword of Bunker Hill," and "Seeing Nellie Home," as rendered by Burdon, became very popular with the regiment, and he is still called out, at our reunions to sing them as he used to sing them in camp. "Last Sunday evening, we all enjoyed very much. Several of us sat in the tent-door enjoying the scene. The air was still, the moon bright, the sky blue, the great trees threw a soft shade, a choir, near us, furnished sweet music, while we discoursed of home and heavenly themes."

"I was reading the other day," says a well-known writer, "that on the shores of the Adriatic Sea, the wives of the fishermen, whose husbands have gone far off upon the deep, are in the habit at even-tide of going down to the seashore, and singing, as female voices only can, the first stanza of a beautiful hymn; after they have sung it, they listen, till they hear, borne by the wind across the desert sea, the second stanza, sung by their gallant husbands as they are tossed by the gale upon the waves, and both are happy.

"Perhaps if we would listen, we too might hear in this desert world of ours, some sound, some whisper borne from afar, to remind us that there is a heaven and a home, and when we sing the hymn upon the shores of earth, perhaps we shall hear its sweet echo breaking in music upon the sands of time, and cheering the hearts of them that are pilgrims and strangers, and look for a city that hath foundations."

Little Abe.

"June 15th. Our mess in Company B has engaged a prepossessing young contraband who boasts the name of Abraham Douglass, to do the singing and wash the dishes, for the modest salary of two dollars and a half per month. We enjoy having him sing and wash the dishes very much indeed. Last evening he sang for us:

'De gospel ship's a sailin'—sailin'—sailin'—
De gospel ship's a sailin'—bound for Canin's happy sho'!

Chorus: 'Den, glory, glory, hallelujah!

"Another of his best ones is:

'Dere's a light in der winder fur thee, brother,
Dere' a light in der winder fur thee!'

"Each member of the regiment was presented with a small, red-covered hymn book, containing the old familiar hymns, which were sung at religious services. In opening my book the other day I found on the inside cover the following beautiful lines written by a private in Stuart's engineer regiment, which made a deep impression on my mind:

'"Halt! who goes there?" my challenge cry, it rings along the watchful line;
"Relief!" I hear a voice reply—"Advance, and give the countersign!"
With bayonet at the charge, I wait—The corporal gives the mystic spell—
With arms aport, I charge my mate: Then onward pass, and "all is well!"

But in my tent that night awake, I ask, if in the fray I fall,
Can I the mystic answer make, when th' angelic sentries call?
And pray that Heaven may so ordain, where'er I go, what fate be mine,
Whether in trouble, or in pain, I still may have "the countersign!"'"

One of the members of another company wrote home: "The men have found a remedy for poor rations, in songs which carry the mind back to the scenes of other days. Here, a group, as the evening twilight gathers, sing the familiar hymns remembered from childhood. Surrounded by the instruments of death, and within reach of the battery's guns, you may hear rising on the air of evening, 'Oh, where can rest be found.' 'Pleyel's hymn,' and 'Jesus, lover of my soul.' Here a band of students revive the memories of 'Brown,' with 'Lauriger Horatius,' 'Here's to good old Prex., drink him down,' while far at the other end of the camp, from the tents of the Ninth Regiment, come to our ears the strains of 'Let me kiss him for his mother.'" "Camp-life has its pleasures, too. If you could hear the manly chorus swelling up from the group of singers before yonder tent, in the broad moonlight, the mingled yet not discordant notes of violin, guitar and banjo, from different parts of the encampment, with here and there a hushed and reverent group, listening in the privacy of their own tent to one who reads the Word of God, you would not think that our life is but a weariness."

"A few from each company are allowed a pass to Washington now and then. The other day a party from Company B were sauntering down Pennsylvania avenue, when a door opened on the opposite side of the street, and there stood General Burnside! They all ran across and claimed the privilege of shaking hands with him on the score of being Rhode Island soldiers. He shook hands cordially with them, and asked where they were stationed, and they left him feeling repaid by this incident alone for the journey to Washington."

"Thursday, June 12th. Our camp was enlivened yesterday by the presence of Maj. Lewis Richmond and wife, and Mrs. General Burnside. Would that the general could run out to see us." A few days after General Burnside made us a flying visit, and was received with warm demonstrations of honor and affection.

General Burnside at Camp Frieze.

A few months later, on September 17th, the battle of Antietam was fought, but sixty miles away from our camp, in which Burnside bore a gallant part. Young Adjt. William Ide Brown, afterwards mortally wounded before Richmond, thus wrote home of Burnside: "O, how I love that general! I would think myself happy if I could be an orderly and follow him from place to place. How I wish I knew him personally! How proud I was to have him speak to me on the night of the battle of Antietam, where I was on duty at the famous Antietam bridge! There may be greater generals than Burnside, but nowhere a more honest, noble, patriotic hero!" Young Brown was the beloved class president of the class of 1862, in Brown University. He fell only a few weeks before the final surrender at Appomattox.

"Senator Simmons and Dr. Okie were also in camp recently, which reminds me of William Okie's experience on guard duty. After a guard has been on two hours he is relieved. When the guard hears the relief approach he calls out, 'Halt! who comes there?' Answer, 'Corporal, with relief.' 'Advance, corporal, and give the countersign.' Young Okie was on guard one night, and, after the answer from the corporal, instead of saying, 'Advance, etc.,' he said, 'You can't come too soon!' Generally after the two hours' duty the men are glad to get back to their tents.

"Ned Brown and Fred Armington received boxes from home last evening. Each of us had a cake from Brown's box, and Armington will have his 'spread' this morning. Later: I told you so. Armington has just passed the doughnuts, and it's jolly to be remembered by the friends at home. As I write, Price lies stretched out before me, and distracts me by asking me to draw his army shoes, but I tell him his 'whangs' are too large to be transferred to this sheet 'life-size!'

"The contrabands brought some nice, soft fresh strawberries into camp this morning, at twelve cents per quart. We sent out for six quarts, and they made a good relish, I assure you. Cost: berries, six quarts, seventy-two cents ; milk, thirty cents ; sugar, ten cents ; total, one dollar and twelve cents, divided by sixteen of us, leaves just seven cents for each man to pay. Cheap enough isn't it? Have some?"

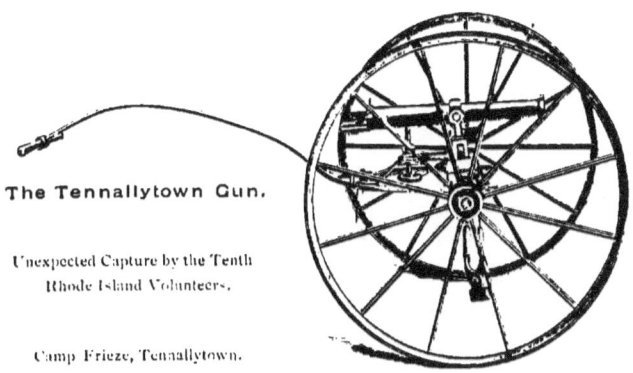

The Tennallytown Gun.

Unexpected Capture by the Tenth Rhode Island Volunteers.

Camp Frieze, Tennallytown.

"June 18th. Yesterday afternoon," wrote the author, "Company B was thrown into quite a flutter of excitement, by the announcement that it had been detailed for a secret expedition, and was under marching orders. We formed in line, as per regimental orders, with equipments and muskets, and left camp at two o'clock, P. M., accompanied by the officers of both regiments, with directions to observe the strictest silence on the march. What was going to happen? Had old Stonewall Jackson again ventured within our lines, and were we to have the glory of surprising and capturing him? Unhappily it proved not, though Stonewall did make a visit to Maryland a few months later, and his progress, and that of the entire rebel army, was arrested only at the terrific pass of Antietam, but sixty miles from camp. After Company B had been marched perhaps two miles, it was halted, and faced, as the boys say, 'eyes right and left,' before a peaceful and unpretending wooden mansion, and awaited an answer to the summons of Colonel Bliss at the front door. It seems that intelligence had reached the colonel, through our own men out foraging, that a rebel cannon was concealed in the barn of a well-known southern sympathizer, and it was considered not improbable that he might turn it some dark night on our sleeping regiments at Camp Frieze. It looked like a very serious piece of business, the boys thought, after hearing the news, and visions of a thirty-two, if not a forty-two-pounder rose before us. The summons for its surrender, however, was met by an indignant refusal from the fair matron who answered the colonel's call, and from the proprietor himself, who now appeared from a neighboring field. He was making off, but was induced to return after a short chase by Adjutant Tobey. Soon a daughter appeared on the scene, fresh from school, and a true 'gray,' and no mistake. She loudly declared that they would *never* give it up. No, never! The choice being now given them to surrender the gun, or take up a family march back to camp, to the tune of 'we won't go home till morning,' they concluded to produce it. And lo, what a disappointment! Instead of a mighty forty-two pounder, or Stonewall Jackson, we beheld a small field howitzer, about two feet long, such as is used in the field by infantry. It was rifled, and carried a ball, weighing a pound, about a mile. But such as it was, it was mounted on its carriage and trailed back to camp by Company B, who thus earned the honor of capturing the *only* rebel cannon taken by the Tenth Regiment Rhode Island Volunteers. It was receipted for by Captain Dyer, and in due time safely arrived in Providence. After many years, through the courtesy of his son, Adjt.-Gen. Elisha Dyer, it has been placed in the museum of the Rhode Island Historical Society."

Contraband Goods.

Resuming the narrative from Company D, we read that: "A little dancing contraband, one of the innocent causes of the war, is now in front of the 'Athenæum' tent, blacking Elisha Mowry's boots. At seven this evening, we form in line for inspection, with equipments, which must be in shining order. Every boot, button, belt, bayonet, and musket, must be polished as bright as rubbing can make them. At inspection every man appears in line, with his musket and equipments, full knapsack, canteen, haversack, cartridge-box, etc., all of which are duly inspected. The blankets being strapped upon the knapsacks, the tents are supposed to be empty, and, of course, their condition, as to cleanliness can be ascertained at a glance."

"One of our first efforts," wrote Captain Dyer, "as quickly as opportunity and 'leave of absence' from camp would allow, was a general reconnoissance of our surroundings, to provide against the liability of being surprised, outflanked, or attacked in the many vulnerable points to which our camp was exposed, by some raiding Jackson or Early. This duty was most faithfully performed."

Resuming, H. T. Chace, of Company D, wrote: "On coming into camp this morning, I noticed some very pretty evergreen boughs, or arbors, in one company's quarters, with arched doors and windows, all displaying excellent taste. The Westerly company have things about right. The boys have dug a well which yields the best water in camp. They have their tables handsomely protected by evergreen boughs."

"The orderly has just appeared at the tent-door, saying, 'Two men of this mess are wanted to bring water for the cook.' Sergeant Brown and the writer responded to the call, and brought several buckets of water from the spring. We then helped peel the po-

WATER SQUAD.

tatoes, and split some wood for the fire. Herman and Burdon are also assisting Mr. Burroughs in the cooking department. I am on police duty again to-day, with George Briggs, to wash the dishes. Returning I saw Robert Paine in the cook's tent, picking over beans. Think of it! and we all have to take our turn! My box arrived this P. M., and has been opened to my satisfaction and that of the mess. We propose dividing the cakes on Sunday evening. We shall have Fred Hedge, Ned Brown, John Cady, William A. Harris, and Fred Armington, participate in demolish-ing it. They are all regular boarders at the 'Athenæum.' They say 'you can't have too much cake for supper,' and if the cake gives out, we shall all relish the gingerbread.

"June 14th. To-day a small party has gone to the Potomac to bathe, three miles away.

"June 15th. Was up before sunrise this morning, and bathed at the spring and went over and admired the battery's new twelve-pounders before reveillé."

Reveille, 4.30 A. M.

"Reveille sounds at half past four. We tumble out for early roll-call, just as we please, as regards our costumes. In the excitement many of the men come half dressed, dragging their muskets after them, completing their hasty toilet after getting into line. The helter-skelter that follows the hasty endeavor to get into the ranks is extremely comical to behold. It gives no time for the adjustment of collars, or tying of neckties or 'whangs.' This morning all our men but one had overcoats on. That one was late, and not having time to dress at all, before his name would be called, he hastily wrapped the drapery of his couch, that is an army blanket, about him, and took his position in line, to our great amusement. Later this morning, we marched over to the quartermaster's tent, and actually received our blue army pants. Such a motley assembly! Some with no pants (only drawers), some with only three-quarter pants, multitudes with dilapidated pants, full of patches and holes, and the balance with blankets to cover them, for respectability's sake. Each man received the pair first handed him, with the instruction to 'try them on,' and if 'no fit,' to change round with some other member of the regiment. If any one could not, after all, succeed in finding a pair which would answer the purpose, he could return them to the quartermaster for exchange. We had a good deal of fun during the operation of 'trying on' and getting fitted.

Thus our 'infant,' a tall six-footer, received a short pair, while Halsey DeWolf, had a pair which came up to his neck. Fred Armington is now hard at work shortening the legs of his trousers, so as not to show the white linings.

"2 P. M. We had a good dinner of beef-soup and potatoes, with strawberries for dessert. Potatoes, thanks to our foragers, are quite plenty now. Seeing Fred Hedge (the Athenæum librarian) staining his hands picking over strawberries, reminds me of a laugh we had at William A. Harris while on the march from Washington. He had a new red silk handkerchief in his cap, and the perspiration soon began to make the color run, so that as he wiped his face with it the color was transferred, which gave him a peculiarly heated and exhausted appearance. When we first noticed it we thought that the march was giving him 'jessy!' We soon discovered, however, that he was only being artificially colored, '*à la* Indian!'

"Tuesday, June 17th. Yesterday, we had plenty of drill, and only six roll-calls. I wish you could hear us, 'break ranks, march!' We just do it altogether, with a will! This morning we had battalion drill, as usual, carrying our muskets and equipments. Our dress, over the uniform, consists of a belt which fastens round the body, and which holds a cartridge-box and bayonet, with a cross-belt. Our muskets after an hour's drill in the hot sun seem a good deal heavier than they did as we proudly handled them at first." "To relieve this difficulty," says the author, "a belt-hook was devised, which attached to the body-belt in such a way that when the musket was at the position of 'carry,' its weight could be easily transferred from the arm to the belt-hook.

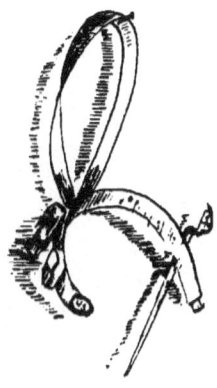
Belt and Belt-Hook.

It immediately became very popular, and worked to perfection, until one unlucky day as we stood in line with our muskets quietly resting on our belt-hooks, the order was suddenly given to 'order, arms!' Down went every other fellow's gun promptly! But mine wouldn't let go of that plaguy belt-hook, and was left suspended high in air! The captain reprimanded me sharply, the boys in the ranks smiled audibly, and all belt-hooks were ordered off promptly. They might afterwards be seen adorning the belts of officers, supporting their long swords, but they no longer supported the firelocks of privates. I was so mortified that I began to feel sorry that I'd come out with the rest of the boys to help save the capital. I felt almost as bad as I did once in a spelling-class at school. I suppose I wasn't paying then the best of attention, when suddenly the teacher called upon me to spell the word. I hadn't any more idea what the word was than if it had been 'belt-hook,' but supposing that the next boy kindly intended to prompt me by whispering, 'lignum-vitæ,' I boldly pronounced, and spelled it, until interrupted by shouts of laughter from the school, in which the teacher himself joined. I looked at the other boy, and realized that he'd given me away, for his sides were shaking. He is an old boy now, and I forgive him, as I hope to be forgiven, for perpetrating some of the same sort of practical jokes. Certainly, I can never forget my experiences with 'belt-hooks' and 'lignum-vitæ.'

"The 'grand rounds?' Yes, well do I remember my first experience. I was guard at the west of the camp, at the foot of the hill, when the 'grand rounds' came along. Captain Smith was officer of the day, and, of course, led the  guard. It had been raining hard, and the water was rushing down the hill, so that my tramp was through mud and water. About midnight I heard stumbling footsteps: 'Halt! who goes there?' 'Grand rounds!' 'Advance, sergeant of the grand rounds and give the countersign!' The sergeant spattered the mud, gave the countersign, and inquired the way to the next rounds, for it was so dark that you could hardly see him. The captain stopped, and said 'Chace, how do you stand it?' I said 'first rate,' and he went on his way rejoicing. He has been on duty every day, although often very tired, and troubled with a cold.

"By the way, we have a man here named Adam. A few minutes ago some one went by our tent calling out, 'John, where's Adam?' and John Cady immediately called out, 'Where's Adam? Gone after Eve!' You would think we needed an Eve if you could see the sleeves of my blouse. I cut them off, and then stitched, basted and sewed the edges; it would puzzle a seamstress to tell which. At this moment we are emptying Corporal Foster's box of ginger cookies.

A few days later, Mr. Chace wrote: "Have just returned from 'dress parade.' All the companies march to the parade-ground, form in two ranks, and face to the front, sergeants in the rear. The order is then given, 'order, arms; parade, rest.' At this rest the right foot is thrown to the rear of the left, the hands crossed in front of the body, left uppermost, thumbs crossed, eyes to the front, every man to remain as still as a statue, even if a fly or a spider walks over his face. The drum-band, five fifes leading, followed by eight snare-drums, then marches in front of the regiment, from right to left, playing in common time, then halts, about face, and marches back quick time. 'First sergeants to the front and centre.' At this command the first sergeants pass to the front of their respective companies, face inward, and marching to the centre of the regiment, take the position, 'front-face.' The sergeant on the right, his piece being at a light infantry 'shoulder,' then salutes, by carrying his left arm across the breast, and reports to the adjutant, 'Company D present, or accounted for.' Each sergeant follows, reporting his company in the same manner. The adjutant who is standing opposite the centre of the regiment, facing it, and in front of the colonel, then orders, 'outward face, to your posts, march.' The sergeants return to their posts. The order, 'parade is dismissed,' then follows. At this the commissioned officers advance to the front, face, march to the centre and report, the band meanwhile, playing. Having reported, the officers return by the shortest route to their companies and take them out of line. Each company is then drilled by its commandant, presenting a lively spectacle. At the same time another company was going through the movement of 'charge bayonets' about a quarter of a mile distant. The yells of the men were exciting to hear. After drilling some time we were again formed in line, and drilled by Lieutenant-Colonel Shaw for about twenty minutes very lively.

"Ned Brown has been cooking a nice custard in his mess-pan. A pint of milk, two eggs, a little nutmeg, and watching the fire for ten minutes, made

Cooking Custard.

a cheap and luxurious dish for a soldier. I am now sitting on a box in front of our tent, and can see down Benefit street beyond the cook's tent. It is amusing to see some of the boys steering for their tents, with bread in one hand and meat in the other, remembering at the same time, how they lived at home.

"Yesterday, the Zouaves, Captain Duckworth, received a big pile of good things, not the least acceptable of which, was a football. Sergeants Brown and Cady went on pass to Washington yesterday. They returned in time for 'retreat' which beats at seven P. M. They brought along a two-gallon coffee pot, and 'K. D.' had a blacking box and brush. Ned also brought coffee and sugar, and we had some coffee in the evening that beat any that we have had since leaving home. We have not as yet been served with either mess-pans, knives or forks. What we have in that line has been 'foraged.' My silver spoon, for which I paid four cents, the other day in Washington, disappeared yesterday. I have made two trips from camp, recently, one to the Potomac, the 19th, and one to Washington, the 20th. In the former tramp, after crossing Chain Bridge, we proceeded along a steep, rocky road, about half a mile, when we came to Fort Marcy, garrisoned by two companies of a New York artillery regiment. The fort mounts thirteen guns (twenty-four-pound Parrott, six-pound field pieces, and twelve-pound brass howitzers). The fort overlooks the Potomac. From Fort Marcy we could see encampments in the distance, and further on in Virginia, Fort Ethan Allen, mounting twenty-five guns. Returning to camp, we reported in good season, tired out. The next day being my chance to go to Washington, I snapped up the offer, and, borrowing a fresh collar, and brushing my hair and boots, was soon ready.

"Brock Mathewson, 2d, was the corporal, and William A. Harris was the other private. We started about 8.15 and walked to Georgetown. On reaching Georgetown heights a beautiful panorama opened before us. Arlington heights, the old residence of General Lee, Fort Corcoran, the Potomac, Long Bridge, the Capitol and Washington Monument. We took the stage for Washington, and pulled the strap in front of the White House." Then follows an interesting description of the places visited: the White House, Willard's Hotel, Patent Office and the Capitol. "The bakery in the basement bakes 35,000 loaves daily for the soldiers. Returning to camp via Georgetown, a carriage passed, and we exchanged salutes with Secretary of War Edwin M. Stanton. Following was a gentleman on horseback, who immediately lifted his hat to us, and we recognized President Lincoln." He was greatly beloved by the soldiers, and more than once interfered with the military powers to pardon some youthful deserter, or sentry who had fallen asleep at his post.

"My business in Washington," says a well known official, "was to secure a pardon for a young soldier who had deserted under rather peculiar circumstances. When he enlisted he was under engagement to a young girl, and went to the front very certain of her faithfulness, as a young man should be, and he made a most excellent soldier, and felt that 'she' would be proud of him. It is needless to say that the young girl being exceptionally attractive, and the war unexpectedly protracted, had another lover, whom she had discarded for the young volunteer, for which the stay-at-home hated the accepted soldier with the utmost cordiality. Taking advantage of his long absence he began to renew his suit with such vehemence, that a rumor reached the young man at the front that his love had gone over to the enemy. He immediately applied for a furlough, which was refused, and, half mad and reckless of consequences, he deserted his post and started for home. He found the information he had received partially true, but he had arrived in time. He married the girl, but was immediately arrested as a deserter, tried, found guilty, and sentenced to be

The Girls We Left Behind Us.

shot. After patiently listening to the recital, and inquiring as to his previous good character, the President at once signed the pardon, saying: 'I want to punish the young man; probably in less than a year he will wish I had withheld the pardon. We can't tell though, I suppose when I was a young man I should have done the same fool thing myself!'"

If ever a man was fairly tested, Lincoln was. General Longstreet, of the South, calls him "the greatest man of rebellious times; the one matchless among forty millions for the peculiar difficulties of the period." There was no lack of resistance, nor of ridicule both at home and abroad, and one of the most touching tributes at his death was the manly recantation of the London *Punch*, which for four long years had pursued him with its slanders:

> "Beside this corpse that bears for winding sheet
> The Stars and Stripes he lived to rear anew,
> Between the mourners at the head and feet,
> Say, scurrile jester, is there room for you?
>
> Yes, he had lived to shame me from my sneer,
> To lame my pencil, and confute my pen,
> To make me own this kind of princes peer,
> This rail-splitter, a true-born king of men!"

Resuming, H. T. Chace wrote: "June 21st. Arriving in camp on our return from Washington, we found rumors current that we are under marching orders. If we move it will be to Virginia. There is another report that we are to be sent to the front. While drilling, to-day, I saw a string of army mules and wagons for the Fourteenth Infantry, passing down the road."

Captain Greene wrote: "Paymaster Jabez C. Knight made us a very acceptable visit during the week just past, and paid over the long talked of bounty money."

H. T. Chace, wrote the same day: "A battalion of regulars is now passing by. I have no idea General McClellan will be defeated on the Peninsula, and rather hope that we may have a chance to assist in crushing the rebellion.

Chaplain A. H. Clapp.

"The chaplain has just looked in and given us a pleasant word. We like him." "We are greatly attached to our chaplain," wrote Capt. A. Crawford Greene. "He is in every way fitted for the duties of his office. He is daily among the sick, and among the soldiers generally, speaking an encouraging word to all. He holds services every night, and on the Sabbath services at eleven A. M. and seven P. M." In his report to the governor of Rhode Island, Colonel Shaw said: "The regiment was particularly fortunate in its chaplain, Rev. A. Huntington Clapp, the honored pastor of the Beneficent Congregational Church in Providence. He was singularly qualified for the duties of his office, and devoted himself with unremitting fidelity to the temporal and spiritual welfare of the men." Indeed, Sir Walter Scott's description of Father Clement might well be applied to our beloved chaplain, "You will think of him as the best and kindest man in the world, with a comfort for every man's grief, a counsel for every man's difficulty, the rich man's surest guide, and the poor man's best friend."

Major Babbitt.

Capt. A. Crawford Greene, wrote June 21st: "Maj. Jacob Babbitt has arrived, and commenced his duties. Our pickets brought in a man this morning who seems wonderfully frightened. He gives no satisfactory excuse for being in the road. He cocked his rifle when about to be taken, but one of our pickets arrested him in time to prevent the discharge. We have every indication judging from preparatory orders that we are to leave Camp Frieze, and pitch our tents, the God of battles only knows where. We hear it rumored that we are to go to Cloud's Mills, Va., near Alexandria. It is also reported that we of the Tenth are soon to receive rifled muskets similar to those of the Ninth. We have just received orders to cook two days' rations, which is another evidence that we are to march. The Tenth Battery has already started for Cloud's Mills, via Washington. Our hospital exhibits this morning about the same number (say seventy-eight) of inmates who are comfortably sick. None are thought to be in a dangerous state. Our advantages for company and battalion drill have been extremely limited at Camp Frieze, and our hope is that we may find our new camp better adapted for general instruction. There seems to be an unusual movement of troops about here, and the supposition is that an important engagement is about to take place. We notice that most of the regiments about us are packed up, with knapsacks on, ready to march at a moment's notice. Our men appear ready for whatever awaits them."

Scene in Hospital.

Regimental surgeon to patient:

"You've got a bad cold, and a fever, sir. Have you been in a draught?"

Patient:

"Drafted, no, sir! They didn't draft me. I was darned fool enough to enlist of my own free will! I thought the war was about over, and if I didn't hurry up I should get left!"

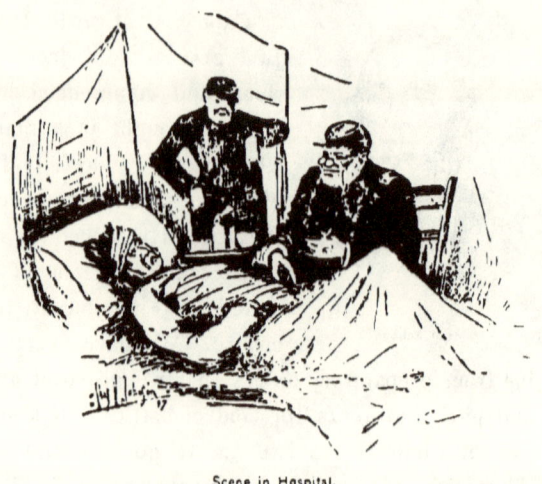

Scene in Hospital.

"A few days ago," wrote Chace, "a soldier went to the surgeon's tent with a sore hand. Seeing that the trouble arose chiefly from a neglect of cleanliness, Dr. Wilcox wrote a prescription, and sent the man with it to the tent where they are prepared. The directions were: 'Four drops in a basin of water, and wash the hands in the mixture, the operation to be repeated four times a day.' The joke was that the vial from which he took the drops contained nothing but pure water. It is needless to add the sores disappeared. Another man went to the doctor, who he saw was simply and purely homesick. He received for his complaint a dose of sugar of milk, and when it leaked out, he also recovered. The general health of the regiment is very good."

Brig.-Gen. Wadsworth.

"Saturday, June 21st. General orders number 19 were read to the regiment.

"June 25th. We expect to be roused at two o'clock to-morrow morning for a march. Our camp is a scene of bustling, stirring activity to-night. The reflection on the trees of the grove from a fire in a neighboring street is beautiful. Tattoo beats earlier than usual, and reveillé at two o'clock A. M."

WAR DEPARTMENT, WASHINGTON CITY, D. C.,
June 24, 1862.

ORDERED, That all applications for passes and permits for persons or property within the lines of the United States forces shall hereafter be made to Brigadier-General Wadsworth, Military Governor of the District of Columbia, and be subject to such terms and conditions as he may prescribe.

Signed, EDWIN M. STANTON.
Secretary of State.

HEADQUARTERS RESERVE ARMY CORPS,

General Orders No. 1.   WASHINGTON, June 24, 1862.

1. Pursuant to instructions from the War Department, the undersigned hereby assumes the command of all the forces in and about the City of Washington, except such as may be required by Brigadier-General Wadsworth, for purposes set forth in the instructions referred to.

2. Such of these troops as are north of the Potomac will hold themselves in readiness to move at a moment's warning.

Signed, L. D. STURGIS,
Brig.-Gen. U. S. Vols.

NOTE. Brig.-Gen. James S. Wadsworth, a most worthy and intrepid officer, was mortally wounded and fell into the hands of the enemy, in the battle of the Wilderness, Va., May 6, 1864.

HEADQUARTERS TENTH REGIMENT R. I. VOLS.,
CAMP FRIEZE, June 20, 1862.

General Orders No. 19.

For the better enforcement of that discipline so essential to the health, comfort, and soldierly bearing of the members of this regiment, the following orders and extracts from the Army Regulations are hereby promulgated:

I. Captains will cause the men of their companies to be numbered in a regular series, including the non-commissioned officers, and divided into squads, each to be put under the charge of a non-commissioned officer.

II. The utmost attention will be paid by commanders of companies, to the cleanliness of the men, as to their person, clothing, arms, accoutrements and equipments, also their quarters or tents. Every man will be required to bathe the whole body at least twice a week. The hair to be kept short, and beard neatly trimmed.

III. The knapsack of each man will be placed at the head of his bed, around the outer circle of the tent, packed and ready to be slung. The overcoat neatly folded inside out, and placed on the knapsack. Boots well cleaned.

IV. Dirty clothes will be kept in an appropriate part of the knapsack. No article of any kind will be put under the bedding.

V. Cooking and mess utensils will be cleansed immediately after using, and neatly arranged in their proper places.

VI. Non-commissioned officers in command of squads, will be held more immediately responsible that their men observe what is prescribed above. That they wash their hands and faces daily; that they brush or comb their heads; that those who are to go on duty put their arms, accoutrements, dress, etc., in the best order, and that such as have permission to pass the chain of sentinels, are in the dress that may be ordered.

VII. When belts are given to a soldier, the captain will see that they are properly fitted to the body, and it is forbidden to cut any without his sanction.

VIII. Cartridge boxes and bayonet scabbards will be polished with blacking.

IX. Arms shall not be kept loaded in the tents, or when men are off duty, except by special orders.

X. Company officers must visit the kitchen daily, and inspect the kettles, and at all times carefully attend to the messing and economy of their respective commands. Soup must be boiled at least five hours, and vegetables always cooked sufficiently to be perfectly soft and digestible. These duties are of the utmost importance and must not be neglected.

XI. Courtesy among military men is indispensable to discipline. Respect to superiors will not be confined to obedience on duty, but will be extended to all occasions. It is always the duty of the inferior to accost or offer first the customary salutation, and of the superior to return such complimentary notice.

XII. When a soldier without arms, or side arms only, meets an officer, he is to raise his hand to the right side of the visor of the cap, palm to the front, elbow raised as high as the shoulder, looking at the same time in a respectful and soldier-like manner to the officer, who will return the compliment thus offered.

XIII. A non-commissioned officer or soldier being seated, and without particular occupation, will rise on the approach of an officer, and make the customary salutation. If standing, he will turn towards the officer for the same purpose. If the parties remain in the same place or on the same ground, such compliments need not be repeated.

XIV. All non-commissioned officers and privates visiting officers' quarters will stand at "Attention," and remain uncovered.

By order of
ZENAS R. BLISS,
Colonel Commanding.

JOHN F. TOBEY,
Adjutant.

HEADQUARTERS STURGIS'S BRIGADE.
General Orders No. 18.
WASHINGTON, June 20, 1862.

I. All commands in this brigade, excepting the Fifty-ninth Regiment New York Volunteers, will be held in immediate readiness for marching orders.

II. The commanding officer of each command will notify the brigade quartermaster, Lieut. Nelson Plato, of the number of wagons requisite for the moving of his command.

By order of
Brigadier-General STURGIS.
HENRY R. MIGHELS,
Capt. and A. A. G.

PARTING SKETCH OF CAMP FRIEZE.

By HENRY T. CHACE, Company D, Tenth Rhode Island Volunteers.

Service Ground, Tenth Regiment.

Company B, Captain Dyer.
Company K, Captain Low.
Company G, Captain Greene.
Company H, Capt. Duckworth.
Company E, Captain Cady.
Company I, Captain Hale.
Company A, Captain Taber.
Company C, Captain Vose.
Company F, Captain Harris.
Company D, Capt. Smith.

Captains' and Lieutenants' Tents.
Colonel, Lieut. Colonel and Major.
Hospital Tents.
Street.

Orderly Starkey's Mess.
Sergeant Tobey's Mess.
Sergeant Dorrance's Mess.
Sergeant Brown's Mess. (Athenæum.)
Corporal Gould's Mess.
Mathewson's Mess.

NINTH REGIMENT.

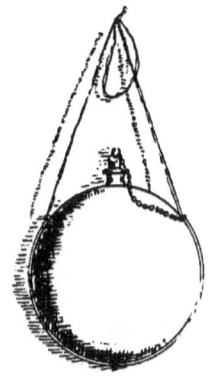

Canteen.

"We are about to start for Cloud's Mills, near Alexandria," wrote one of the men. "Already our noble battery has thundered off, and we shall soon follow them, leaving our familiar avenues, our evergreen bowers and shady resorts for chatting and smoking, to the spiders and wood-ticks, the tree toads and fire-flies, whose domain we have invaded. We may find in some respects a better, but surely not a more picturesque camping ground."

HEADQUARTERS TENTH REGIMENT R. I. VOLS.,
CAMP FRIEZE, June 25, 1862.

General Orders No. 21.

I. The regiment will move from its present camp to-morrow morning.

II. Knapsacks must be packed and marked, and canteens and haversacks filled, and all provisions and articles on hand in the cook-tent and not immediately required, packed in the wagons by evening.

III. Reveillé will sound at two o'clock A. M., to-morrow. Company cooks will prepare breakfast and hot coffee, and serve them out at that time.

IV. The regiment must then be ready to strike tents and march.

By order of

ZENAS R. BLISS,
Colonel Commanding.

JOHN F. TOBEY,
Adjutant.

Packing knapsacks meant compressing all our housekeeping into a space so that it could be carried on our backs. Now we had so many things on hand—good to eat and to wear—that it became very hard to decide which to take and which to leave.

"June 26th. As per orders," wrote the author, "we broke up our old camp shortly after midnight this morning. At two o'clock came the rattling 'rap-a-tap-tap' of the reveillé. It was a grand sight, as the beautiful grove with its stately oaks and tented avenues was suddenly illuminated with blazing bonfires, as if by magic. The long rows of glistening bayonets shone up and down the camp, the sparks filled the air and shot upward to the sky; which with the falling tents, the men hurrying to and fro, with shouts and laughter, and the army wagons rumbling off, full of stores and baggage, produced a scene of rare enchantment. After roll-call we were ordered to pack knapsacks and be ready to march at daylight. It is astonishing how heavy a knapsack gets on the march, even if there isn't much in it. The knapsack opens like a carpet bag, with a great pocket in one side, and a loose flap with straps on the other. It is strapped to the back by a novel arrangement of straps and buckles. Some stuffed everything into their knapsacks regardless of the weight. One of them contained the following articles: 'Two pairs of drawers, a pair of thick boots, four pairs of stockings, four flannel shirts, a blue blouse, a looking-glass, a brush and comb, a razor, razor strop and brush, a box of blacking and a blacking brush, a can of preserves, a bottle of pain-killer, and cough mixture, a small bag of sugar, a piece of chalk, several towels, a Bible, besides postage stamps and writing

Knapsack.

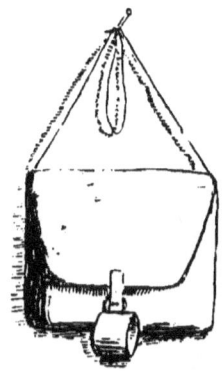
Haversack.

materials. On top of the knapsack was stuffed a double woolen blanket and a rubber one.' Fortunately, there was extra wagon-room, and the men were allowed to pile in their knapsacks, instead of strapping them on their backs."

"We left Camp Frieze," wrote H. T. Chace, "at six o'clock in the morning, with three rousing cheers and a Narragansett! The regiment stepped off at a lively gait in the fresh morning air. We carry muskets, haversacks for rations (mine was supplied with lemons); canteens (mine was filled with tea), and cartridge boxes, with ten and twenty rounds of ammunition. Our rations were served last evening and consist of beef and hard-tack."

Says Lieutenant Phillips: "Our route of march lay through Washington, where General Scott's fine residence was pointed out. As we approached Willard's Hotel Colonel Bliss requested us to strike up 'John Brown ;' a thousand voices responded, the ladies thronged the balconies, and, recognizing the colonel, they waved their best wishes, as we went marching on." Between nine and ten the regiment passed over Long Bridge, making the old wooden structure shake with its measured tread. Tramp, tramp, tramp, how many thousands crossed this 'bridge of sighs' never to return! The day was oppressively hot, as we tramped on, past rifle-pits, fortifications and earthworks. We hadn't been in 'ole Virginia' an hour before we realized that there wasn't so much fun in it after all. We marched, and marched, and marched till we reached Alexandria. After a further tramp of several miles, we finally halted about two o'clock P. M., on a vast, elevated plain, under the guns of Fort Ward, near Fairfax Seminary. A man who lives here told me that we marched twelve miles this side of Long Bridge, or twenty miles in all."

Captain Hale, Company I, wrote, "That the length of the march had been variously estimated, according to the

Cooling Off.

length of limb and strength of muscle of those who participated, ranging from eighteen miles (about the actual distance), to thirty or forty; while Corporal Stump declares that he must have traveled at least a hundred and fifty miles! Somebody asked him on the road what regiment it was, and he promptly responded, 'the One Hundred and Tenth Rhode Island!'" An old soldier wrote home after such a tramp, "I'm all right except the dog-gorned blisters on my feet, and I hope these few lines will find you enjoying the same blessings!" Surely, the monks who used to put peas in their shoes, as a penance, did not suffer more than some of us did on that march. I recall the celerity with which I kicked off my "whangs," and getting a refreshing drink of cold water from the well at Fort Ward, I dropped on the ground and dropped off to sleep in the twinkling of an eye.

Making Coffee.

We were somewhat rudely awakened toward sunset by the orders to "pitch tents," which we soon accomplished to the satisfaction of the officers. Hard-tack and coffee were then served for supper, and didn't they go good, particularly the hot coffee from the old iron kettles;

" The old coffee kettles, the iron bound kettles,
The old coffee kettles that hung on a pole."

"The Ninety-ninth Pennsylvania Regiment," wrote H. T. Chace, "came into camp to-night too late to pitch tents till morning. Some of them came over to our tent, tired out and hungry. Fortunately our canteens had just been filled, and they speedily emptied them." What hospitality ever equaled that of comrades in the days when "we drank from the same canteen!" How we all slept that night! "Phat a blessing," said Pat, "that noight niver comes in till late in the day, when yer all toired out, and couldn't march no more, anyhow, at all, at all, not even if it was mornin!" The morning dawned at length and found us a good deal refreshed, but somewhat stiff and sore. It proved to be another scorching day, "with a sky of brass, an earth of ashes, and the air of a furnace." Captain Hale wrote home: "To distinguish it from our last camp, 'Camp Frieze,' we designated it 'Camp Scorch,' although no special order was issued to that effect.

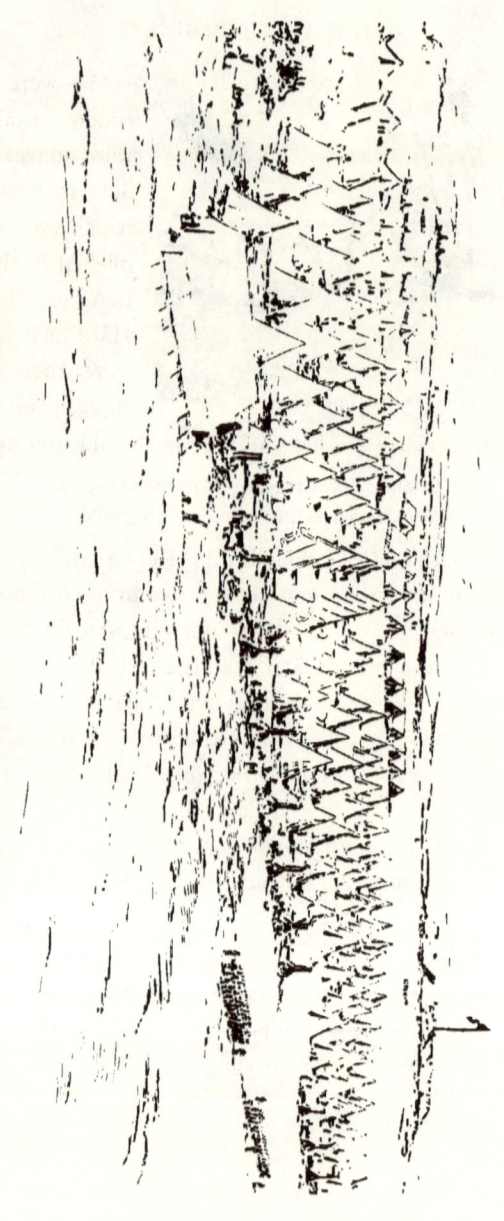

Camp Scorch, alias Camp Misery, alias Camp Desolation.

I should judge from appearances that this particular portion of the sacred soil has undergone the effect of the last great conflagration. I was about to say, prematurely, but more properly, in advance of the rest of the world. Barren desolation marks it as far as the eye can reach, and Corporal Stump, after scouring the plain with a critical eye, remarked, 'that the most nimble of grasshoppers could not cross it unless he carried three days' rations on his back.' The country has been even stripped of its fences and hedges to remove every cover for the enemy, and everything has a grim, ravaged look." Our camp became generally known as "Camp Misery," while the members of the Ninth Regiment, which arrived the following day, Saturday, preferred to call it "Camp Desolation," a very appropriate name.

"Our present camp," says H. T. Chace, "is in one respect, at least, superior to the old one, viz.: in the evenness of the temperature. The nights are not so cold or damp as at Tennallytown. We have more company around us, also. It is evident that a large number of troops are being concentrated on this great plain at 'Seminary Hill.' Between ten thousand and twenty thousand are already here. This famous camping-ground, over two hundred acres in area, recently witnessed the stately march of the grand army of the Potomac, on its departure for the Peninsula. We hear that the various regiments and batteries assembling here are to be consolidated into a division. Every hill top is crowned with the inevitable fort; near us are forts Ward, Worth, Blenker, and Ellsworth. Fort Ward is a large earthwork mounting several thirty-two pounders, and rifled field pieces. It commands the roads to Fairfax Court-House, and Leesburg."

"Seminary Hill takes its name from a group of handsome brick buildings partly hidden in a grove on its southeastern slope, known as Fairfax Seminary. Here Messrs. Bancroft, Wheeler, and Hoffman studied. In yonder grove they have many times walked. We are now fairly entered on a soldier's life, and expect a rough time. Breakfast, this morning, consisted of hard-bread and coffee, without sugar or milk. I was on guard from 'five to seven o'clock,' and had a pleasant time enjoying the view. Before me was Fort Ward; off to the left oblique Munson's Hill; to the right oblique was Washington and the Capitol, while the unfinished Washington Monument loomed up, plainly visible."

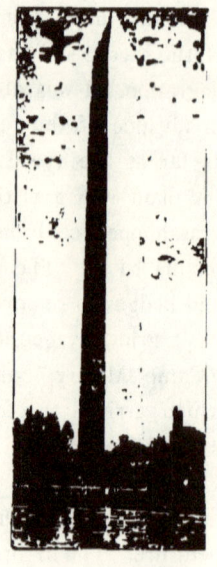

Washington Monument.

"As we marched through Washington, down Fourteenth Street, we passed near the monument, which was on our right hand." At that time it was but partially built, and was but little more than a staring mass of marble blocks, covered with mighty derricks and scaffolding. It was also surrounded by the government cattle yards and slaughter-houses, and presented anything but an inviting appearance. Corp. Nathan H. Baker, of Company B, tells a good story of being detailed with a squad of men from Camp Frieze, to get a supply of beef for the regiment, at the monument stock yards. After performing this duty, Baker accompanied by Nelson W. Aldrich, of Company D, made a visit to the

Capitol, and as Congress had not assembled for the day, they proceeded to the desk of Representative George H. Browne, of Rhode Island, and decked it with some spring flowers. They then retired to the gallery to await the result. Soon Colonel Browne entered the chamber, noticed the floral decoration of his desk, and was well pleased with this mark of attention and respect. The next year Colonel Browne buckled on his sword and rendered good service in his country's defence. A few more years passed, peace and union were restored, and Nelson W. Aldrich, the young volunteer of the Tenth, became a representative of the House from his native state.

The Washington Monument is a granite shaft faced with white marble, six hundred feet high, fifty-five feet square at the base, and thirty feet square at the top. Under the auspices of the Washington National Monument Society, the construction of the monument was begun in 1848, on the very spot selected by Washington himself for a memorial of the American Revolution. Funds amounting to nearly $250,000 were contributed by the people of the United States of all ages and from all quarters of the Union, and the construction continued until 1856, when it reached a height of over one hundred and fifty-six feet. The financial embarrassments of the time led to the discontinuance of the work, and it was not until 1877 when, by act of Congress, its completion was authorized, and it was finally dedicated, in the presence of President Arthur and his cabinet, on the 22d of February, 1885. The address of the occasion was written by Robert C. Winthrop, who in 1848 had delivered an oration on the laying of the corner-stone.

THE ARMY MULE.

Sweet Bye and Bye.)

"You may sing of your
beans and hard-tack,
Of bad water you drank
from the pool;
Of tin cup, tin canteen,
haversack,
But you must not forget
the old mule!

The Army Mule.

Chorus: Good old mule, army mule.
Both your ears were so graceful and long;
You were true to our flag,
So we'll praise you in story and song!"

"Shortly after crossing Long Bridge," wrote Chace, "on the Virginia side, we noticed a large drove of mules, herded together by the road-side. They numbered upwards of two thousand." The motive power of an army wagon usually consisted of six of these long-eared creatures, although horses were substituted when available. It requires special training to be a good mule driver. Mules are stubborn things,—when you will, they won't; and when you won't they will! After being kicked by a mule, with both fore and hind feet, a young volunteer mule-driver was glad to withdraw in disgust. I heard of a Virginia mule which lived in a coal mine nine years after the war, without seeing daylight. The old fellow was hoisted up the other day, and his first act was to kick a boy sky-high. Nine years in a coal mine won't make a mule anything but a mule.

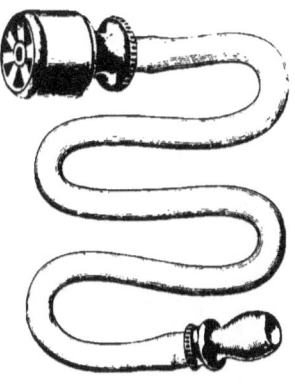

Water Filter.

June 27. H. T. Chace, says, "At ten o'clock we fell in for drill which ended in our marching two miles to Hurd's Run, and all bathing, which was truly refreshing. When on the march some of the men are provided with filters, an ingenious device for straining the water and relieving it from the presence of insects and impurities. On the way we passed several farms, one located on a rising knoll with large trees affording a pleasant shade. Near by, at the top, were the ruins of an old mansion-house, while at the entrance by the roadside two gate-posts still stood like grim sentinels. A fine meadow extended to the right and left, with a crop of rotting, ungathered grass, presenting a sad picture of war's desolation. To have been obliged to leave such a home must have been painful indeed; but trees, fences, and houses, are all swept away. Briggs and I were detailed, before dinner, to go to Fort Ward, for bricks, to repair the cooks' fireplaces, many of which were left here by the regiments preceding us. We obtained a good supply by boldly venturing under the guns of the fort, where we found a great many lying scattered about on the ground. It was an inspiriting sight to see the various batteries drilling and hurrying from point to point, in quick response to the bugle-calls, with an occasional race, by way of diversion. All these things enliven us, and add the spice of variety to a soldier's life.

"Foraging appears to be reduced to a science here. Even in pitching tents we had to look out for our axes and mallets. If we happened to lay them down for a moment, just to turn round, we were very likely to find them missing. The contrabands, also, are great foragers, and the chickens and the ducks have to suffer accordingly."

Old Decatur, an aged African, was recently found late at night in the vicinity of a neighbor's hen-yard, when he was thus interviewed by the proprietor:

"It's pretty damp, Decatur, for a person with rheumatism to be prowling around here at this time of the night."

"Mebbe so, massa, but it's de doctor's advice."

"What, do you mean to tell me that the doctor advises you to be out here nights?"

"No sar, not 'zactly dat way, sar—but he says, 'Catur, you mus' hab' chicken brof, whedder or no!'"

"Our bill of fare at dinner to-day, was as follows," says Chace: "*Soup — chicken, mock-turtle, oyster. *Roast — beef, lamb, turkey. Fried — bacon, hard bread. Entrées — olives, sardines, pickled shrimps. Dessert — nuts, raisins, figs. Drinks — water."

NOTE.—The items marked * were unfortunately overlooked by the cook, and we were consequently reduced to fried bacon, hard bread, and water.

Tempting Game.

"Corp. Nathan H. Baker went out on a little foraging expedition yesterday afternoon," wrote the author in a letter home, June 27th, "and calling me out, on his return, displayed a single, solitary chicken. It was safely landed in the High School tent, where it was secretly stowed away, and in due time Corp. William P. Vaughan undertook to construct a chicken stew for the whole mess, consisting of seventeen hungry recruits. He said he could do it, and had never failed us on good coffee, but it proved to be 'fowl play' in this instance. He proceeded to fill one of our large iron mess buckets with water, prepared and placed the chicken therein. He then used up about all our stock of pepper and salt for seasoning, and after so many minutes by the watch, and a *pretended* tasting, he said 'fall in for chicken stew.' So we all fell in, and each had his share, as he found, *unduly* seasoned; for he immediately passed his cup along to the next victim, with a wry face. There was plenty of stew for all, and a good supply left for the college boys. Our cook says, 'next time draw a little *less* water and *more* chicken!'"

"This afternoon," resumed Mr. Chace, "Cady and I are on guard. We are on the second relief, two hours on, and then four hours off. As we were on, the Ninth Rhode Island came marching into camp. They left Camp Frieze at five o'clock this morning, June 28th, reaching here about twelve, traveling by a shorter route than we did. The weather is very warm, and for some time the men came straggling into camp, tired out. The surveyors are now laying out the quarters of the Ninth, adjoining ours."

"Judging from the variety we have thus far had," wrote Chace, of Company D, "a soldier's life is about the spiciest of any." It is well illustrated by the following excellent poem by Prof. W. Whitman Bailey, another high private of Company D, Tenth Rhode Island Volunteers:

A Day in Camp.

"Faintly sounds the 'reveillé,' and now it louder thrums;
We hear the music of the fife, the tapping of the drums,
And mutter 'you must louder beat before this private comes!'

What! calling to 'police' the camp, is that our duty, too?
To sweep and dust with mop and broom, like common 'biddies' do;
And not a taste of coffee yet? This work is somewhat new!

There's 'peas upon a trencher,' the breakfast call, they say,
Our cup and pan we haste to seize, and gladly speed away,
To take our meagre little third of 'rations' for the day.

'Guard-mounting' after breakfast comes, parade turned inside out,
Just watch the major of the drums how he doth strut about;
The greatest man upon our side, of this there is no doubt.

Then comes the call for morning drill, our 'cap' a man is he,
Who posted up the night before on his 'Revised Hardee,'
Just 'boned'* his tactics like a man, from 'taps' to 'reveillé.'

You cannot stick him, don't you try, and questions will not do;
The guard tent, lo, adjacent stands, in front of it a crew
Of myrmidons to execute, the insubordinate few.

The morn is spent in drilling, but 'roast beef' sounds at last,
The salt-junk motions us to come to our sublime repast,
Ere envious harpies from on post descend to break their fast.

"*'Boned,'" a West Point cadet word for hard study.

THE TENTH REGIMENT

A pipe, and then more tactics, to help the captain out,
That he may know to-morrow how best to 'face about,'
Or form 'a line of battle,' ere the rebels knock us out.

Battalion drills and lots of things in time, will interpose,
To let us feel that martial life is not 'coleur de rose,'
Nor idling all the time away, as most recruits suppose.

At dress parade the soldier, if he has a bit of pride,
Steps gaily forth, a gallant man, of all the earth espied,
And holding in his single hand his country's welfare wide,

Melodiously the bugle is sounding the 'retreat;'
The weary work of day is done; there's rest for tired feet,
The 'briar woods' will offer soon the night's supreme treat.

Ah! what is like those old-time nights around the flaring blaze?
What comrades like the ones we met in yonder vanished days!
Old time will keep their memory green and fresh for us always.

But hark! that surely is 'tattoo,' how quick the time has sped!
Now hasten every soldier true to unroll his 'little bed,'
For 'taps' will soon be beating, and a day in camp be fled."

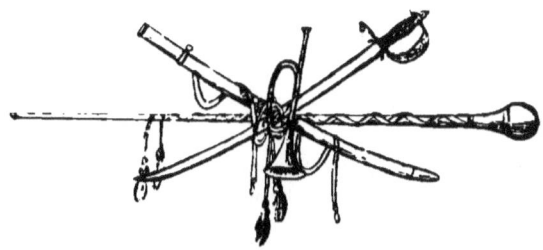

HEADQUARTERS RESERVE ARMY CORPS,
General Orders No. 3.   WASHINGTON, June 26, 1862.

All commands of the Reserve Army Corps south of the Potomac, not garrisoning fortifications will constitute a Division to consist of two Brigades.

The first brigade to be under command of Brigadier-General Cooke, and to be stationed at Cloud's Mills, Virginia, and will comprise the following commands:

Fourteenth United States Infantry,	MAJOR WILLIAMS.
Seventeenth United States Infantry,	" "
Nineteenth United States Infantry,	" "
First and Eleventh United States Infantry,	" "
Sixty-ninth New York Infantry,	COLONEL BAGLEY.
Sixth New York Cavalry,	COLONEL DEVIN.
Ninth New York Cavalry,	COLONEL BEARDSLEY.
Second Pennsylvania Cavalry,	COLONEL PRICE.
Company L, Sixth United States Cavalry,	CAPTAIN BRISBIN.
Detachment Fifth United States Cavalry,	LIEUTENANT FOSDICK.
Sixteenth New York Battery.	CAPTAIN LOCKE.

The second brigade to be under command of Col. Zenas R. Bliss, Tenth Regiment Rhode Island Volunteers, and to be stationed near the Fairfax Seminary, and will comprise the following commands:

Battery L, Second New York Artillery,	CAPTAIN ROEMER.
Sixteenth Indiana Battery,	CAPTAIN NAYLOR.
Battery C, First New York Artillery,	CAPTAIN BARNES.
Second Excelsior Battery,	CAPTAIN BRUEN.
Tenth Regiment Rhode Island Volunteers,	COLONEL BLISS.
Ninth Regiment Rhode Island Volunteers,	LIEUT.-COL. PITMAN.
Thirty-second Massachusetts Volunteers,	LIEUT.-COL. PARKER.
Twelfth Pennsylvania Cavalry,	COLONEL PIERCE.

The above troops will report at once to their respective commanders. The quartermaster will furnish the necessary transportation.

Official: S. D. STURGIS,
WILLIAM C. RAWOLLE,   *Brig.-Gen. Commanding.*
    Captain and A. D. C.

HEADQUARTERS, ARMY OF VIRGINIA,
WASHINGTON, June 27, 1862.

General Orders No. 1.

In accordance with instructions from His Excellency the President of the United States, the undersigned assumes command of the forces comprising the late departments of Major-Generals Fremont, Banks, and McDowell, together with the forces in and around Washington, now under command of Brigadier-General Sturgis. The headquarters of this command will be established for the present in Washington.

General Orders No. 2.

Col. George D. Ruggles is announced as Assistant Adjutant-General and Chief of Staff at these headquarters.

Official: JOHN POPE,
Maj.-Gen. Commanding.

HEADQUARTERS, SECOND BRIGADE,
STURGIS'S DIVISION, June 28, 1862.

General Orders No. 1.

In obedience to instructions contained in General Orders Number Three, Headquarters Reserve Army Corps, Washington, D. C., the undersigned hereby assumes command of the Second Brigade, Sturgis's Division.

Official: ZENAS R. BLISS,
Col. Tenth R. I. Volunteers
Commanding.

JOHN F. TOBEY,
Adjutant and
Act'g Ass't Adj't Gen'l.

HEADQUARTERS RESERVE ARMY CORPS,
ALEXANDRIA, VA., June 29, 1862.

General Orders No. 5.

I. The Ninety-ninth Regiment Pennsylvania Volunteers, the Ninety-first Regiment Pennsylvania Volunteers, the Fifty-ninth Regiment New York Volunteers, and the Thirty-second Regiment Massachusetts Volunteers, will move at once, provided with one hundred rounds of cartridges and five days' rations to embark at Alexandria, Virginia. The quartermaster will furnish the necessary transportation.

II. The Tenth Regiment Rhode Island Volunteers (Col. Zenas R. Bliss), will take immediate possession of the forts to be vacated by the Fifty-ninth Regiment New York Volunteers. The colonel commanding is directed to send an officer and a sufficient force in advance, to receipt for and take charge of all Government property in said forts.

III. The Ninth Regiment Rhode Island Volunteers (Lieutenant-Colonel Pitman), will take immediate possession of the forts on the east branch of the Potomac, extending from Fort Meigs to Fort Greble.

IV. The colonel commanding is directed to send an officer and a sufficient force in advance to receipt for and take charge of all Government property in said forts.

V. The Sixty-third Indiana Volunteers (Lieutenant-Colonel Williams commanding), will take the place of the Ninety-first Pennsylvania Volunteers, as provost-guard, in Alexandria.

By order of

Brig.-Gen. S. D. STURGIS.

HENRY R. MIGHELS,
Capt. and A. A. G.

HEADQUARTERS RESERVE ARMY CORPS.
ALEXANDRIA, VA., June 29, 1862.

General Orders No. 8.

I. The following announcement of the staff of the general commanding is made for the information of all concerned:

    LIEUT.-COL. J. A. HASKIN, Inspector-General:
    CAPT. H. R. MIGHELS, Assistant Adjutant-General;
       "   NELSON PLATO, Chief Quartermaster:
          F. E. BERRIER, Chief Commissary:
          WILLIAM C. RAWOLLE, Aide-de-Camp:
       "   I. K. CASEY,   "
       "   H. B. STURGIS,
       "   J. S. GRIER,

II. Col. J. A. Haskin is placed in charge of fortifications north of the Potomac; his headquarters will be established in Washington City. All reports and returns of the troops north of the Potomac intended for these headquarters will be made to his office.

                By order of
                    Brigadier-General STURGIS.

                          H. R. MIGHELS,
                            Capt. and A. A. G.

HEADQUARTERS RESERVE ARMY CORPS,
ALEXANDRIA, VA., June 30, 1862.

Special Order No. 9.

Col. Zenas R. Bliss, Tenth Rhode Island Volunteers, is hereby relieved from duty as Acting Brigadier-General, Second Brigade, Reserve Army Corps.

                By order of
                    Brigadier-General STURGIS,

                          H. R. MIGHELS,
                            Capt. and A. A. G.

HEADQUARTERS TENTH REGIMENT, R. I. VOLS.,
SEMINARY HILL, VA., June 30, 1862.

Second Lieutenant William C. Chace, Tenth Rhode Island Volunteers, is hereby detailed as Acting Assistant Quartermaster for the Tenth Rhode Island Volunteers, and will report immediately to these headquarters for instructions.

ZENAS R. BLISS,
*Col. Tenth R. I. Vols.
Commanding.*

HEADQUARTERS RESERVE ARMY CORPS,
ALEXANDRIA, VA., June 30, 1862.

COL. ZENAS R. BLISS,
    Com'g Tenth R. I. Vols.

You will proceed at once to Fort Pennsylvania, Tennallytown, D. C., with your entire command, the Light Battery included.

By order of
    Brigadier-General STURGIS,

HENRY R. MIGHELS,
    Capt. and A. A. G.

SEMINARY HOSPITAL, GEORGETOWN, D. C.,
June 29, 1862.

SIR: I have to inform you of the death, this day, of Private William F. Atwood, of Company A, Tenth Regiment Rhode Island Volunteers. Disease, peritonitis. His funeral will take place at four o'clock to-morrow.

Very respectfully,
    Your obedient servant,
        JOSEPH R. SMITH,

To the Adjutant and Captain of　　　　*Ass't Surgeon U. S. Army*
Company A, Tenth Regiment R. I.　　　　　*in charge of Hospital.*
Vols., Camp at Seminary Hill, Va.

The sudden death of Fred Atwood produced a universal feeling of sorrow. He was greatly beloved for his manly qualities.

June 15th, only two weeks before, he had written home that he was well, and had been into Washington "to see the sights." He then described his visit to the Capitol, and of going in to listen to the debate in the Senate. "I also went," he continues,

Washington's Treasure Box.

"over the Patent Office, and among the millions of curious things, the most interesting to me were the articles that belonged to General Washington. There were his coat, vest, and knee-breeches, which he wore when he resigned his commission at Annapolis. There was his iron treasure box, sword, lantern, chairs, tent-poles, fire bucket, etc. That room contained enough to interest me for a month. I then visited the White House, and went into the reception room, which is furnished splendidly. I wish that you and I could stay here a week and go around as much as we liked. We have but little sickness. I am in as good health as I ever was. We will have to give up the good times we were going to

Fire Bucket.

have, for the present, but if I get back at the end of the three months, we will make up for lost time." Just two weeks later came the sudden and startling intelligence of his death. He left the noble example of a brave and spotless manhood.

"Early on the morning of Monday, June 30th," wrote Lieut. Winthrop DeWolf, "came the order assigning the Tenth Regiment to garrison duty in the seven forts and three batteries hitherto occupied by the New York Fifty-ninth, constituting that portion of the defensive chain which protects the capital on the northwest. A lieutenant, sergeant, and twelve men from each company, under command of Lieut. Samuel H. Thomas, of Company B, were detailed to march at once and take possession of the several posts, in advance of the main body, so as to expedite the departure of the Fifty-ninth, ordered to join McClellan on the Peninsula, who was then fighting and retreating to a new base on the James river. The detachment of one hundred and forty men reached Tennallytown soon after noon, with only twelve miles marching. At Fort Pennsylvania, near by, our several posts were assigned us. Much to my satisfaction our little party were sent to Chain Bridge to occupy Battery Martin Scott, commanding that important approach to Washington. Here we remained three days, seemingly forgotten by the world, for no familiar face presented itself; no army wagon with rations crept down the long, steep hill; no newspapers, no mail, nobody came to see if we were dead or alive. Yet do not grieve for us. We lived on the fat of the land—and the water too. From the Potomac we had shad, herring, and catfish; by energetic foraging in the neighborhood we obtained milk, butter, eggs, chickens, corn-bread, sugar, and coffee, and a dilapidated stove found near by sufficed to cook them. On the whole we were rather sorry when the message came from headquarters that Company D was occupying Fort De Russey, where we were to report forthwith."

Marching Orders.

Captain Hale, Company I, under the *nom-de-plume* of Matthew Bagnet, wrote: "It is related somewhere in profane poesy that:

'The king of France, with forty thousand men,
Marched up the hill, and then marched down again.'

Well, the gallant Tenth have imitated his illustrious example, on a somewhat more extended scale in point of distance, if not of numbers. In short we have made a forced march —at least, I suppose that is what they call it—for it was a march, and we were forced to make it. After marching up the hill, we were scarcely settled in our new location, had scarcely drawn the vinegar bottle out of our stocking, and the pepper-sauce from our shirt-sleeves (where they had been placed for safe transportation), had just filled to overflowing our eyes, ears, noses, mouths, lungs, and epidermis, with the dusty exhalations of 'Old Virginny,' when the order came for us to move, and here was where 'we marched down the hill again.'

"Early Monday morning, June 30th, tents were struck in a hurry, baggage-wagons loaded at the double-quick, and we were ready to resume the march, at a run if necessary, anything to escape Camp Misery, Seminary Hill, Fairfax County, Virginia." A three mile march brought us to Alexandria, where we marched by the Marshall House, singing "John Brown" and "Ellsworth's Avengers," led by Levi Burdon, of Company D, who stood on the hotel steps. The headquarters of Acting Brig.-Gen. Zenas R. Bliss, was also serenaded. "At length the regiment halted on a long wharf, facing the Potomac. After the usual, and, of course, necessary delay, we were packed, bag and baggage, men and guns, on board some transports bound to Washington, where we arrived about dusk, and, unfortunately too late to unload our baggage. So, after a weary rest on Sixth street, we resumed our march for Tennallytown, at 10.30 P. M., reaching that memorable locality about 2.30 A. M., and a very cool and penetrating A. M. at that. Here we bivouacked, without tents or blankets.

"Bivouac is a word of French extraction, and I am sorry that the use of it is not confined to that volatile nation. But it is not, so we bivouacked in a ten acre lot, without even a rail fence to keep the cold out. Tired and foot sore, we lay down on the cold ground, with the sky for our nearest covering, and the horizon for the sides of our bed. I secured a handful of straw and tried to fashion it into a luxurious couch, but the straw was obstinate and wouldn't be fashioned. Corporal Stump tried to cover himself with his gun, but found he couldn't tuck in the sides, and so didn't go to sleep for fear he should fall out of bed. Some crawled into hay-ricks and some into barns, while the corporal, after vainly trying the protection of his musket, betook himself to the shelter of an empty flour barrel, which fitted him to a nicety, and where he slept the sleep of innocence.

"Between dozing and shivering, the hours dragged slowly on. Now nodding off into fancied comfort, and now waking up in real discomfort; now trying to soften the hard bosom of mother earth, and then in a sleepy delirium trying to pull the edge of a ten acre lot over one for a coverlet; such is bivouacking." To counteract the effects of the damp night air, whisky rations were issued to stimulate the flagging zeal of the men who were getting faint at heart, weak in the knees, and lame and sore in body. "At early dawn, July 1st," Capt. Elisha Dyer wrote, "the regiment was in motion, and hungry, weary, and dispirited, marched to the headquarters at Fort Pennsylvania. At noon a piercing northeasterly storm came upon us, without tents or other protection, except such as was afforded by the quartermaster's store-house and other lesser buildings left by the Fifty-ninth New York. On the floor, among boxes and barrels, our men lay huddled together for hours without food or relief of any kind. The result of this last trying march from Virginia, was an addition to our sick list, upon which the writer's name appeared for a few days. Our camp equipage, knapsacks, and stores, at length arrived, and company quarters were assigned and marching orders given. Companies B and K, Captains Dyer and Low, to Fort Pennsylvania, the regimental headquarters; Company A, Captain Taber, to Fort Franklin; Company C, Captain Vose, Batteries Cameron and Martin Scott; Company D, Captain Smith, Fort De Russey; Companies E and I, Captains Cady and Hale, Fort Alexander; Company F, Captain Harris, Fort Ripley; Company G, Captain Greene, Fort Gaines; Company H, Captain Duckworth, Batteries Vermont and Martin Scott."

FORT PENNSYLVANIA.
Regimental Headquarters, Tenth Rhode Island Volunteers, and Tenth Light Battery, July and August, 1862.

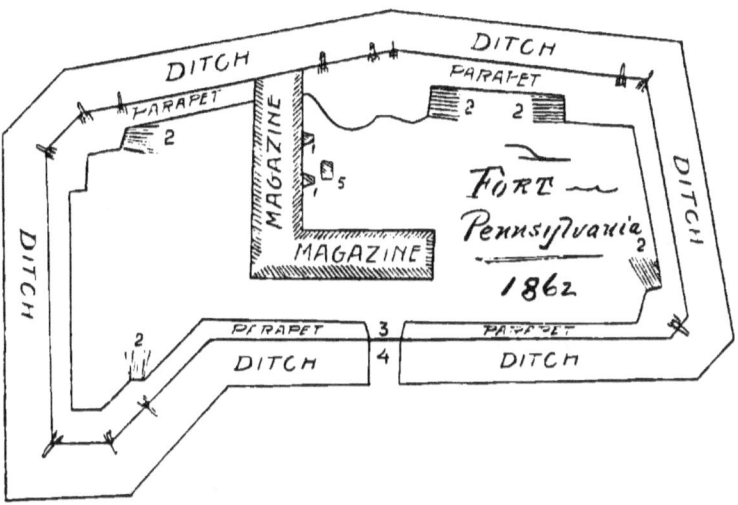

Plan of Fort Pennsylvania.

Fort Pennsylvania mounted three Parrott siege guns and nine 24-pounder barbette guns ; Fort Gaines, four 32-pounder barbette guns ; Fort De Russy, three 24-pounder and four 32-pounder barbette guns ; Fort Alexander, seven 32-pounder barbette guns ; Fort Franklin, six 32-pounder barbette guns ; Fort Ripley, six 24-pounder barbette guns ; Battery Vermont, three 32-pounder barbette guns, and is mounting more ; Battery Cameron, two 42-pounder barbette guns ; Battery Martin Scott, one 32-pounder barbette gun and two mountain howitzers ; total, fifty guns. These forts and batteries extends over a space of six or eight miles, from Battery Cameron on the left, near the Potomac, to Fort De Russy on the right, near Rock Creek, commanding the view at and near Chain Bridge, and the roads to Harper's Ferry and Rockville.

A brief review of the military situation in Virginia, in June, 1862, is necessary in order to understand why our forces around Washington were ordered into Virginia, and a week later were ordered back, or, how we resembled the soldiers of another army, who "marched up a hill, and then marched down again!"

On to Richmond

Notwithstanding the success achieved at Fort Oaks, June 1st, the situation of the Army of the Potomac besieging the Confederate capital, was becoming critical. And, although on the following day, the advance under Hooker pushed forward within sight of the steeples of Richmond, McClellan declared that he could accomplish nothing further until his right was reinforced by McDowell's Corps, which had been withheld for the defence of Washington. On the twelfth instant, McDowell advised McClellan: "For the third time I am ordered to join you, and hope this time to get through. . . . McCall's division goes in advance by water. I will be with you in ten days with the remainder via Fredericksburg." To support this forward movement to the Peninsula, a general advance was ordered of all the forces around Washington to concentrate at Seminary Hill and Cloud's Mills, in Virginia, and, in a few days, an entire division under the command of General Sturgis, was in position, the Ninth and Tenth Rhode Island Regiments and Battery being assigned to the Second Brigade, Col. Zenas R. Bliss, acting brigadier-general, commanding. As we pitched our tents on Seminary Hill, on the afternoon of June 26th, it was generally believed that at last we were on our way to Richmond, perhaps to aid in making an end of the Confederacy. Not much was said about fighting, but doubtless a good deal of thinking was done on that tender subject.

But at that very hour, the turning-point of the Peninsula campaign was reached. Jackson had escaped the combined pursuit of Fremont, Banks, and McDowell, and joined the main army of Lee at Richmond. By his masterly movements he had prevented the reinforcement of McClellan's exposed right, by McDowell, and now interposed his own corps of thirty-five thousand men between them. He had so completely puzzled the authorities at Washington, who appear to have been directing, or misdirecting the campaign, that it seemed to them that Jackson was more likely to be sweeping down the Shenandoah Valley than to be marching back to Richmond. For this cause they held back the reinforcements, and McClellan was left to meet the impending attack, unaided. On the 25th, the Secretary of War telegraphed him, "Neither Banks, Fremont, or McDowell, have any accurate knowledge of Jackson's whereabouts." On the 26th, McClellan reported that Jackson was on his right, driving in his pickets. At three o'clock that afternoon, as the Tenth Rhode Island Volunteers were quietly pitching their tents at Seminary Hill, the battle for Richmond was set in motion at Mechanicsville. The next day, the 27th, Jackson took command of the left wing of the enemy, and attacked McClellan's right with such overwhelming force at Gaines's Mills as to turn his position and cause his retreat to the James river. The order to withdraw was especially bitter to Hooker, on the left, who had pressed forward to the very gates of Richmond, where the prize seemed almost within his grasp. On the same day, June 26th, when McClellan reported the arrival of Jackson in his front, after outmanœuvring and outmarching, the combined forces of Fremont, Banks, and McDowell, these heretofore three independent commands were consolidated into one army, called the Army of Virginia, and Maj.-Gen. John Pope, whose success in the west had given him reputation, was assigned by the President to the chief command. Two days later, when the news of McClellan's retreat to the James reached Washington, all orders for the advance of troops were countermanded, and, with other forces, the Tenth Rhode Island Regiment and Battery were ordered back to the vicinity of their old camps.

The following is the order creating the Army of Virginia:

General Orders No. 103.   WASHINGTON, June 26, 1862.

I. The forces under Major-Generals Fremont, Banks and McDowell, including the troops now under Brigadier-General Sturgis, at Washington, shall be consolidated, and form one army, to be called the Army of Virginia.

II. The command of the Army of Virginia is especially assigned to Major-General Pope as commanding general.

The troops of the Mountain Department, heretofore under command of General Fremont (after Fremont's resignation General Sigel was appointed), shall constitute the first army corps, under the command of General Sigel.

The troops of the Shenandoah Department, now under General Banks, shall constitute the second army corps, and be commanded by him.

The troops under the command of General McDowell, except those within the fortifications and the City of Washington, shall form the third army corps, and be under his command.

By order of the Secretary of War.

E. D. TOWNSEND,
Assistant Adjutant-General.

Back to Tennallytown!

July 1st. Fortunately the author escaped the night march to Tennallytown, for he wrote, "I was appointed on the rear guard to remain at Washington and look after the stores and baggage on the transports. There was no room for us either in the cabin or forecastle, so we tried to find a soft bed in the hold. Sleep was difficult, however, among the boxes and barrels and smells which surrounded us, and we were glad when the morning came, and we could mount up on deck and get a supply of fresh air. After getting the baggage loaded on the army wagons, we started for camp. Two of us were put in charge of a sutler's provision wagon, and after marching a while we climbed in behind, and, being almost famished, feasted ourselves on bologna sausages, greasy pies, cakes, doughnuts, and cookies. The doughnuts were either hand made or machine sewed, but we have become pretty well 'seasoned' for anything during our short campaigning, and we managed to 'get away' with quite an allowance of the sutler's pastry." It was the only time we had pie enough in the army. Fortunately the road was rough, and we were well shaken up, else we might have died from the graspings of indigestion.

The author had been in camp only an hour or two when he was summoned to the officers' quarters, and informed that he had been detailed from the regiment under the following orders:

                        HEADQUARTERS RESERVE ARMY CORPS,
COL. ZENAS R. BLISS,   WASHINGTON, D. C., July 1, 1862.
    Com'g Tenth R. I. Vols.

The General Commanding directs me to say that you detail two intelligent non-commissioned officers or men as clerks to Col. George D. Ruggles, headquarters of General Pope, at the War Department.

                            WILLIAM C. RAWOLLE,
                                  Captain and A. D. C.

               HEADQUARTERS TENTH REGIMENT, R. I. VOLS.,
                   FORT PENNSYLVANIA, July 1, 1862.
Special Orders No. 14.

Company B will detail one non-commissioned officer or man for service as clerk to Colonel Ruggles, headquarters of General Pope, at the War Department, who will report to these headquarters forthwith for instructions.

            By order of
                    ZENAS R. BLISS,
JOHN F. TOBEY,   *Colonel Commanding.*
   Adjutant.

               HEADQUARTERS TENTH REGIMENT R. I. VOLS.,
                   FORT PENNSYLVANIA, July 1, 1862.
Special Orders No. 15.

Company D will detail one non-commissioned officer or man, for service as clerk to Colonel Ruggles, headquarters of General Pope, at the War Department, who will report to these headquarters forthwith for instructions.

            By order of
                    ZENAS R. BLISS,
JOHN F. TOBEY,   *Colonel Commanding.*
   Adjutant.

Gen. John Pope in 1862.

General Pope had just arrived in Washington, from the west, and assumed command of the Army of Virginia. A fortnight was spent in organizing his personal staff, and two men were detached from the Tenth Rhode Island Volunteers for special service at headquarters, the author from Company B, and Charles H. Wildman from Company D, and the following orders were issued:

Special Orders No. 16.   HEADQUARTERS TENTH REGIMENT R. I. VOLS.,
FORT PENNSYLVANIA, July 2, 1862.

Privates William A. Spicer, of Company B, and Charles H. Wildman, of Company D, are hereby detailed for service in Washington as clerks to Col. George D. Ruggles, Chief of Staff, at the headquarters of General Pope, and will report at the War Department for duty forthwith.

By order of ZENAS R. BLISS,
JOHN F. TOBEY, *Colonel Commanding.*
Adjutant.

HEADQUARTERS TENTH REGIMENT R. I. VOLS.,
COLONEL RUGGLES, FORT PENNSYLVANIA, July 2, 1862.
A. A. G. and Chief of Staff.

I have the honor to report that in accordance with orders yesterday received, the bearers, Privates William A. Spicer and Charles H. Wildman are detailed for service as clerks in your department.

Very respectfully, your obedient servant,

Signed, JOHN F. TOBEY,
Adjt. Tenth R. I. Vols.

Our Ambulance Ride.

Letter from the author: "Headquarters Army of Virginia, 232 G Street, Washington, July 3, 1862. Don't be startled because I've turned up in another new locality. Sunday night, June 30th, was our last at Camp Misery, in Virginia. Monday night, July 1st, I slept on board a transport at the Washington Navy Yard, and Tuesday afternoon reported at Fort Pennsylvania. Things were in a tipsy-topsy, hurly-burly state on my arrival." "Unfortunately," says Captain Dyer, "that curse of the army, whiskey, found its way among our men and confusion reigned." One of the men always got drunk on pay-day, in order, as he said, that he could see double, and thus, in imagination, get double pay. Another man was wiser, who kept sober, but always put on his spectacles when eating cherries, so that the fruit might look larger and more tempting.

"Tuesday afternoon, June 2d, I had spent but an hour or two in camp, at Fort Pennsylvania, when I was officially informed (see orders inclosed), that two of us, had been detailed for special service at the War Department, with orders to report at once. Hurriedly packing our knapsacks, and loading all our personal effects into an army ambulance, we bade our comrades good-bye, and started for Washington about half past two P. M. The rain was descending in sheets, as we halted at the War Department, and we got our feet thoroughly soaked in transferring our baggage from the ambulance to the corridor of the War Office.

Gideon Welles
Secretary of Navy.

"We found, on inquiring, that it was past office hours, so we walked twice in the pouring rain to Colonel Ruggles' residence. He received us kindly, and gave us a note to General Wadsworth, the military governor of the district. After scanning us pretty sharply he gave us an order on the superintendent of the Soldiers' Retreat, the place where we stopped when we first arrived in Washington, and from which we were glad to retreat. As it was fully two miles away, in a drenching storm, and no umbrellas even hinted at, we determined to beat a retreat to the War Department, and see what would turn up. We told our story to the night janitor, a kind hearted Irishman, and he at once became interested in our behalf, and obtained permission for us to occupy Adjutant-General Thomas's office for the night. Mr. Welles, with long, white beard, the efficient secretary of the navy, was pointed out to us. We then stepped across the street to a restaurant and enjoyed the first square meal we have had since leaving home. On returning to the War Department we had the great pleasure of seeing President Lincoln walk down the corridor. He carried an old fashioned umbrella big enough for two, and appeared anxious and depressed. It was the day after the battle of Malvern Hill, and the campaign against Richmond had ended in failure." During these disheartening days Mr. Lincoln spent much of his time at the war office.

"I am glad to report that we slept soundly last night in the office of Uncle Sam's Adjutant-General, which we think is quite an honor for boys of seventeen! I am now writing at General Pope's Headquarters, No. 232 G Street, near the War Department. It is a good place to see the leading officers. Generals Sturgis and Banks called this morning. General Pope is in citizen's dress. We think we shall like our duties first-rate. Our rations have been commuted at seventy-five cents per day, with forty

At Headquarters.

cents additional for our services at headquarters. We are to sleep here to receive night dispatches, and take our meals close by the office. Wildman and I propose to make our beds on the carpet in the general's office. To-morrow is the glorious Fourth of July! How I would enjoy spending it at home! There will be no public celebration here, but we are to have a holiday, with passes from General Pope giving us permission to go about the city independent of the provost guards. My pass reads as follows :

          HEADQUARTERS, ARMY OF VIRGINIA,
Pass Number 1.   WASHINGTON, July 3, 1862.

The bearer, William A. Spicer, is employed as clerk at these headquarters, and will be permitted to pass to any part of the city, at all times.

     By command of Major-General POPE.
          GEORGE D. RUGGLES,
         Colonel, A. A. G., and Chief of Staff.

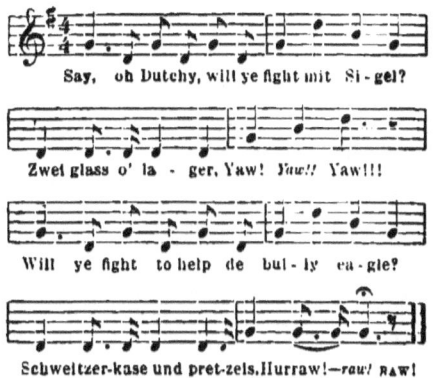

I read in the Providence *Journal* of June 27: "The appointment of General Pope to the command of the Army of Virginia will be regarded as news almost as welcome as that of a victory." "It does look as if he meant to 'push things.' He has kept us busy sending military dispatches in all directions. What we don't know about what is going on, isn't worth knowing. When the general arrived, a few days ago, he found the forces under Fremont, Banks, and McDowell, widely scattered. Then Fremont resigned, and General Sigel was appointed in his place. His two division commanders are Generals Schenck and Schurz. All this is very gratifying to the German soldiers. Sigel is ordered to cross the Shenandoah Valley at Front Royal, and take post at Sperryville. Banks is ordered to take up his position at Little Washington, a few miles northeast of that place. One of the divisions of McDowell's Corps has been ordered forward to Waterloo Bridge, on the line of the Rappahannock, a few miles southwest of Warrenton, while his other division is held at Fredericksburg, by direction of the government. The total effective force, including cavalry, is about fifty thousand. The whole plan of the campaign is changed by the movement of the Army of the

Potomac to Harrison's Landing, which leaves the entire army of General Lee interposed between that of the Army of the Potomac and the Army of Virginia."

"July 6th. General McDowell called at headquarters, this morning. I spent nearly all the forenoon carefully copying a long personal letter from General Pope to General McClellan, at Harrison's Landing, James River, headquarters Army of the Potomac, fully stating his plans and position, and the disposition of the troops under his command. He requests General McClellan in all good faith and earnestness to write him freely and fully his views, and to suggest any measures which he thinks desirable to enable him to coöperate with him and promises on his part to render all assistance in his power. He writes, ' I am very anxious to assist you in your operations, and I will run any risk for that purpose.' In conclusion, he says, 'I therefore request you to feel no hesitation in fully stating your plans, and, so far as in my power, I will carry out your wishes with all the energy, and with all the means at my command.'" The only reply to this cordial communication was a very formal note from General McClellan, very general in its tenor, and proposing nothing whatever toward the accomplishment of the purposes suggested by General Pope. It became apparent, therefore, that there was to be no harmonious coöperation between the Union commanders in Northern and Southern Virginia, so necessary for the success of the campaign. "Later in the day I forwarded a military telegram to General Banks, stating that the critical condition of affairs near Richmond, renders it highly probable that the enemy will advance upon Washington, in force."

"July 15th. By direction of General Pope, I copied yesterday, an important address to the Army of Virginia, for the government printer. A copy will be forwarded to the Ninth and Tenth Rhode Island Regiments and Battery."

HEADQUARTERS ARMY OF VIRGINIA,
WASHINGTON. D. C., July 14, 1862.

To the Officers and Soldiers of the Army of Virginia:

By special assignment of the President of the United States, I have assumed the command of this army. I have spent two weeks in learning your whereabouts, your condition, and your wants; in preparing you for active operations, and in placing you in positions from which you can act promptly and to the purpose. These labors are nearly completed, and I am about to join you in the field.

Let us understand each other. I have come to you from the West, where we have always seen the backs of our enemies; from an army whose business it has been to seek the adversary and to beat him when he was found; whose policy has been attack and not defence. In but one instance has the enemy been able to place our western armies in defensive attitude. I presume that I have been called here to pursue the same system, and to lead you against the enemy. It is my purpose to do so, and that speedily. I am sure you long for an opportunity to win the distinction you are capable of achieving. That opportunity I shall endeavor to give you. Meantime I desire you to dismiss from your minds certain phrases which I am sorry to find much in vogue amongst you. I hear constantly of taking "strong positions and holding them," of "lines of retreat," and of "bases of supply." Let us discard such ideas. The strongest position a soldier should desire to occupy is one from which he can most easily advance against the enemy. Let us study the probable lines of retreat of our opponents, and leave our own to take care of themselves. Let us look before us, and not behind. Success and glory are in the advance; disaster and shame lurk in the rear. Let us act on this understanding, and it is safe to predict that your banners shall be inscribed with many a glorious deed, and that your names will be dear to your countrymen forever.

JOHN POPE.
Major-General Commanding.

HEADQUARTERS MILITARY DEFENCES,
    NORTH OF THE POTOMAC,
        WASHINGTON, July 15, 1862.

To COL. ZENAS R. BLISS,
    Tenth Reg't R. I. Vols.

By direction of General Sturgis, commanding, the firing of blank cartridges at the forts
garrisoned by the companies of your regiment will be discontinued.

Signed,   J. A. HASKIN,
        Lieut.-Col. A. D. C.,
In charge of defences north of the Potomac.

Lieut.-Col. J. A. Haskin.

The firing of the big guns on the forts had been done for artillery practice, but it disturbed certain nervous people in Washington, and was discontinued for military reasons. One of the men wrote: "Colonel Haskin is a brave and accomplished officer, who left his arm at Chapultepec, but who still preserves a certain cheerful manliness which wins the admiration of all who meet him."

Colonel Shaw's report says: "The transfer from camp to garrison was anything but agreeable to the regiment. It compelled us to forego all hope of perfecting ourselves in infantry tactics, and to commence with the rudiments of artillery, with which we were entirely unacquainted. Commendable progress was soon made with our new arms; but extended as we were over so long a line of fortifications, the garrison at each post was necessarily small, and the duties severe. In addition to other duties, a detail of forty men was required to report daily at Battery Vermont, to complete the extension of that work."

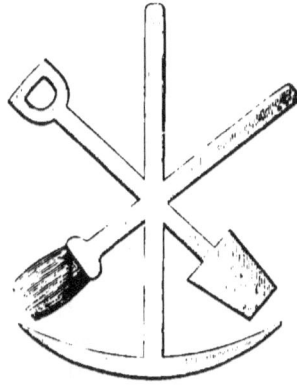
Outfit for Battery Vermont.

"Building forts is one of those heroic but unobstrusive occupations for which our soldiers got little credit. I took an orderly's horse in front of headquarters, and rode out to Tennallytown, to see the boys at Fort Pennsylvania. They appeared glad to see me back again. They say that between heavy artillery drill, garrisoning old forts, and building new ones, their time is pretty well used up. You should see them, hand-spike in hand, heaving at the wheels of those forty-two-pounders. The latest conundrum is, 'Why are the boys of the Tenth in such good company now, at the forts?' 'Because they are closely associated with so many big guns!' But they say they would rather heave at those heavy guns, or make another long tramp into Virginia, and even fight a little than to wear their lives away these hot days, shovelling sand. There doesn't appear to be anything very exciting or inspiring about it, and the patriotism of the boys is at a low ebb. Some of them wear a badge made of lead, consisting of a pick-axe, spade, and broom in combination, to represent their new employment at Battery Vermont. It has been very warm at the fort. In one of the tents the thermometer registered 102 degrees, so that you can imagine how nice and cool it is here. The boys are all pretty well browned, and a good many, I noticed, will go home adorned with a beard which they did not support when they left home."

Company A, Corp. Albert C. Winsor, furnishes the following interesting article on "The Fourth," at Fort Franklin: "The anniversary of National Independence was made a marked occasion at Fort Franklin by a presentation of colors to Company A, Capt. William E. Taber, the gift of the ladies of the Fifth Ward in Providence. Comrade Wendell P. Hood presented the flag, in a neat and patriotic speech, Captain Taber gracefully acknowledging the gift in behalf of the company. Patriotic speeches were also made by First Lieut. Joseph L. Bennett, Jr., Company A; Captains H. B. Cady, Company E; William M. Hale, Company I, and others, and at eleven o'clock the flag was hoisted to the head of the staff greeted by nine rousing cheers and the singing of the 'Star Spangled Banner.' This will be a memorable day to the members of Company A, also, from the fact that a large sized box arrived at the fort last night, well filled with lemons, sugar, tonics, cigars, and tobacco, the gift of the store-keepers and friends in the vicinity of South and Point streets, to enable the 'Blue Pointers' to celebrate, and remind them that they were not forgotten by the friends at home. The boys had remembered their part, and after dinner the camp was visited by a party of the Seventy-first New York Regiment, who were encamped about two miles from Fort Franklin; the comrades were welcomed, and generously entertained, toasts were given, and the camp resounded with patriotic songs; fun and sociability were then in order and greatly enjoyed, as many of the boys will testify by the mementos that were exchanged in caps, buttons, and figures. As the guests left the camp nine cheers were given for New York and Rhode Island."

The following letter of acknowledgment from the chaplain, to the ladies of the Fifth Ward, will be interesting :

FORT PENNSYLVANIA. D. C., July 17. 1862.

REV. C. H. FAY, *Providence*.

MY DEAR BROTHER: Please excuse the long delay in answering yours, which accompanied the beautiful standard presented to Company A (Captain William E. Taber), by the ladies of our Fifth Ward.

The delay has arisen from a little misapprehension, the captain supposing that I had answered it, while I thought *he* had done so.

As the ladies have heard, a debilitating illness made it impossible for me to go to Fort Franklin on the 4th of July. and present the standard, as desired by you, in their behalf.

It was a grievous disappointment not to have that privilege: although, as far as the company and the donors were concerned, nothing was lost; Mr. Hood, a member of Company A, having made the presentation in terms which the ladies would have regarded as eminently befitting the occasion.

They may rely on it, that nothing since we left home has given Company A so much pleasure as this token of remembrance and of confidence from their lady friends of the Fifth Ward.

I will guarantee, moreover, that the Stars and Stripes will never be dishonored at the hands of that noble company.

I knew them at home. I have known them far more intimately here: and I assure you that both officers and men are, as a body, of the right stamp to be entrusted with the beautiful emblem of our country's liberty and greatness.

Please express to the lady donors the thanks of the company; assure them that their gift is appreciated, and will be sacredly preserved as an honored trust: and if borne into battle, will be defended to the last—upborne by no coward's hands.

Please, also, to thank the ladies for the honor they conferred on myself. in selecting me to make the presentation: and, believe me,

Ever, sincerely. yours,

A. HUNTINGDON CLAPP,
Chaplain Tenth R. I. Vols.

Company B, Fort Pennsylvania, July 4th: "Perhaps you would like to know," wrote comrade James F. Field, "how we celebrated the day. The first thing was breakfast, consisting of beefsteak, white bread, and coffee. At half past nine, Companies B and K were formed in line and marched to the colonel's headquarters to listen to a literary feast. An oration was delivered by Joshua M. Addeman, and a poem was read by Henry S. Latham, both of Company B. After the exercises we had a very spirited speech from Mr. Sheffield, one of our representatives in Congress. Soon after we were dismissed, a large box of good things arrived from the Ellsworth Phalanx (High School company). It was quickly opened and the contents were very much appreciated. Your box was also very welcome, especially the cookies. After a few minutes not a vestige of them remained. They tasted tip-top, much better than the first lot, which got mixed up with the catsup from the broken bottle. At half past two dinner was served. Roast beef, potatoes with gravy, beets, onions, peas, and, to crown all, lemonade—and the best of all was, there was enough to 'go around, and around.'

"It was intended that the Declaration of Independence should be read as a part of the exercises, but it had to be omitted, as one of our company, Nathan H. Baker, rode all over the neighboring country in vain, to procure a copy. He did at last succeed in finding one framed, but it was in such fine print that he gave it up as a bad job. At twelve o'clock a salute was fired by the Tenth Rhode Island Battery. During the day and night previous there was firing from the forts on the other side of the Potomac, but we have had orders not to fire any more, for military reasons."

"Toward night, yesterday, July 3d, we had one of the most terrific thunder-storms I ever saw. I happened to be out in it for a few minutes, so I know, and got completely soaked through. The wind blew almost a hurricane. You probably are aware that in a fort the magazine is in the centre, and that the top is somewhat higher than the surrounding embankment. A guard or picket is stationed on this magazine all the time. In order to hold the fort, during the terrific storm of wind and rain, he had to stick his bayonet in the ground the whole length, and then brace himself against it. As it was, he came near being blown off the magazine. But he held on all through the pelting storm, which continued at least half an hour."

Mrs. Partington says, she pities the poor soldiers who have to stay out *on pickets in the scorching rain*, especially when the *pickets are driven in!*

"Companies B and K," wrote Private Edwin B. Fiske, "are still in a flourishing condition, and we can say in the language of a distinguished statesman, 'We still live!' Others have written and told you of the glories of camp-life and its romantic associations, which are welded in a soldier's mind, never to be erased; and he who is permitted to return to his home after the conflict is over, will have as many stories to tell, and stirring incidents to relate to fire the hearts of the young, as fired our hearts when listening to the tales of the old Revolutionary patriots, when our fathers waded through blood and fire to rescue our country from the tyrannical heel of Great Britain. And more, we labor to secure the establishment of our government upon a broader and freer system than has heretofore existed."

Com.-Sergt. James O. Swan was a capable and hard working official. His constant care and vigilance helped bring about a much needed reform in the quality of our rations. He had then, the same quiet, convincing way, to make things move right along — that distinguish him now in his official duties at the City Hall. Some of the boys thought on account of his stern and dignified air that he must have a hard heart. They were mistaken; he always had the interests of the regiment in mind, and demanded the fullest consideration for the men from others, to the extent of his authority.

Com.-Sergt. James O. Swan.

Private Fiske continues: "Allow me to say a few things about ourselves in and around Fort Pennsylvania. The fort is built upon a hill, in a commanding position, and if properly manned could not easily be taken. General McCall's division was encamped in this vicinity last winter. These troops were badly cut up in the late battles before Richmond. Fort Pennsylvania is now garrisoned by Companies B and K, of our regiment, and the Tenth Light Battery. The avenue of Company B is called Dyer Avenue, and that of Company K, Low's Avenue, in honor of the company captains. Here you find 'University Hall' with the students from 'Brown;' the 'Martin Box,' named after the chief of the mess; 'Tiger's Retreat, &c. As you pass down Dyer Avenue, the first tent is that of Orderly Phillips, called by the boys the 'Dioclesian Tower.' It appears that the 'orderly' used to advertise his store near Grace Church, Providence,' 'as the great skate and floral depot directly opposite the Dioclesian Tower.' He is a very lively and efficient officer (just the same), and has a prompt way of calling the men into line with the order, 'Fall in B's!' 'Lively B's!' On the opposite side of Dyer Avenue you see the sign, 'Whang Hotel,' the quarters of the High School mess, Charles L. Stafford, sergeant. The ages range from sixteen to twenty. At dress parade last night, General Pope's stirring address was read, and the resignation of our quartermaster, Lieut. James H. Armington, with a general order from Colonel Bliss complimenting him for the efficient management of his department. Lieut. William C. Chace, of Company B, is now acting-quartermaster, and is a model one. We live much better than we did at Camp Frieze; there it was tough enough! Some of the tents look more like express offices than anything else, by the number of boxes piled up in them, showing that our boys are not forgotten by the friends at home."

Occasionally the opening of a box revealed an unwise selection, or careless packing. A case was opened one morning, smooth and polished without, and neatly jointed, when an overpowering odor filled the air, and drove everybody from the neighborhood. The intolerable stench proceeded from "concentrated chicken," which had been badly prepared. The box had been for some time on the journey, and the nicely cooked "concentrated chicken," had become a mass of corruption. "Be Jabbers!" said Irish Jimmy, the drayman, as he wheeled the box away, "I hope the leddies—God bless 'em! won't send enny more of their '*consecrated* chicken' this way, for it smells too loud intirely!"

Light after "Taps!"

"While Companies B and K were encamped at Fort Pennsylvania," wrote Corp. Joseph E. Handy, of Company K, "my friend and comrade, Carlo Mauran, says, 'Corporal, I have found a hen-house, with hens in it. Will you go with me to-night, and visit the hen-roost?' I told him I would go with him, so after dark we started out, through the brush. 'This is somethin' like huntin' squirrels, ain't it,' said Carlo, as we groped our way along, but at length we arrived at the coop. I went in, while Carlo stood guard outside. It was a dark night, and darker still inside the hen-roost, so I felt round all over the place, but couldn't find anything. Then I stooped down, and felt along on the ground, and found a large hen hovering a brood of chickens. The hen is a kind mother, but still she sits on her children! I took the hen and passed her out to Carlo, who retired a short distance, wrung her neck and plucked her feathers. We then returned to our tent, and, after dressing the fowl, we got one of the cook's mess kettles, and began cutting it up to cook, when 'taps' were sounded; but we kept on, just the same, peeling our potatoes, and then seasoning the stew. Soon Capt. Frank Low came along in front of the tent. 'Put out that light,' he said. Carlo replied, 'Corporal Handy is sick!' 'All right,' said the captain, 'be as quiet as possible.' 'Yes, sir,' said Carlo. When all was done and ready to cook, we put out the light. (A bayonet stuck in the ground, holding a candle in the socket, provided us with a convenient and portable light.) In the morning we turned the chicken over to the company cook, George A. Whelden, and he made us a first-class chicken stew. I then took a portion of it up to Captain Low, steaming hot, for his breakfast. He scanned it carefully, looked at me, and said, 'So this accounts for your sickness last night, doesn't it?' I smiled audibly in the affirmative. 'Well,' said the captain, 'whenever you happen to be taken sick again for chicken stew, let me know, and I will let you keep your light burning as long as you wish!'"

This story from Company K is almost as good as that of a soldier in a Pennsylvania regiment, encamped near some country village, like Tennallytown, who trained his cat so that she would go regularly to a neighboring grocery and steal mackerel for him out of a tub. She didn't lie about it, though.

"Dr. Briggs, United States Medical Inspector, paid us an official visit yesterday, examining closely, our tents, and the grounds, to see if everything was kept neat and clean. He seemed apparently well-pleased and satisfied, for he said that everything was O K around here.

"A few days ago one of the teamers of Company C, Captain Vose, had his horse run away, and by some means got entangled in the reins, and fell from his horse. One of the wheels passed over his head, bruising it badly; the other passed over his shoulder, breaking his collar bone. At first, his life was despaired of, but by the skill of Dr. Wilcox, he is getting better."

"Our new rifles have arrived, and the remainder of the clothing due us. We have built quite a dam across a small stream near our camp, which affords a nice place for bathing (with the water up to our knees), which is a great luxury."

"Fort Alexander, July 23d. In arranging our new camp," wrote Captain Hale, "some generalship was required in selecting the best location, both on sanitary and cautionary grounds. If we were quartered inside the fort, we should be less exposed to marauding parties of the enemy who could only get at us after passing the abattis, ditch, and parapet. But if we were compelled to run at last, we should have no where to run to except to run away, and that is sometimes considered discreditable in good soldiers. Besides, a close inspection of the barracks showed that marauding parties already held possession of them, and that they made up in numbers what they lacked in size.

"On the other hand if we had pitched our camps outside the fort and were compelled to evacuate it, we could run into the fort, and if finally compelled to run from there, we should become so accustomed to running as to do it with perfect ease and considerable rapidity, and thus secure *a double base of retreat.*

"So we chose for our quarters a beautiful grassy slope, overlooking the broad Potomac, fringed with wild flowers, and commanding a fine view of the hills and vales of Virginia. Here we set up our tents, and our tin-ware, and thanked God that we had found such comfortable quarters after all our weary wanderings. But human happiness is liable to sudden reverses, and ours did not differ from the common lot of man, for we were scarcely settled in our new quarters, when we discovered that they had previously been selected as a place of meeting of an immense entomological convention, with delegates from every part of the world of bugs. The convention holds uninterrupted session of twenty-four hours' duration, the importance of their business being such as to admit no intermission. In the discharge of their duties, they enter our noses, skirmish about our ears, and commit forays upon our unprotected eyes. Having discovered that shirts and drawers are not the natural covering of man, they penetrate their recesses, and institute minute examinations, and no doubt make elaborate reports upon the formation and texture of the human skin. Many of them, like other distinguished savants, fall martyrs to the cause of truth, especially when they turn their attention to the nature and quality of our food, in which branch of inquiry they are as zealous as the best of our human conventions.

"Occasionally, I take the liberty to interfere with their proceedings, by covering such parts of the anatomy as are particularly open to their inspection. I am not versed in the fly dialect but am fully satisfied that on such occasions they make use of very profane language. For I can hear a confused buzzing, that sounds like 'Here he is, *confound him*, if we could only get at him,' 'He's playing 'possum, *blast his eyes*,' etc., etc., when the crowd retire in disgust to visit my fat lieutenant, who presents a much broader and deeper field of inquiry than I do.

"At dusk, they are relieved by the moths, crickets, and woodticks, and other insects, nameless and innumerable. The crickets remind one of the female orators at an anti-slavery meeting, by making a noise entirely disproportionate to their size.

"Since the settlement here of Companies E and I, we have been practising at heavy artillery and rifle drill. I suppose the two are combined to compensate for each other and establish a general average. We handle the heavy guns in the morning to settle our breakfasts, and the rifles in the afternoon to give us an appetite for supper. Both proceedings are eminently effectual. In regard to the big guns, the amount of sponging and ramming, heaving, pointing and firing that we have accomplished, ought to be sufficient to quell a moderate size rebellion, if done in earnest."

Colonel Shaw says: "The exceeding kindness of Col. J. A. Haskin, Inspector of Fortifications, in instructing our officers and men in their new duties should be honorably mentioned. I have seen him leave his desk and go to the door to show a private soldier his way of doing it."

"Perhaps the most instructive, if not agreeable feature of camp life at Fort Alexander, is displayed in the administration of the culinary department. The 'Army Regulations,' *allow* a cook, but unfortunately they don't *furnish* one, so that each 'mess' is obliged to look out for its own. We found ours in a sable gentleman of the African persuasion, who came to us on a broiling July day, with an oleaginous smile. We had been living for some time, 'at loose ends,' and thought him a valuable acquisition. He was said to be highly recommended, but I have never been able to ascertain who said it. He could cook anything from an egg to an elephant; either with or without fire or water. We have not had a chance to try him on the elephant, but he has certainly failed on the egg. There is a pleasurable excitement and delightful uncertainty in our relations with the cook. It is like Tom Pinch and his sister in their first efforts at housekeeping. You never know whether your beef-steak pudding will turn out a pudding or something else. In our case, it frequently doesn't 'turn out' at all. Judging from the results accomplished, I should say that our cook followed some simple receipts not laid down in the ordinary cook-book. The following are quoted for the benefit of the uninitiated:

"Eggs are liable to be soft, unless boiled from five to fifteen minutes. (If the cook is busy, they may remain a while longer.)

"Fried eggs should be done *black* on the under side, to give them a relish.

"Salt cod-fish is freshened by being soaked in water. All aqueous exposures are therefore to be avoided.

"Corn-bread, hoe-cake, johnny-cake, and corn dodgers, are made of meal and water, carefully dried by a slow fire. Any sudden heat is liable to brown them, and is therefore to be avoided.

"Army beef is made tender by long boiling, and is thereby made eatable. But, as it is not designed to be eaten, it should be only half cooked.

"It is the chief duty of the cook to look out for number one, and to see that volunteers do not become enervated by delicate viands. He will therefore devour all tit-bits and choice morsels, to keep them out of the way of temptation.

"Our cook is great at foraging. Foraging is procuring necessary subsistence by buying when you can't steal it, or stealing when you can't buy it,—or stealing, *per se*, whether you can buy it or not. The last is the favorite mode in this section. Starting off after an early breakfast, the cook is gone for the best part of the day, foraging. The result of a day's active exertion may be summed up in a pair of meagre chickens and a lank cod-fish. The chickens are put into a coop to fatten, but after being carefully and bountifully fed, there is just enough of them to flavor a stew. By some singular casualties they are generally minus legs or wings, or both, when served by our cook, who is never able to account for the deficiency. I am happy to say, however, that no such misfortune befalls the cod-fish, which always come to the table, complete in all its parts. One specimen of our cook's biscuits will suffice. We tried one, and then had the balance piled up like cannon balls. If not used as projectiles against the enemy, they will be distributed among the various cooking schools of the country, carefully labelled, 'Not to be eaten on pain of death.' Early applicants can secure choice specimens by paying freight and charges. N. B.—Two postage stamps enclosed, will entitle the sender to the best specimens, with the cook thrown in.

"We are still practising artillery drill, rifle drill, battalion drill, company drill, and squad drill, and if we don't succeed in coming home thoroughly *drilled*, we shall certainly be partially *bored*."

Battery Vermont, July 20th, Corp. B. F. Pabodie, wrote: "All our visitors concur in saying that Company H has the most inviting spot of any occupied by the regiment. Our little battery of three 32-pounders, is situated on the south side of the roads leading to the Potomac, and about half a mile from it. It is built partially on the site of an old stone house. From the appearance of the ruins, the growth of shrubbery, and the remains of a large stone barn below it, it must have been a country seat of no mean pretensions. On the opposite side of the road, stands our quarters, consisting of one frame, and two log-houses. A yard in front, is nicely shaded by two rows of locust trees. This is a part of the aqueduct property, and belongs to the government. The reservoir from which the supply of water from Washington and Georgetown is taken, lies near us at the foot of the hill."

Fortunately a fine sketch of "Headquarters, Company H," is still preserved, engraved by Sergt. Charles P. Gay, on the bottom of his mess-pan. It is evident that his hand was as steady as at the target shoot of the Burnside Zouaves in August, 1861, when he bore off the first prize, a silver cup, which was presented to him by Governor Sprague. He has a good record as a soldier, serving not only in the Tenth, but afterwards as a lieutenant in the Fourteenth Rhode Island Heavy Artillery.

A Memorable Mess-Pan.

Resuming, Corporal Pabodie wrote: "The work of enlarging Battery Vermont has been commenced. Details of men from each company, amounting to forty, have been at work for several days, and when the addition is finished, and another 32-pounder mounted, the battery will present quite a formidable appearance Our diet at present consists mainly of blackberries and milk."

Sergeant Gay tells the following story of their milk supply:

Milking the Cow.

"Job Armstrong was one of the advance guards of Company H who first took possession of Battery Vermont. He was also a great milk forager, and had a wonderful faculty in deluding the cows of the neighborhood into the belief that he was one of their own calves. A cow would stand placidly, chewing her cud, while Job with a persuasive 'So bossy,' would milk with all his might. One day after he and another comrade had filled pails and canteens, and drank the milk foaming fresh from the cow, they hurried back to camp, and concealed a large pan of milk under Job's bunk. Soon the farmer's wife arrived and complained to Captain Duckworth, that some of his men had milked her cows. Nobody knew anything about it, and Job, who had overheard everything, declared with much warmth, that he didn't believe there was a man in Company H mean enough to do such a thing, but he'd make it his business to go through every tent, and if he found anybody with milk in his possession he would report him. Thus assured, the woman departed. A few minutes later Job called me to the orderly's quarters, and there under the bunk was a large pan full of milk. 'Now,' says Job, 'I want you to help me get rid of it, among the boys; they'll find it just bully with their blackberries."

Let us visit the room occupied by Orderly-Sergeant Winchester and his mess. "They have fitted it up in imitation of a steamboat cabin, with bunks arranged one above the other, several tiers high. One night, recently, a private was allowed to occupy the upper berth, and as he slept he dreamed that he was peacefully reposing in his own cot at home, where he heard voices appealing to him :

'Stay, stay with us,—rest, thou art weary and worn!
And fain was their war-broken soldier to stay :—'

But just at that moment he started up and rolled out of the top berth, and struck the floor with a sound that aroused the other sleepers with the impression that a bomb-shell had been dropped in their midst, or that Stonewall Jackson was upon them. The poor disappointed private felt hurt in more respects than one, and murmured something about 'being at home,' and 'seeing stars.' After a vigorous rubbing of his sore places, he climbed back into his perch, and turned over against the wall. The next day he was able to report for service, and went through the usual drill, but evidently with a good deal of difficulty.

"There is an interesting member of the orderly's mess who goes by the name of Richard Swiveller, Esq. He it is who soothes the orderly's troubled nerves (when disturbed after the day's arduous labors), with the musical notes of the flute.

"The extreme hot weather, the numerous drills, and the work at Battery Vermont begins to affect the troops unfavorably. The health of the regiment is not as good. Hospital accommodations have been largely increased, but the sicknesses do not appear to be alarming ; they are generally slow fevers.

"Since we have become settled here, many letters and delicacies from home, have continued to pour in upon us. We have received from the Burnside Zouaves two dry goods packing boxes, and one pickle-keg full of things good to eat and to wear. The ex-press charges are enormous, but the disposition here appears to be to charge soldiers fifty per cent. more than anybody else. Captain Duckworth is a soldierly and efficient officer, and under his direction we have made quite an advance in company and also artillery drill. The other night one of our sentinels fired at what was supposed to be an approaching rebel, but which proved, on investigation, to be an innocent weed on the parapet, which nodded and bowed to the guard, as it was swayed by the night wind. Governor Sprague made us a flying visit yesterday. Secretary of War Stanton and family, are spending the summer near by, on the banks of the Potomac. Blackberries are in great quantity on the surrounding hills, while fish and eels in the canal and reservoir afford us an opportunity of varying our otherwise rather monotonous life. There is a nice fruit orchard right across the road where we can get our pie apples for nothing. Next door, the farmer never locks up his kindling wood. In fact, it's a very good neighborhood. One of our number, a mason by trade, has built a brick oven, in which we have already had baked beans and brown bread, and bread and hasty puddings."

Home Messages.

"Fort De Russy the headquarters of Company D," says Lieutenant DeWolf, "is situated two miles east of Tennallytown, upon a high knoll in the midst of farms cultivated with more than usual care. With a short amount of labor, guided by engineering talent of a high order, our camp was first laid out upon an adja-

Fort De Russy, from the West.

cent knoll, tents pitched, floors leveled, trenches dug, everything in apple-pie order, when a one-armed gentleman of critical aspect, known as Colonel Haskin, of the Engineers, came round, and told us to move nearer the fort. Now it seemed to us that in case of attack we could get there at least as soon as the enemy could, but the colonel didn't think so, and somehow the minority rule prevailed. We now occupy a narrow terrace just under the walls, very strong, very stumpy, and rather buggy. Before many hours, however, the stones had been removed, the stumps transformed to seats and writing desks, and the bugs—well, the bugs, the spiders, the lizards, *et id omne genus*, still roam through their accustomed haunts, the ants build catacombs beneath our beds, the mosquitoes hum playfully about our ears, the wood-ticks

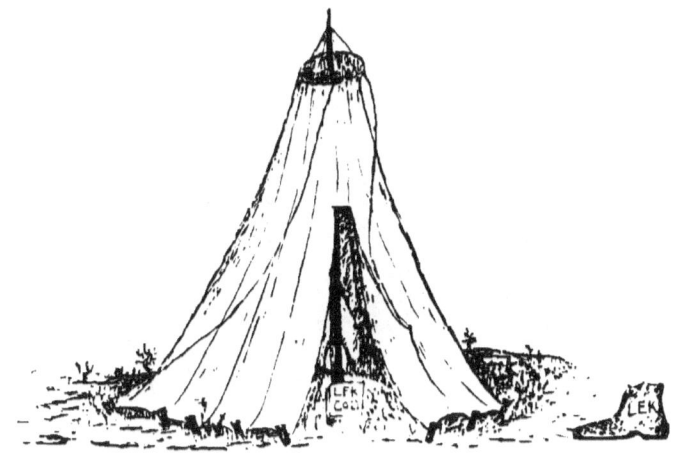

Sibley Tent—Company D.

climb up the tent walls, and by the light of our solitary candle, gaze curiously upon our little group, selecting the most promising victim." The best remedy we found for getting rid of bugs was the liberal use of *Pennyroyal*, one of the old lady's three P's for getting rid of all her troubles, as narrated on page 168.

July 7th, H. T. Chace wrote: "Some of the boys call our tent the 'Smithsonian Institute,' on account of the variety of bugs and insects it contains. In reference to the proposed trip to

Washington, one said there was no use to spend any time at the 'Smithsonian' there, as we have all the specimens of ants, flies, bugs, and lizards, in our own quarters. 'That's so,' was the reply, 'We not only have ten-ants, here, but a thousand ants.' Sergeant Mathewson has a pretty terrier, black and tan, named 'Lutitia' called for short 'Titia,' a good and playful creature. Speaking of the army and navy at breakfast this A. M., one of the mess broke in with the sage remark, 'There are many strong arms in the navy, and many strong knaves in the army.'

Guard House—Fort De Russy.

"We shall soon commence heavy artillery drill. I am now in the guard-house in the fort, being on duty till nine o'clock to-morrow morning. The house is built of logs, and twelve by eighteen feet in size. Cady and I were on guard duty last night. When our turn came to be off, I placed my cartridge-box on the floor, and, throwing my cape over my head, and folding part of it on the box for a pillow fell asleep without other covering. Cady had no overcoat, so he took my blanket, and placing his cap on a piece of an inch and a half plank for a pillow, and throwing himself on the hard floor was soon asleep."

"We are to have no bell ringing or gun firing, here to-day," wrote Chace, "but still realize it is the Fourth of July. Six of us were on guard in the fort, and at 2.30 this morning, we drew lots to see which three should be relieved for all day. I was one of the three relieved, and we will have to-morrow to ourselves just the same. For breakfast we had each two slices of bread, beefsteak, and coffee, from 'J. B. Chace's.' Adjutant Tobey

Entrance to Fort De Russy.

was in our camp to-day. We all like him. He is a pleasant officer and appears to understand his business. We have celebrated in our mess to-day, on soup, peas, fish, coffee, custard with cake and lemonade, and have ordered three pecks of peaches and three dozen eggs for our mess for the glorious Fourth! Some milk will also be brought in. We have been gladdened to-day, by the return of George Briggs. He will soon be all right. Armington is also better. He is one of the quiet, uncomplaining, obliging fellows, that it is hard to do without. A little leaven leavens the whole lump.

"July 8th. Our little mess-darkey was telling one of his friends what a glorious dinner was given him on 'the Fourth,' 'ham, an' peas, an' custard, an' cake, an' cocoa, an'—,' when the other interrupted him, 'You talks like a fool, you does. Folks would know you never had a good dinner befo'! Oh !!! (long.) You just ought ter be where I used to live on P'nsivania Av'nu'! We could look right ober de heads of de white folks, we could, and frow ham and chick'n away, ev'ry night!'"

Elevated Contraband on Pennsylvania A. e.

"Thursday, July 10th. Before 'tattoo' last night we had one of those pleasant hours which relieve so much the monotony of camp life. A guitar accompaniment, and an improvised choir did the business. They treated us with 'Let me kiss him for his mother,' 'Way down in my old cabin home,' 'The old folks at home,' 'Larboard Watch,' and several college songs, all very finely rendered. From another post, a writer says, 'Notwithstanding the hardships of a soldier's life, we do not lack for amusements. Two evenings we have been entertained by a negro fiddler, with dancing by both negro men and women.'"

On Guard.

"Fred Armington, George Briggs, Sam Brown, and John Cady, are on guard to-day, from our mess. Privates N. W. Aldrich and George W. Adams are detailed from the company, to report for duty to the adjutant, at Fort Pennsylvania. Howard Sturgis has just gone over with the mail. It is very warm here. The perspiration runs when one is standing still. According to general orders, the regiment will have battalion drill three times per week, in a field near Tennallytown. The drill is to commence at nine A. M., and continue for two hours. The companies which are located at Forts Alexander, Franklin and Ripley will have a hot march of over three miles. Have just had a visit from three of my a(u)nts; did not receive them very graciously, but expelled them in a hurry as soon as made aware of their presence. Never saw flies and things so tormenting as at this post. Yesterday afternoon Company D marched to Fort Pennsylvania to receive the new Enfield rifles. We went in single file over a narrow foot-path through the woods, with the trees often meeting overhead. We not only received our weapons, with straps and tompions, but also mess-pans, spoons, knives and forks. We shall really begin to live like civilized nations. This noon we had blackberries, which are now plenty here, served in our new tin mess-pans. All our men are better, and Mason has returned, greatly to our satisfaction. Lieutenant-Colonel Shaw now quarters with company D. The men gave him a hearty welcome when he arrived at Fort De Russy."

"Wednesday, July 16th. We are progressing rapidly with the heavy artillery drill," wrote Chace. "This A. M. I acted both as gunner and as chief of the piece. There is one chief, one gunner, and four cannoneers to each gun. The cannoneers load, the gunner tends vent (that there may be no premature discharges), inserts the friction-primer, and sights the gun, and the chief then sees that it is correctly done. To-day we went over the names of the different parts of the gun-carriage." An amusing incident is re

The Magazines—Fort De Russy

ported by Private Yerrington, of Company G. One day during artillery target practice at Fort Gaines, Lieut. James H. Allen had just sighted the piece, when Colonel Haskin, Inspector of Forts, stepped up, and said, " Lieutenant, your aim is too low, let me assist you." After the gun was fired, the shot went over the target, and made some contrabands scatter in the wheat-fields beyond. The colonel enjoyed the joke at his expense, and went on showing us how to do it, just as if nothing had happened. He was a veteran in the military service, having won distinction in the war with Mexico. He was a very obliging officer, and was much respected by our officers.

"July 20th. Yesterday Briggs and I were occupied most of the day in laying floors for Lieutenant-Colonel Shaw's and Captain Smith's tents. Both officers expressed themselves well satisfied with the work done. At dress-parade we marched in front of the new flag-staff (just raised by the boys) when the company having halted, Lieutenant-Colonel Shaw run up the 'Stars and

Raising the Flag at Fort De Russy.

Stripes.' I never heard more hearty cheering than was then given. Never before had the sight of the flag excited such feelings as then. We felt as though with that flag in sight, and with such comrades, we could march or fight in its defence. Colonel Shaw made a few appropriate remarks, to which the men responded with three cheers. He then drilled the company for about fifteen minutes, after which we were dismissed for rations.

"Yesterday another box arrived, from the Second Ward folks. It contained ginger snaps, soda powders, soap, writing paper, envelopes, etc., sugar, sardines, lemons and other eatables and drinkables. Briggs has dug a hole under the head of his bed, and when he wishes to keep things cool he puts them *down-stairs*. Another change in our cook department to-day. Corporal Kelley goes out, Levi Burdon is in. We enjoyed, yesterday, the luxury of some home-made gingerbread. Have some?

"July 20th. George Briggs had a box from home last evening. Some of the articles were nicely packed in a tin-pan, and a little coffee-pot. The sight of the pan caused visions of bread and rice puddings to pass before our minds. All we lack are the eggs.

"July 23d. At the afternoon drill Lieutenants Amos D. Smith, Jr., Samuel A. Pearce, Jr., Henry Pearce, and Sergt. Philip B. Stiness, of the Tenth Battery, were present. A detachment selected from our company was put on one of the thirty-two-pounders. They loaded and fired, running the gun from battery, out in full length, once in sixty, and once in fifty-seven seconds. A few days since we fired in fifty seconds. Mrs. General Burnside, Mrs. Richmond, and Miss Gardner were in camp this noon. Lieut.-Col. James Shaw has his wife and his little Ted with him. The mail just in has brought Sergt. Tom Tobey a commission as lieutenant in the Seventh Rhode Island Regiment. We heartily congratulate him; he will make a good officer, and will treat his men like men. At 'retreat' this evening official orders from General Pope were read. One prohibits the soldiers of his army leaving their camps. Now we cannot go to Georgetown or Washington without a special pass from his headquarters."

"Room Boys, Room, By the Light of, the Moon."

"After sunset," wrote DeWolf, "on these glorious July evenings, our own band assembles, two violins, guitar, banjo, tamborine, triangle and bones, accompanied by a dozen manly voices, and song follows song, with an occasional interlude, during which the negro field-hands from the neighboring farms, indulge in a regular Virginia 'hoe down,' with 'walk round,' and 'double shuffle' embellishments. Our evening assemblies usually wind up with the strains of sacred or patriotic song." What time so welcome in camp as the still evening hour, and what influence so potent as music, to cheer and refresh the drooping spirits of those whose roving tents were pitched far from home and kindred.

> 'Yes, music is the prophet's art;
> Among the gifts that God hath sent,
> One of the most magnificent!'

"July 22d. Our battalion drills near headquarters, are conducted sometimes by Colonel Bliss, and sometimes by Lieutenant-Colonel Shaw. The latter has recently finished his labors at the general court martial, of which he was president. One of the boys said he 'thought a little battalion drill went a great way,' to which another replied : 'Yes, and we have to go a great way to get a little battalion drill !'

"July 23d. While going through 'inspection of arms,' two of the darkey boys joined in. It was too comical for a soldier's gravity to see them gravely bring their sticks to the 'right shoulder' and pass them to the man for 'inspection.'

"Thursday, July 24th. At the drill this afternoon, we used powder, shot and shell. A target was placed nearly a mile distant at the edge of a piece of woods. The shots fell very near, and the shells exploded over it. We are much pleased with the success of the shell practice.

"I remarked to one of the boys, 'I believe your forte is exaggeration.' Cady immediately rejoined, 'My fort(e) is Fort De Russy!' Our relief on from two to four A. M., was not relieved until 4.30, for which error the sergeant of the guard will have to 'take it.' He was asleep. We are glad to hear that General Twiggs is dead. May many more of the Confederate leaders follow his example; and the sooner, the better.

"July 27th. After 'retreat' last evening, we were entertained with drumming by Master James Shaw, 3d, and he certainly did exceedingly well for a boy of his age. Yesterday we had a report that the night before, fifty guerillas had attacked Fort Slocum, not far from us, and were driven off. It may only have been some men on a drunken frolic, but it has had the effect to keep us on the alert. Later: The party of guerillas proved to be a squad of Union cavalry, bearing dispatches to Secretary Stanton. Rev. Mr. Woodbury was in camp to-day.

"Just after taps, one night, Fred. Hedge said, 'Boys who will occupy this fort after we leave?' We couldn't tell so he informed us. 'I suppose the bugs will be left tenants (lieutenants).' He was immediately told to go to sleep. Between our fort and Fort Pennsylvania, lives an old colored woman, who has invited some of the boys to stop at her 'humble *fabrication*,' when they go by. We are to have fish-balls to-night, William A. Harris, chief cook."

"Fort Alexander, July 18th. Companies E, I, F and A, form the second battalion of the Tenth Rhode Island, under Major Babbitt. We are encamped upon the heights of the Potomac, about eight miles from Washington, under the walls of Forts Alexander, Ripley, and Franklin, which crown as many hills and form a triangle. The river, more than a hundred feet below us, makes a short bend before reaching this point, and the small sweep visible, being studded with islands, many of which resemble stacks of bullrushes, has more the appearance of a frog pond than of that Potomac of which we have heard so much. But it is magnificent at sunset, where, after a smoky, hot day, the sun goes down like a ball of fire; and when we have retired to our tents and our blankets, the noise of its waters as they rush over the rocks which obstruct its channel, sounds not unpleasantly. We are pleased with our location and its duties—pure air, spring water, wood, cut and dried; excellent drainage, good bathing facilities, little policing, hardly more guarding, and a drill which gives a pleasant change,—heavy artillery in the afternoon, rifle drill in the morning.

"A change has come over the spirit of this battalion. Perhaps I ought not to write it, but a week ago grumbling and indifference had begun to be too prevalent in camp. And for this reason: We had no muskets, save the same worthless ones which we brought from Providence; we, or at least not a man of Company E, had a cap-box; our belts were old and rotten; the sergeants had no swords : bed-ticks and rubber blankets few possessed ; and most of all, we had not, and for that matter still have not, an ensign of the Republic to revive our tired patriotism, and to

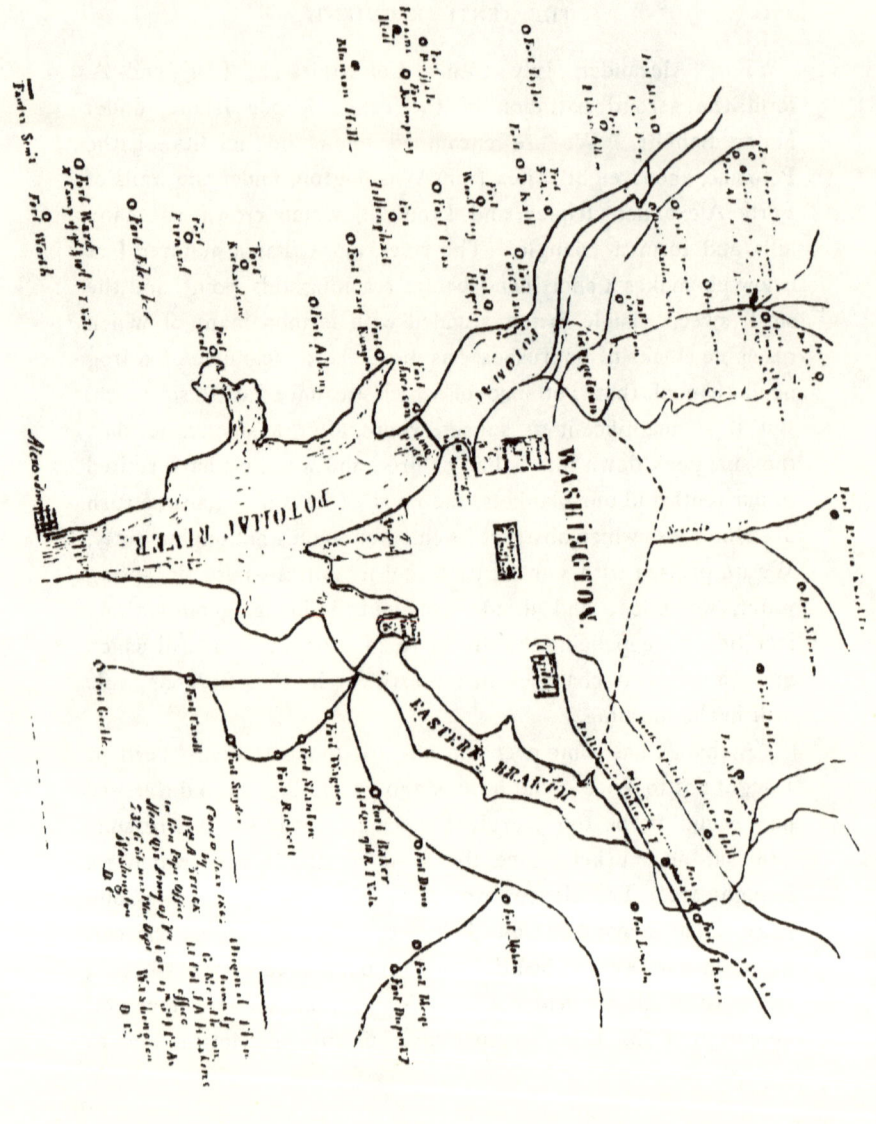

symbolize the land and the laws that we are helping to uphold. Last Saturday, however, we received our splendid, new Enfields, and the other 'fixings' wanting previously, and now we feel that we play the soldier no longer. Increased attention at the drills, stricter obedience, and, if I may so say, a revival of the whole regiment is the result. The health of the company is good.

"An order has been issued offering to muster all those who will enlist again in the Seventh Regiment for three years. That some will reënlist is certain. Major Babbitt will return, ere long, to take his position as major of the Seventh and expects to raise a company from this battalion alone. Saturday, we were under arms to receive His Excellency Governor Sprague."

Christopher A. Cady, of Company E, was detailed as "orderly" for Major Babbitt, at Fort Alexander, and carried the mails and other dispatches to headquarters at Fort Pennsylvania. Starting late one dark night, he lost his bearings at a point where a small stream was forded by a log, and fell into the water—mail and all, but succeeded in scrambling out without loss of correspondence. He was afterwards furnished with a horse, and continued to serve as orderly till Major Babbitt left for home to take the position of major of the Seventh Regiment. One morning on his way for the mail, as Cady was riding through an apple orchard, he stopped to fill his saddle-bags with fruit for the boys, when the owner suddenly confronted him. Not desiring any complaint, he turned over the apples, and rode on. A few days after, as he was riding through the same locality, a musket shot whistled close to his ear. He turned but could see no one. The matter was investigated by the major, but nothing ever came of it.

In his official report to Governor Sprague, Colonel Shaw says: "About the first of August, an epidemic or malarial fever broke out in Fort De Russy (Company D), and twenty men were on the sick list at one time. Subsequently the fever appeared at Fort Pennsylvania, and prevailed so generally in Companies B and K, that for some time after the daily details were made, not half a dozen men from both could be mounted for cavalry drill." Dr.

Dr. George D. W...
A recent picture.

George D. Wilcox, our efficient surgeon, assisted by Dr. Albert G. Sprague, very faithfully attended to the needs of the sick, all of whom, save one in Company B, recovered.

"Fort Gaines, August 7th," Capt. A. Crawford Greene wrote: "The extreme heat under which we have been laboring for the past two weeks has prevented our doing any extra duties; but to-day I have mustered courage, although the mercury on the thermometer stands at about 100°. As I wrote you last, we are continuing the drill in heavy artillery, and consider ourselves pretty familiar with that arm of the service. We can load or discharge our forty-two pounders at the rate of forty-five seconds each round. Battery Vermont and Fort Gaines are engaged in mounting more guns. The boys are not quite so fond of the engineering department as we expected to be when first detailed for that business. Many of us have never been used to handling the pick and shovel, but considering it is our first attempt building forts I think we are making marked progress.

"One week ago next Monday morning, Company G raised the stars and stripes over Fort Gaines, when speeches were made by Chaplain Clapp, Adjutant Tobey, Captain Gallup, of the Battery ; Captain Duckworth, Lieut. J. H. Allen, Lieutenant Pierce, Dr. King, Sergt. A. J. Manchester, and others. Cheer after cheer was sent up for the old ensign and for the speakers. It was the first flag raised over Fort Gaines.

"Colonel Bliss left us yesterday, to return to Rhode Island, to take charge of the Seventh Regiment, now being mustered into the service."

The following order was read to the regiment :

HEADQUARTERS TENTH REGIMENT, R. I. VOLS.,
FORT PENNSYLVANIA, August 6. 1862.

General Orders No. 36.

The colonel commanding having been ordered to report immediately in Rhode Island to take command of the Seventh Regiment Rhode Island Volunteers, is obliged to leave his present command this day. Being unable in the haste of departure to visit each post of his command, he takes this method of expressing his regret at parting with the Tenth.

He begs each of his officers and enlisted men, to accept his thanks for the cheerful faithfulness with which they have discharged all duties required of them, and to receive assurances of his entire satisfaction with their conduct, while under his command. To the Field and Staff especially, the Colonel commanding tenders his thanks for the kindness which has made his intercourse with them uniformly agreeable. His regret at parting with them is tendered with the certainty of life-long memories, of this brief but most pleasant association.

It is a pleasure to the colonel commanding to feel that though personally separated from this command, he will be still united with them, in the service of our honored State, the defence of our common country, and the triumph which is speedily to crown our cause.

Signed,   ZENAS R. BLISS,
Colonel Commanding.

HEADQUARTERS TENTH REGIMENT R. I. VOL.,
FORT PENNSYLVANIA, August 6, 1862.

General Orders No. 37.

The undersigned hereby relinquishes command of the Tenth Regiment Rhode Island Volunteers.

Signed, ZENAS R. BLISS
Colonel Commanding.

"August 6th. The following resolutions were read to our Battalion this afternoon at dress parade, when the companies composing it (E, A, I, and F) joined heartily in adopting them and in giving nine rousing cheers for Colonel Bliss. Many of us hope to see him once more, and join hands again in crushing the rebellion :

"WHEREAS, The exigencies of the service have required the recall of Col. Zenas R. Bliss from this command, to assume his post at the head of the Seventh Regiment, it is due to him as an officer and a man, that we tender to him some slight testimony of our respect: therefore, be it

"*Resolved,* That during our short intercourse with Colonel Bliss, we have learned to esteem him for the many high qualities which distinguish him, both in his official and private relations; for the soldierly bearing that mark the former, and for the kindly heart and social disposition which have made the latter so pleasant to us.

"*Resolved,* That in parting with him, we are deprived of the services of an officer who has done all in his power to improve us in drill and discipline, and whose longer connection with us would have brought us to the highest state of efficiency.

"*Resolved,* That we congratulate the Seventh that they will be led to the field by so gallant and accomplished a commander, and that we tender to him the best wishes of each officer and soldier in this command for his future welfare, happiness and prosperity."

Tennallytown Church, 1862.

"In Tennallytown, near Fort Pennsylvania, where we had our first camp (Camp Frieze) there is a small, meeting-house, which we used at first for quarter-master's stores. When the Anderson Zouaves were there they used it for a guard-house, and tore out the pulpit, and destroyed the Sabbath School library. Quartermaster-Sergeant Lysander Flagg learning about it, sent to the Methodist Sabbath School in Pawtucket, and the Baptist Sabbath School in Central Falls, and informed them of the facts, and they immediately sent a large collection of their books to the little Sunday-school of Tennallytown. The books we presented last Sabbath. Both teachers and scholars were greatly pleased with this remembrance from the children of the New England schools."

Comrade R. W. Chappell, of the Ninth Rhode Island Volunteers, says, "that the old meeting-house at Tennallytown, was the last building in which John Brown preached on his way to Harper's Ferry, in October, 1859, where in an effort to free the slaves he lost his life, 'but his soul is still marching on.' "

HEADQUARTERS TENTH REGIMENT R. I. VOL.
FORT PENNSYLVANIA, August 6, 1862.

General Orders No. 38.

The undersigned hereby assumes command of the Tenth Regiment Rhode Island Volunteers.

    Signed, JAMES SHAW, JR.,
           Lieut.-Col. Commanding.

HEADQUARTERS NORTH OF THE POTOMAC
WASHINGTON, August 6, 1862.

To the Colonel of the Tenth Rhode Island Volunteers:

SIR: If you have not one hundred rounds of cartridges per man in addition to forty rounds in cartridge-box, please send in requisition, at once.

I am very respectfully, your obedient servant,
        CHARLES H. HALL,
         Captain and A. D. C.

HEADQUARTERS TENTH REGIMENT R. I. VOLS.,
FORT PENNSYLVANIA, August 11, 1862.

GEN. S. P. STURGIS.

DEAR SIR: I would respectfully request, if possible and consistent with the interests of the public service, that this regiment may be released from the daily details of laborers for Battery Vermont.

I have thirty-three men on my sick report this morning, nearly all of them have a slow fever caused by hard work and exposure to the sun; with the thermometer varying as it has done from 100° to 130° in the sun, during the past week, it is impossible for them to do the work effectually, and if attempted at all, it is daily adding to my sick list. I have placed the detachment under command of a commissioned officer, and if they cannot be released, I will see that they do all that it is possible for them to do.

I am, Sir, very respectfully, your obedient servant,
    Signed, JAMES SHAW, JR.,
          Lieut.-Col. Commanding.

"A verbal reply was received through Lieutenant-Colonel Haskin, A. D. C., saying that a requisition had been made for 'contrabands,' but they had not been obtained, so that the regiment would be expected to do all the work they were able. The details were therefore continued until the regiment was ordered home. It was a thankless task, which the men felt that idle hands in Washington might better have been employed to do. Still the orders were promptly obeyed, and a large amount of work was performed."

August 11th. Capt. William M. Hale, of Company I, was promoted to be Lieutenant-Colonel, and First Lieutenant Samuel H. Thomas, of Company B, was promoted to be Captain of Company I. These were two of our most efficient officers.

"Fort Alexander, August 13th," Lieutenant-Colonel Hale wrote: "Thanks to our many friends, yesterday was a gala day with the 'What Cheer Guards,' Company I, Tenth Regiment. It is marked with a white stone in our calendar, for we received such a supply of good things from our friends at home, as will cheer our hearts, to say nothing of our bodies, for the remainder of our campaign. Such fat living, such unctuous hams, such bursting bolognas, such creamy cheese and pungent pickles, such golden lemons, such fragrant tobacco, such crispy crackers, and soothing sweet bread, my feeble pen in vain essays to describe. After the solids were duly distributed among the messes, the liquids, among which are included the lemons, were compounded into lemonade, which, for a short time, claimed the undivided attention of the entire command. Resolutions were then passed, toasts were drank, speeches were made, and songs were sung."

"The following were rescued from the wreck :

"*Resolved*, That Capt. Thomas W. Hart is a tall man, with a heart l ge enough to reach from Rhode Island to the banks of the Potomac.

"*Resolved*, That Lieut. Calvin Fuller is pure 'old government Java' to the backbone.

"*Resolved*, That we tender our sincere thanks to all the friends who have contributed so bountifully to our comfort.

"*Resolved*, That when we get home, we will defend the Third Ward to the last drop of our blood, against all foes, internal and external.

"Short and pithy speeches were made by Major Babbitt, Dr. Sprague, Lieutenant Thurber, and others, which would undoubtedly have brought down the house, if we had occupied one, but as we were under the 'broad canopy of heaven,' they brought down 'all out-doors.'

"Corporal Stump, during the course of his remarks had frequent occasion to 'return to his subject,' which seemed to be contained in a pint cup, near by, of standard measurement."

August 11th. First Sergeant Charles F. Phillips, of Company B, was promoted to second lieutenant Company B, and William C. Chase, second lieutenant Company B, to first lieutenant Company B, Tenth Rhode Island Volunteers.

"August 14th." Corp. O. S. Alers wrote : "A part of Company I went over to the quarters of Company F, Capt. Benjamin W. Harris, and gave them a serenade, which was greatly appreciated.

"August 17th. We had a grand review to-day, Capt. Hopkins B. Cady, of Company E, acting as colonel, and Lieut. Peter Read, of Company I, as adjutant. The battalion showed a great improvement in discipline and drill."

Ex-Mayor Henry R. Barker.

Ex-Mayor Henry R. Barker, of Providence, was at this time one of the youthful sergeants of Company I, and was much esteemed by his comrades. Since the war he has served in various positions of official trust. He was a member of the Common Council from the Ninth Ward, from June 1873 to January 1880, and president in 1879; alderman, 1880 to 1883; president in 1882; mayor, from 1889 to 1891. He has also been Commander of Slocum Post, No. 10, G. A. R., and Department Commander of Rhode Island.

Lieutenant-Colonel Hale resumes: "Having completed one term of service, we propose to return to the land of our nativity, and make such a display as has never greeted the eyes of the quiet dwellers at home. The regiment will be so formed as to represent an entire *corps d'armée*. First: The ambulance wagon, drawn by our reliable switch-tailed horse, will represent the cavalry, with the sharpshooters about the wheels and shafts, deployed as skirmishers. Next, the mountain howitzer, borne in triumph by its captors, will form the light artillery, having the 'stars and stripes' floating gloriously from the vent, while the Confederate flag is dragged in disgrace from its depressed muzzle. After that the main body of the regiment will appear divided into light and heavy infantry, dismounted huzzars and chasseurs, and the heavy artillery, selected from the most ponderous men of the regiment, armed with as many thirty-two and sixty-four pounders as possible. Captain Duckworth's Zouaves will close the column, acting as the rear-guard, with instructions to close upon the main body at the double-quick at the first instruction of danger.

"We shall bring home few trophies and less scars. We shall bear no tattered, shot-rent banners from the bloody field, nor shall not be entirely destitute of tatters, if we are of banners, and feeling that we have done what we have been ordered to do in our limited sphere of action, shall not be ashamed to expose our bared soles for public inspection."

August 20th. We have received the following order

HEADQUARTERS, DEFENCES OF WASHINGTON,
WASHINGTON, August 20, 1862.

General Orders No. 1.

I. In virtue of Special Orders No. 196, from the headquarters of the army, dated Washington, August 19, 1862, Brig.-Gen. J. G. Barnard assumes the command of the fortifications of Washington and troops assigned to the defences.

II. The fortifications and troops on the south side of the Potomac will remain under the immediate command of Brig.-Gen. S. W. Whipple; those on the north side, under charge of Lieutenant-Colonel Haskin, A. D. C., through whom all orders will be transmitted, and to whom commanding officers will make their usual reports.

III. Capt. J. Brice Smith is announced as assistant adjutant-general to this command, and Lieut. T. M. Farrel, Fifteenth New York Volunteers as A. D. C. to the General Commanding.

J. G. BARNARD,
Brigadier-General,
Commanding Defences of Washington.

August 21st. A note was received by Colonel Shaw from Lieutenant-Colonel Haskin, asking if the regiment would be willing to be sworn in for an extra term of from two to four weeks, until relieved by another regiment. The following is his reply:

> HEADQUARTERS TENTH REGIMENT R. I. VOLS.,
> FORT PENNSYLVANIA, August 22, 1862.

COLONEL: Yours of the 21st requesting the regiment to remain two weeks or one month after the expiration of their term of service is received, and has been laid before the regiment. I regret to say it has not met their approbation, although when all the circumstances are considered I am not surprised at the result. You will remember that the regiment started from Rhode Island at twenty-four-hours' notice, coming simply for the emergency, and expecting to be released within a month. Many of them left important business matters, and permanent situations, that they feel must be attended to. They will have staid on the 26th inst., the longest time as they understood it, when they left home, that would possibly be required of them, and have made their arrangements expecting to be at home at that time. We have many amongst us who are expecting positions in the regiments to be sent from our State, and many that wish to obtain the large bounties that are now being offered by many of the towns. These all wish to go. The epidemic fever which now prevails at Fort Pennsylvania has a great influence. Sick men always wish to get home. Under these circumstances, I trust you will do the regiment the justice to believe that its disinclination to stay is not from any lack of patriotism or desire to comply with every wish of the government. So much, we think, was manifested by the readiness with which they volunteered for what then appeared immediate, active service, and the cheerfulness with which they have served through the longest time mentioned as the limit of our stay. I trust that our reply when thus explained will meet the approbation of General Barnard.

I am, Sir, very respectfully, your obedient servant,

Signed, JAMES SHAW, JR.

To COL. J. A. HASKIN, *Colonel Commanding.*
A. D. C.

"This reply and the action of the regiment I was assured by Colonel Haskin was perfectly satisfactory. He did not think the regiment should have been called on to stay, and said that had General Barnard (who had just assumed the command) understood the circumstances, as he did, he would not have made the request.

"On the 22d inst., the One Hundredth and Thirteenth New York Volunteers arrived and encamped on our old ground of 'Camp Frieze,' and the next day the following order was issued

HEADQUARTERS DEFENCES OF WASHINGTON
WASHINGTON, August 23, 1862.

General Orders No. 2.

1. EXTRACT. In pursuance of orders from the War Department, all regiments of three months' volunteers within this command, will be mustered out of service at the points where they organized respectively.

They will be placed *en route* for the rendezvous, so as to arrive there one or two days before the expiration of their time.

By order of Brigadier-General BARNARD.

Official: Signed, J. B. SMITH.
J. A. HASKIN,   J. J. G.
   A. D. C.

"On the 24th of August, the One Hundredth New York Volunteers took their post at the several forts and batteries, and on the 25th we took up our homeward march to Washington."

"Returning to the peaceful pursuits of life," says our worthy and valiant Matthew Bagnet, "We sheathe our sword, hang our armor on the wall, and return our 'Bagnet' to its scabbard, until our country again calls us to her defence."

General-in-Chief.

During the months of July and August, 1862, when the Tenth Rhode Island Regiment was quietly holding the forts near the capital, an entire change had taken place in the military situation in Virginia. The retreat of General McClellan to the James River, July 1st, and the bitter feelings and controversies which it occasioned, led General Pope to ask to be relieved from the command of the Army of Virginia. Instead of granting the request, President Lincoln, who appeared to lack confidence in McClellan's ability, decided to appoint Gen. Henry W. Halleck, general-in-chief. To bring this about, Governor Sprague, of Rhode Island, was sent July 6th, on a confidential mission to Corinth, General Halleck's headquarters. On the 11th, General Halleck was appointed general-in-chief. General Pope favored this course, and united with Secretary Stanton and General Scott in advising that McClellan should be superseded and Halleck placed in charge of military affairs at Washington. Unfortunately General Halleck did not arrive in Washington and assume command till July 23d, nearly two weeks after his appointment. After looking over the situation in Virginia, he determined to withdraw the Army of the Potomac from the James river and unite it with the Army of Virginia. General McClellan remonstrated in vain, General Halleck replying: "I find the two armies hopelessly separated, with the Confederates between, and I propose to reunite them."

What proved to be a singularly just criticism of the capacity of General Halleck appeared in the Providence *Journal* of July 19th, just a week after his appointment, and is doubtless from the pen of Senator Anthony, the senior editor, and also our accomplished senator. He said, "The general impression is that the talent of General-in-Chief H. W. Halleck is more conspicuous *in the council, than in the field*. Doubtless he has admirable qualities *as a military counselor*." In his subsequent efforts to direct the movements of our armies in Virginia, from his office in Washington, he proved no match for Lee and Jackson, in the field. Senator Anthony was always an honored guest at the headquarters of the Tenth.

Senator Henry B. Anthony

Henry B. Anthony was governor of Rhode Island from 1849 to 1851, and a senator of the United States from March 4, 1859 till he died in Providence, September 2, 1884. His eloquent words spoken for another, are his own fitting eulogy: "The State that he served so faithfully and so well, in the time of her emergency proudly lifts his name and inscribes it on the roll of her honored and remembered sons. And the history of that State cannot be fairly written without honorable mention of his character and services. The Senate which he informed with wise counsels, which he adorned with dignity of manners and with purity of life bears equal testimony to his abilities and to his virtues, and to his honor to his memory."

July 23d. Author's correspondence: "Headquarters Army of Virginia, Washington. General Halleck, from the West, arrived to-day, and is now general-in-chief of the army. Colonel Ruggles, chief of Pope's staff, says that arrangements to leave for 'the front,' cannot be completed with General Halleck before Friday, 25th inst. An important movement is now on foot, General Hatch of General Banks corps, is with the advance at Culpeper. He has a large cavalry force with orders to move south to Gordonville, destroy the railroad to Lynchburg, and the James river canal, if possible, the two sources from which the Confederates, at Richmond, receive their supplies. General Pope says if Hatch is successful, the President will make him a major-general, and that the evacuation of Richmond must follow.

"Charles Wildman and myself (Tenth R. I. Vols.), have been summoned before General Pope to answer a charge of appropriating his fancy cigars. You know we sleep at the office. Pope is very violent and profane at times. This was one of his times. We finally got in a sockdolloger by proving that we didn't smoke. Now Gen. Samuel P. Sturgis is the cigar forager. We have seen him walk in to the office, step up to the mantel, and take a good handful at a time,—but we thought that was *his* business—if he could forage without being caught.

"July 24th. All quiet on the Potomac. I had my bunk last night on top of an old shoe-case. I got to dreaming, and rolled off on the floor. I jumped up quickly, thinking we were attacked, but found it was only a 'change of base.'

"July 25th. General Pope is becoming vexed and impatient at the continued delays. His letters and dispatches are harder than

ever to make out. In a message to
President Lincoln, he says: 'I am
becoming anxious and uneasy to join
my command in the field.' Generals
Burnside and McDowell called at
headquarters to-day. Officers in gold
lace and gilt buttons are thick here.
There are brigadier-generals enough
on Pennsylvania Avenue, if not at
'the front.' I met Hon. William H.
Seward, to-day, Secretary of State,
out for a walk. It was Mr. Seward,

Wm. H. Seward, Secretary of State.

who, at the opening of the war, spoke of the antagonism between
slavery and freedom as an 'irrepressible conflict.'

"A cavalry expedition recently went within thirty-five miles
of Richmond, to Beaver Dam Creek Station, tearing up the
railroad, destroying the depot, and taking a Confederate officer
and three privates, prisoners. Well, these prisoners were at
'headquarters' to-day, for examination. We had quite a talk
with them when the officers got through. They were a rough
looking crowd, no two dressed alike. The stuff their clothes
were made of, looked just exactly like that old bagging up
in the attic. Were they scared? Not any, I can tell you; nor
would they give a particle of information to anybody. They
wanted to know how quick they could be exchanged, as they
wanted to get right back to the Confederacy. One of them, an
adjutant of the First Virginia Cavalry, said to me, 'You uns will
find it will take the North a right smart while to whip the South.'

General Hatch's great cavalry expedition to Gordonville was a failure. It is claimed that Hatch didn't obey orders, and Pope has relieved him from command. But other officers say that the trouble was that Stonewall Jackson got there first, with fifteen thousand of his foot cavalry.

"July 26th. The President has issued an order communicating information of the death of Ex-President Martin Van Buren. As a mark of respect for his memory, the Executive Mansion and the several Departments, except of the Army and Navy, will be placed in mourning, and all business will be suspended, to-day, during the funeral. By order of the Secretary of War, suitable military and naval honors will be paid to the memory of the illustrious dead. The national flag will be displayed at half staff, the troops paraded, the orders read to them, and minute guns will be fired. The following order has been issued here:

"HEADQUARTERS, ARMY OF VIRGINIA,
WASHINGTON, July 25, 1862.

To Brigadier-General Sturgis:

The Secretary of War directs by an order received at these headquarters that the preceding orders of the President and Secretary of War be carried into effect to-morrow, by the troops in this district.

Signed,   GEORGE D. RUGGLES.
Colonel and Chief of Staff.

"Later, July 26th. Pennsylvania Avenue Hotel, near Georgetown (a small family hotel). I am confined to my bed with a severe attack of malaria. But I am in good hands. The headquarters' surgeon is looking after me, and a lady stopping here is very kind, who says I remind her of an absent brother. It was fortunate for me that I wasn't sent to a hospital."

"At this time the city was full of sick and wounded soldiers, and more were arriving daily from the Peninsula. Many private buildings and public halls were taken for their accommodation,—where they could receive better care and treatment. Hundreds of the loyal women of the North came to Washington to minister to the sick soldiers, and many a poor man lives to be grateful to them for their cooling drinks and cheering words. Their devotion touched Mr. Lincoln's heart, and in a speech which he made about this time at the close of a soldiers' fair, he said : 'I am not accustomed to the language of eulogy ; I have never studied the art of paying compliments to women, but I must say, that if all that has been said by orators and poets since the creation of the world in praise of woman were applied to the women of America, it would not do them justice for their conduct during this war. God bless the women of America!' Much good was accomplished also, by those who remained at home, in corresponding with the sick and wounded soldiers in the hospitals. In addition to many home comforts furnished, the sweet influences of home were continued and cherished, by many kindly messages of advice and encouragement. Here are a few which have been preserved:

"'Dear Soldiers. The little girls of —— send this box to you. They hear that many of you are sick, and some of you have been wounded in battle. They are very sorry, and want to do something for you. They cannot do much, for they are small ; but they have bought with their own money, and made what is in here. They hope it will do some good, and that you will all get well, and come home. We all pray to God for you night and morning.'

"In another case, on a pillow was pinned the following note:

"'My dear friend. You are not *my* husband or son; but you are the husband or son of some woman who undoubtedly loves you as I love mine. I have made these garments for you with a heart that aches for your sufferings, and with a longing to come to you, to assist in taking care of you. It is a great comfort to me, that God loves and pities you, pining and lonely in a far off hospital, and if you believe in God, it will also be a comfort to *you*. Are you near death, and soon to cross the dark river? Oh, then, may God soothe your last hours, and lead you up "the shining shore," where there is no war, no sickness, no death. Call on Him, for He is an ever present helper.'

"'Dear soldier. If these socks had language they would tell you that many a kind wish has been knit into them, and many a tear of pity for you has bedewed them. We all think of you, and want to do everything we can for you, for we feel that we owe you unlimited love and gratitude, and that you deserve the very best at our hands.'

"Here is another of a different character:

"'My dear boy. I have knit these socks expressly for you. How do you like them? How do you look, and where do you live when you are at home? *I* am nineteen years old, of medium height, of slight build, with blue eyes, fair complexion, light hair, and a good deal of it. Write and tell me all about yourself, and how you get on in the hospital. Direct to ——.

"'P. S.—If the recipient of these socks has a wife, will he please exchange with some poor fellow, who is not so fortunate?'

"'My brave friend. I have learned to knit, on purpose to knit socks for the soldiers. This is my fourth pair. My name is ——, and I live in ——. Write to me, and tell me how you like the foot-gear, and what we can do for you. Keep up your courage, and bye and bye you will come home to us. Won't that be a grand time, though? And won't we all turn out to meet you, with flowers and music, and cheers, and embraces? "There's a good time coming, boys!"'

"Very many of these notes were answered by the soldiers who received them, and a correspondence ensued, which sometimes ended in life-long friendship.

"A nicely made dressing gown, in one of the boxes, had one pocket filled with hickory nuts, and the other with ginger-snaps. The pockets were sewed across to prevent the contents from dropping out, and the following note was pinned on the outside:

"'My dear fellow: Just take your ease in this dressing-gown. Don't mope, and have the blues, if you *are* sick. Moping never cured anybody yet. Eat your nuts and cakes if you are well enough, and snap your fingers at dull care. I wish I could do more for you, and if I were a man I would come and fight with you. Woman though I am, I'd like to help hang Jeff Davis higher than Haman,—yes, and all who aid and abet him, too, whether North or South!'

"There was exhumed from the depths of one great box, a bushel of cookies tied in a pillow-case, with this benevolent wish tacked on the outside: 'These cookies are expressly for the sick soldiers, and if anybody else eats them, *I hope they will choke him!*'

"A very neatly arranged package, of second-hand clothing, but little worn, was laid by itself. Every article was superior in quality, and in manufacture. Attached to it was the following card:

"'The accompanying articles were worn for the last time by one very dear to the writer, who lost his life at Shiloh. They are sent to our wounded soldiers as the most fitting disposition that can be made of them, by one who has laid the husband of her youth—her all—on the altar of her country.'

"Thus we can realize the passionate interest in the soldiers, felt by the women of the North. They toiled, retrenched, economized, to furnish the necessary supplies for the hospitals, and hallowed them with their patriotic and religious spirit. Like their grandmothers of the Revolution, they flung heart and soul into the labor of willing hands.

"Here are a few of the directions on boxes for the hospitals:

"'For the love of God, give these articles to the sick and wounded to whom they are sent!'

"'He that would steal from a sick or wounded man, would rob hen-roosts, or filch pennies from the eyes of a corpse!'

"'Surgeons and nurses! Hands off! These things are not for you, but your patients,—our sick and wounded boys!'

"'Don't gobble up these delicacies, nurses! They are for the boys in the hospitals!'

"We close these sketches with a scene at the Washington barracks:

"'A pale and sick, but good looking soldier, ready for transportation, and an anxious young lady nurse, in search of a subject:

"*Lady nurse.*—'My poor fellow, can I do anything for you?'

"*Soldier* (emphatically).—'No, ma'am! Nothin'!'

"*Lady nurse.*—'I should like to do something for you? Shall I not sponge your face and brow for you?'

"*Soldier* (despairingly).—'You may if you want to, very bad! but you'll be the fourteenth lady as has done it this blessed mornin'!'"

Author's correspondence at "Headquarters" resumed:

"July 28th. Before General Pope left Washington, to join his army in the field, at Warrenton, Va., General Halleck announced his purpose to withdraw the Army of the Potomac, from the James, and unite it with the Army of Virginia, via Fredericksburg; that army (under Pope), to advance promptly to the Rapidan, keeping the approaches to Washington covered, and oppose and delay any advance of the enemy northward to the last extremity. On the next day (the 30th), General Halleck ordered General McClellan to send away his sick, and on the 3d of August he telegraphed, 'It is determined to withdraw your army from the Peninsula to Aquia Creek.' General McClellan again protested against this movement, as did Generals Dix, Burnside, and Sumner. General Halleck replied: 'There is no alternative, I have taken the responsibility.' The movement began at once. Between the 1st of August and the 16th, 14,159 sick and wounded soldiers were sent away, many of them necessarily to the North. The first troops arrived at Aquia Creek within seven days, and the last of the infantry within twenty-six days after the receipt of the order.

"On the other hand, to meet the advance of Pope, Stonewall Jackson with his own and Ewell's division, was at Gordonsville. General Lee says in his official report : 'The army at Harrison's Landing (McClellan's), continuing to manifest no intention of resuming active operations, and General Pope's advance having reached the Rapidan, Gen. A. P. Hill's division was ordered on July 27th to join General Jackson, as it seemed that the most effectual way to relieve Richmond was to advance upon General Pope.' This was promptly done, and as soon as General Lee became aware of the movement withdrawing the Army of the Potomac from the Peninsula, he turned his whole army northward, choosing between the danger of losing Richmond, the crushing of Pope's army and the capture of Washington."

"July 30th." Author resumes : "Headquarters Army of Virginia, in the Field, Warrenton, Va. We arrived here yesterday afternoon. I was hardly fit to come, being still weak from an attack of malaria ; but when I found that headquarters were really off, I insisted on going, also. So, here I am, in Warrenton, right side up, I guess, only a little the worse for wear. It took us about two hours to get here, *via* Alexandria, Manassas and Catlett's Station. The road was very rough, and the cars were rickety. Headquarters are established at the Young Ladies' Seminary, a large brick building, pleasantly located. Our office is in the main school-room, and we now occupy the school desks. I hardly expected to attend school 'down in old Virginny !' As everything here is contraband of war, we went through the desks this morning, in search of information for General Pope, and succeeded in capturing quite a quantity of female correspondences.

The young ladies of this school appear to be in a very rebellious state of mind, judging from these little rebel billet doux, fancifully folded, three cornered and otherwise, they were evidently intended for parting gifts, when the school broke up in a hurry. One young lady, after enlarging on her music lessons, and a recent serenade, adds: 'I hope the Yankees won't get my letter!' Another, addressed to 'My Dear Eloise,' is more pathetic, and expresses a sort of melancholy foreboding. She says: 'That was a *very* sad accident, was it not, which befell our beloved General Ashby? It does seem as though all our distinguishd men were being taken! Oh! if we could only have *piece* once more, how delightful it would be!' (The loss of General Ashby was greatly mourned in the South. He was one of the leading cavalry commanders of Stonewall Jackson's army, and was killed in the battle of Cross Keys, Va., June 6th) Another letter captured by my comrade Charles Wildman, of the Tenth, was signed, Hattie P. Beauregard, Corinth, Miss. He was very choice of it, pretending to believe that it had come direct from General Beauregard's headquarters, and was probably the production of one of his fair daughters. They all indicated a scarcity of envelopes, being directed like the inclosed on coarse brown paper wrappers. Probably home communication will be more difficult from here than from Washington. I don't suppose that we will remain here long, as General Pope means to push on.

The Author at 7, "at Headquarters, in Warrenton, Va.

"The Confederate prints indicate the spirit of the Southern women: 'Messrs. Editors, I see that General Beauregard has called for bells, to be manufactured into cannon. I send mine as a beginning.' Another says, 'I send you the weight which was attached to the striking part of our clock, with the hope that every woman in the Confederacy will do likewise.'

"The members of one of the regiments stationed here have 'good mouths for music.' Here is their programme for to-morrow night:

NINTH NEW YORK REGIMENT SOCIAL UNION.

Warrenton Hotel, Thursday Evening, July 31, 1862.

PROGRAMME.

PART FIRST.

Grand March: "Norma."	BAND.
Old Musketeer,	GRAHAM & Co.
Ballad.	LODEN.
Comic Song.	BARNES.
Recitation,	HOWARD.
Ballad.	JOYCE.
Virginia Rose Bud,	GRAHAM & Co.

PART SECOND.

Storm Galop,	BAND.
Happy Dreams,	ATKINSON.
Recitation: "Lady of Lyons."	LIEUTENANT HUBBARD.
Comic Song,	ADJUTANT TUTHILL.
Ballad: "Miller's Song,"	GRAHAM.
Duett: "Larboard Watch."	ATKINSON AND GRAHAM.
Fairy Bell, chorus,	THOMPSON & Co.
Limerick Races.	ATKINSON & Co.

"Warrenton is a pleasant Virginia town. It is at the terminus of the Warrenton branch of the Orange and Alexandria Railroad, and nine miles from Warrenton junction. It appears to be a place of considerable importance, and before the war had a population of about eight thousand. Most of the men are in the Confederate service, the once celebrated Black Horse Cavalry having been principally recruited in this vicinity. The people remaining are entirely secesh, and several of our men have been shot at from the windows. The churches are occupied for hospital purposes. The streets are bordered with fine shade trees. Near by is the former elegant residence of the Confederate general, Gustavus W. Smith.

"August 2d. Great numbers of our troops are constantly passing here for Culpeper Court House, and the roads are literally blocked." As we watched them they appeared more like an army of boys on a holiday excursion than soldiers who within a brief week would be tried in the fierce encounter at Cedar Mountain. Yet the official record shows that the younger men stood the test of marching and fighting far better than the older comrades. The Union Army was made up mainly of very young men. It averaged a little under twenty-two years of age The "walk-soldiers," as the cavalrymen called them, looked with envious eyes upon the officers, booted and spurred, as they galloped gayly ahead with their clinking sabres, and many a foot-soldier, like our own worthy Gen. Horatio Rogers, won his horse and spurs by faithful and gallant service. General Rogers's motto when a foot-soldier, with which he earned his way to deserved promotion, was "a horse or a hearse."

"August 2d, later. Headquarters are ordered to Sperryville to-day, and by advice of the surgeon, I have been ordered back to Washington for proper care and treatment. The fact is that hard fare, hard travelling, and hard work, has brought about a slight relapse of fever." It was a bitter disappointment, I remember, to be left behind, and witness the gay departure of officers and comrades, as they rode rapidly away towards Sperryville; but subsequent events proved it to be a kind Providence which interposed in my behalf. From that day General Pope's headquarters were chiefly in the saddle, "somewhere on the Warrenton road." His advance, under General Banks, met the enemy under Stonewall Jackson, August 9th, at Cedar Mountain, and although repulsed with heavy loss, he succeeded in maintaining his position, until the main army, under Pope, arrived, when an advance was made to the Rapidan River, the movement being to delay and retard the advance of the enemy, until Pope's army could be reinforced from the Peninsula. Soon after the Union army fell back slowly from one position to another towards Washington, Pope successfully delaying his assailants, but unable to hold them in check. Daring and successful raids were made on his train on the night of August 22d, by Gen. J. E. B. Stuart, at Catlett's Station, thirty-eight miles from Washington, and by Stonewall Jackson, August 24th, at Manassas, twenty-seven miles from Washington, which caused him to fall back more rapidly. The Federal army fought bravely and suffered severely a second time at Bull Run, on the 30th of August, but by stubbornly disputing the way, General Pope had gained time for McClellan's army to reach the scene of action, and thus Washington was saved.

On the evening of August 2d, my comrade of the "Tenth" and at "Headquarters," C. H. Wildman, wrote me from Little Washington, Va.: "We are now encamped in a fine place in the woods. We have wall-tents, and only three in a tent. We shall fare well, and have a colored cook from the cavalry. By orders just issued we expect to come in contact with old Stonewall Jackson very soon." Again on the 10th, he wrote me from headquarters, at Culpeper, Va.: "We started from our camp at or near Little Washington, on Thursday morning. We encamped that evening about seven miles from Sperryville, by the side of a wood. That evening one of General Banks's men, was out in the woods, looking round, when a party of guerillas appeared and shot him. General Pope sent out a company of cavalry, but did not find them. We arrived at Culpeper yesterday morning, and went about a mile from the town, and stopped at a house, on a large farm. Of course you remember General Pope's address: 'We, in the West, have always seen the *backs* of our enemies! Let us look before, and not behind us! No modes of retreat, etc.' But I notice, though, that we retreated yesterday on the double-quick, without stopping to look behind us! Old Stonewall was within three and a half miles of headquarters yesterday, and I tell you we just pulled up stakes and travelled for Culpeper humming. We went away out of the town, and had just got things into shape, and tents up, when troop after troop of cavalry came

Picketing the Rapidan.

General Pope's Headquarters at Cedar Mountain.

down the road pell-mell, till in a few minutes it was completely blocked with them. Come to find out, Jackson had crossed the Rapidan in force and driven our pickets, and we, having cavalry only, and he plenty of artillery, we were obliged to retire in a hurry. On the way back, we met the brigades going out. They appeared full of fight, and some were singing and others laughing at each other's jokes. There are between twenty and thirty thousand of our troops."

August 16th, from headquarters near Cedar Mountain, he wrote: "On Saturday afternoon, August 9th, the ball opened here. It was a terrific encounter. General Banks bravely held his ground against vastly superior force of the rebels. Our loss was over fifteen hundred, killed, wounded and missing. General Pope and staff arrived on the field about seven P. M. They would not let the clerks go, but I could not see it in that light, and went out in the evening with the surgeons. I shall never forget that night. There were hundreds of killed and wounded men,

The battle was over, but an artillery fire was kept up till midnight. I went out again on Tuesday, 12th instant, and saw the old devils, just as the last of them skedaddled for the Rapidan. I came near getting my old head knocked off, too. I tell you that was quite a little fight (Cedar Mountain, 9th instant). Colonel Ruggles, Chief of Staff, had a horse shot under him. Colonel Morgan, who signed your last pass, got a bullet through his hat, and, in fact, Pope and the whole staff came near being captured. We shall move forward again to-morrow, to the Rapidan, to join the advance. Our pickets watch that river from Raccoon's Ford to the base of the Blue Ridge. We now have a colored cook, and have ordered cooking utensils forwarded here from Washington."

But on that very day August 16th, a party of Confederate cavalry was captured, with orders from General Lee, which disclosed the plan that he was moving northward, by forced marches, with the main Army of Richmond, to attack Pope's little army with overwhelming force before he could be reinforced by the troops from the Peninsula. In consequence of this information, General Pope hastily broke up his camps on the Rapidan and on the 18th and 19th, retired to a new position behind the north branch of the Rappahannock, in the hope that by holding the fords, sufficient time would be gained for the Army of the Potomac to come to his relief. But Lee and Jackson had pressed forward with such vigor, that General Halleck soon found, when it was too late, that the line of the Rappahannock was too far forward for the union of Pope's and McClellan's armies. The troops which had not been landed were conveyed to Alexandria, and assembled in time to assure the safety of the capital.

Catlett's Station in 1862.

On August 22d, when General Pope was watching the line of the Rappahannock, Gen. J. E. B. Stuart, the noted Confederate cavalry leader, made a daring raid in his rear, with fifteen hundred horsemen, to interrupt his railroad communications with Washington. Stuart crossed the Rappahannock at Waterloo Bridge, and marching rapidly *via* Warrenton, arrived at Catlett's Station, General Pope's camp, after dark. My comrade, Wildman, of the Tenth, says : "The rain poured in torrents, and the sudden attack at midnight was a complete surprise. Everyone at headquarters was startled from sleep by the firing of volley after volley in their midst, and all started up in the darkness, in the endeavor to find a place of safety, 'I escaped,'" he said, "but had a hard tramp through the mud, rain, and darkness, —but I am thankful to get off alive." Fortunately for the author, his brief leave of absence from headquarters, to recover his health, was perhaps the means of saving his life, as he could hardly have withstood, in his physical condition, the perils and exposures of that night attack. Stuart and his horsemen remained, gathering up the spoils till a little before daylight, when they departed southward, *via* Warrenton Springs. They carried off about two hundred horses, General Pope's uniform, baggage, and important dispatches, several of his clerks and staff officers, and about two hundred prisoners. A few were killed on both sides. All the sick men were taken from the hospitals, and many of them were put on the Confederate horses to ride. All this happened in the rear of General Pope's army, within thirty-five miles of Washington, on the night of August 22d.

Encouraged by the success of Stuart's raid, Stonewall Jackson with his own and Early's division, started a day or two later, made a grand circuit to Pope's right, through Thoroughfare Gap, and on the night of the 25th, struck the Orange and Alexandria Railroad, at Manassas Junction, capturing an immense quantity of army supplies. This movement caused Pope to abandon the line of the Rappahannock and his communication with Fredericksburg, and concentrate his whole army in the neighborhood of Warrenton and Gainesville, to reopen the railroad to Washington, and, if possible, crush Jackson. But Longstreet succeeded in making a junction with Jackson *via* Thoroughfare Gap, on the morning of August 29th, on the same field on which the first battle of Bull Run was fought in 1861. Then followed the second battle of Bull Run. The Union army fought bravely, and General Pope showed his usual energy, but on the following day, the 30th, the Confederates succeeded in driving his army across Bull Run to Centreville, from which they retired in good order to the defences of Washington, but General Pope had succeeded in gaining time for the Army of the Potomac, to assemble for the defence of Washington.

Brooklyn Suspension Bridge.

One of the officers of General Pope's staff, in the campaign of July and August, 1862 (who has since won a national reputation as a civil engineer), was Washington Augustus Roebling. Under his direction a suspension bridge was constructed across the Rappahannock River, early in 1862, and later another across the Shenandoah, at Harper's Ferry. He served till January, 1865. His greatest work is the building of the Brooklyn suspension bridge, which was begun in 1869, and completed in 1883. This structure, built by him, is the largest suspension bridge in the world, and cost about $13,000,000. The picture shows it incomplete, as it was in 1877, when the writer crossed it by the picket foot-path attached to the cables suspended from the tops of the towers. Its total length, including approaches, is about 6,000 feet, or one and one-eighth miles.

Charles H. Wildman, of the Tenth Rhode Island, from General Pope's headquarters, rejoined the regiment at Washington, August 25th. As he told the story of the night attack and escape at Catlett's Station, on the night of the 22d, he became the centre of interest. He agreed that the order for "cooking utensils for Cedar Mountain," might safely be countermanded, and was glad to let General Pope's "line of retreat" take care of itself.

We regret to record the death of Private Mathew M. Meggett, of Company B, who died of typhoid fever, in the hospital, at Fort Pennsylvania, August 18th. He was a young man greatly beloved by his companions, and was a student of Brown University. A sketch of his life is given on page 30.

The Tenth Regiment and Battery arrived home, via Baltimore, Harrisburg, and Elizabethport, N. J., on the morning of August 28th, and was received with a national salute, and escorted by the Marine Artillery and the First Ward Light Guards, led by the American Band, to Exchange Place, where it was dismissed to the several armories to receive the hospitalities and congratulations of its friends.

The Providence *Journal* of the 18th thus welcomed its return:

> The Tenth Regiment and Battery, which have completed their term of service, sailed from New York yesterday, at one o'clock, in the steamer *Bay State*, which probably anchored in the bay during the night.
>
> The gallant fellows will come up as soon as the tide allows, and several of the companies will have special receptions by the companies of the National Guards, to which they respectively belonged. And all will be most cordially welcomed home by their friends and neighbors. These brave men went off on the shortest notice, at the time that Washington was supposed to be in danger, after Banks's retreat down the Shenandoah Valley. They went in the closing days of May. It has so happened that they have not been called into active service on the battlefield. But they went prepared and expecting to meet the foe. It was not their fault that they did not meet him. They have been engaged most of the time in most exhausting labors. They have been constructing, altering or strengthening forts, and have performed the most wearying tasks. They have discharged their duties with credit to themselves, and to their state. We rejoice that we can now take them by the hand and bid them a hearty Welcome Home!

September 1st. The several companies of the Tenth Regiment were mustered out of service and paid off this morning. The following farewell order from Colonel Shaw was read to the companies :

HEADQUARTERS TENTH R. I. VOLS.,
PROVIDENCE, September 1, 1862.

Special Order No. 48.

The term for which this regiment was called into the service of the United States has now expired, and the Colonel Commanding takes this opportunity to return to each and every officer, and every man of his command, his thanks for the courtesy and kindness that have marked their intercourse.

Suddenly called from the quiet pursuits of private life to the hardships and dangers of the camp, you have vindicated the character of the National Guard of Rhode Island, and shown that the citizen soldier can be depended upon when the country is in danger. The dispatch of the Secretary of War to our Governor, saying that General Banks was completely routed, and that the enemy was advancing on Washington, reached this city at midnight. At nine o'clock the next morning, you were called on to assemble and to volunteer for the defence of the Capital. At 7.30 o'clock the same evening, your Commandant had the honor of presenting six hundred and thirteen names to the Governor, as ready to respond to his call; within thirty hours from the first call, you were armed, equipped, and ready to proceed to Washington, with every expectation of immediate active service.

Starting from home in the midst of a pouring rain, crowded in the cars on your long and tedious journey, packed in the barracks at Washington, marching to Tennallytown under a burning sun, then drenched and chilled by the heavy rain that greeted your arrival in camp; these, with the cold and stormy weather of the next three weeks, were experiences to try even older soldiers.

Breaking camp on the morning of the 25th of June, you marched to Fairfax Seminary, eighteen miles, in six and a half hours, with every man in his place in the ranks. Three days after, while yet foot-sore and weary from your last march, you were ordered to return and garrison the fort near your old camp. Arriving there at two o'clock the next morning, after working and marching for twenty-two hours, you came into your cheerless bivouac with a cheerful song. Well did our Colonel say, "A better regiment I never saw." Separated from each other, with so many batteries and forts to garrison, your duties were necessarily more numerous and severe, while the extra work at Battery Vermont, was well calculated to tax your patience to the utmost.

A kind Providence has spared you from the dangers of the battlefield, but judging from the manner in which every other duty was performed, the call for battle should have met with a ready response.

Sickness has visited your camp, and three of your members have been taken away from you by death, leaving the legacy of a bright example of soldierly faithfulness, to a regiment that will ever cherish their memory.

Of the character and conduct of the regiment, your Commandant could not speak in too high praise. It has been all that could be asked, and the guard-house has been almost a useless institution. And, now, as you close your labors, you can carry with you the consciousness of having faithfully performed every duty, and you will receive, as you deserve, the thanks of your fellow-citizens.

By order.

JAMES SHAW, JR.,
Colonel Commanding.

JOHN F. TOBEY,
Adjutant.

Mustered Out.

THE TENTH REGIMENT.

Lieut.-Col. William M. Hale.

The portrait of Lieutenant-Colonel Hale, has just been received. He was the captain of Company I, until August 11th, when he was promoted to lieutenant-colonel. He was an ideal officer, and the author of the interesting letters in the *Evening Press*, from the Tenth Regiment, signed Mathew Bagnet.

The fine view of Fort Alexander, on the opposite page, will be appreciated by the members of Companies E and I, of the "Bloody" Tenth Rhode Island, as it was christened in 1862. It was reproduced from a larger sketch furnished by Hon. Henry R. Barker, formerly a sergeant of Company I.

Some of the more familiar bugle-calls will touch responsive chords in the memory of the old comrades:

The Reveille.

FORT ALEXANDER.

Headquarters Companies E and I, Tenth Rhode Island Volunteers, July and August, 1862.

The General.

Boots and Saddles.

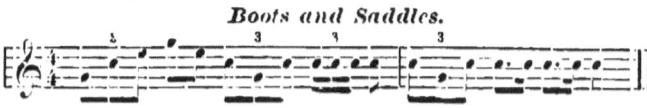

To Horse.

The Assembly.

To Arms.

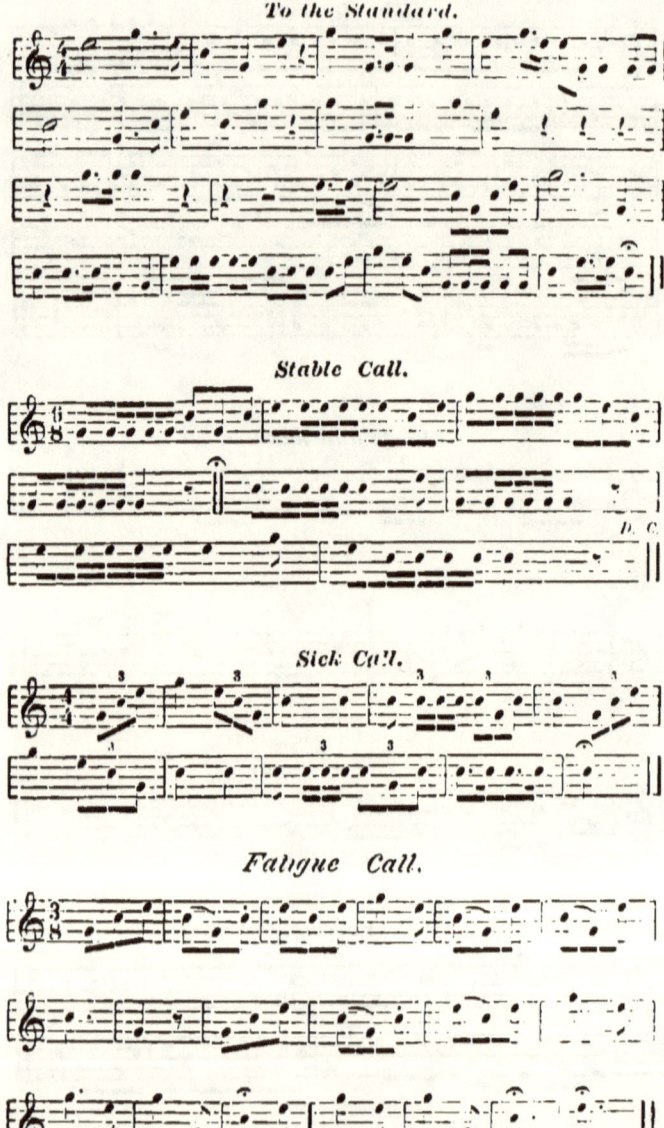

TENTH R. I. VOLUNTEERS.

FIELD AND STAFF.

Colonels—ZENAS R. BLISS, JAMES SHAW, JR.
Lieutenant-Colonels—JAMES SHAW, JR., WILLIAM M. HALE.
Majors—C. H. MERRIMAN (Acting), JACOB T. BABBITT.
Surgeon—GEORGE D. WILCOX.
Assistant-Surgeon—ALBERT G. SPRAGUE.
Chaplain—A. HUNTINGTON CLAPP.
Adjutants—B. F. THURSTON (Acting), JOHN F. TOBEY.
Quartermasters — JAMES H. ARMINGTON, WINTHROP DEWOLF, CHARLES W. ANGELL.
Sergeant-Majors—JOHN F. TOBEY (Acting), EDWARD K. GLEZEN.
Quartermaster-Sergeant— LYSANDER FLAGG.
Hospital Steward— CHARLES G. KING.
Commissary-Sergeant—JAMES O. SWAN.

COMPANY OFFICERS.

COMPANY A.

Capt. WILLIAM E. TABER, 1st Lt. JOSEPH L. BENNETT, JR.,
2d Lt. LEANDER C. BELCHER.

COMPANY B.

Capt. ELISHA DYER,
1st Lt. SAMUEL H. THOMAS,   2d Lt. WILLIAM C. CHASE,
" WILLIAM C. CHASE,   " CHARLES F. PHILLIPS.

COMPANY C.

Capt. JEREMIAH M. VOSE,   1st Lt. JOHN E. BRADFORD,
           2d Lt. CALEB B. HARRINGTON.

COMPANY D.

Capt. CHARLES H. DUNHAM (Acting),   Capt. WILLIAM S. SMITH,
1st Lt. JAMES H. ARMINGTON,   2d Lt. WINTHROP DEWOLF,
   "   WINTHROP DEWOLF,   "   CHARLES W. ANGELL.

COMPANY E.

Capt. HOPKINS B. CADY,   1st Lt. STEPHEN THURBER,
           2d Lt. MOSES O. DARLING.

COMPANY F.

Capt. BENJAMIN W. HARRIS,   1st Lt. ORVILLE P. JONES,
           2d Lt. GEORGE W. FAIRBANKS.

COMPANY G.

Capt. A. CRAWFORD GREENE,   1st Lt. JAMES H. ALLEN,
           2d Lt. EBEN BURLINGAME.

COMPANY H.

Capt. CHRISTOPHER DUCKWORTH,   1st Lt. NICHOLAS B. BOLLES,
           2d Lt. WILLIAM H. MASON.

COMPANY I.

Capt. WILLIAM M. HALE,   1st Lt. CHARLES H. MUMFORD,
   "   SAMUEL H. THOMAS,   2d Lt. PETER ALEXANDER REID.

COMPANY K.

Capt. G. FRANK LOW,   1st Lt. JOHN F. TOBEY,
           2d Lt. WILLIAM G. PETTIS.

COMPANY L.

Tenth Light Battery Rhode Island Volunteers.

THE OLD COFFEE KETTLE.

(*Tune:* "The Old Oaken Bucket," or "Araby's Daughter.")

NOTE.—In singing these ten line verses to the printed music, sing twice the notes in second line (or bar) of music before D. C. or return to beginning for the music for last two lines of each verse.

How dear to our hearts are the days when we soldiered,
  As fond recollection presents them to view;
The long line of earthworks, the deep tangled thicket,
  And every rough spot that our army life knew.
The long parks of artillery, with harness and saddle,
  The picket roped horses oft trying to roll;
The cook-house, the guard tent and the muskets stacked nigh it,
  And the old Coffee Kettle that hung on a pole;
    That old Coffee Kettle, that welcome old kettle,
    The old Coffee Kettle that hung on a pole.

How dear to this day are the forms and the faces,
  Of those who stood with us in those trying times;
So many are gone from their ranks and their places,
  It mightily shortens the original lines;
Hard camping and marching we all well remember,
  And everything trying to body and soul;
Yet one thing we had that was genuine pleasure,
  'Twas the old Coffee Kettle that hung on a pole,
    That old Coffee Kettle, that welcome old kettle,
    The old Coffee Kettle that hung on a pole.

TENTH LIGHT BATTERY

R. I. VOLUNTEERS.

Battery on Drill.

THE Tenth Battery Rhode Island Volunteers was raised simultaneously with the Ninth and Tenth regiments of infantry, for three months' service in Washington. It was mainly recruited from the Providence Marine Corps of Artillery, under the supervision of Col. Edwin C. Gallup, and other officers of this organization, who went into service as officers of the Tenth Battery, taking position as they stood in the home organization, as follows: Captain, Edwin C. Gallup; Senior First Lieutenant, Samuel A. Pearce, Jr.; Second Senior Lieutenant, Amos D. Smith, Jr.; Junior First Lieutenant, Frank A. Rhodes; Junior Second Lieutenant, Henry Pearce.

On the 24th of May, 1862, Governor Sprague received a dispatch from the Secretary of War, announcing that the little army under command of Gen. N. P. Banks had been routed, that the

Capt. Edwin C. Gallup

enemy were advancing on Washington, and calling upon the Governor to send all his available militia to the defence of the capital.

Under special orders from the adjutant-general's office of Rhode Island, Colonel Gallup was directed to organize a company of artillery, and assisted by his fellow officers, he immediately commenced the formation of the Tenth Battery.

On the 29th of May, Lieut. Samuel A. Pearce, Jr., started for Washington with a detachment of ninety men and three officers. Lieutenants Frank A. Rhodes and Amos D. Smith, Jr., went with this detachment, which arrived in Washington on Sunday morning, May 31st, and reported to Governor Sprague, who had preceded his troops to the capital.

The detachment of the battery was immediately ordered to Tennallytown, a village seven miles from Washington, where it arrived at noon and reported to Col. Charles T. Robbins, of the Ninth Rhode Island Infantry. The detachment was received with cheers from the Ninth and Tenth Rhode Island Regiments. The first camp was located at the right of and in front of the Tenth Regiment and was called Camp Frieze.

The arrival of the detachment was unexpected and no provision had been made for the men by the quartermaster and commissary departments, but through the energy and obliging disposition of Quartermaster George Lewis Cooke all were soon made comfortable. Colonel Robbins was particularly attentive and furnished the men with cooked rations from his regimental stores. Sunday afternoon was occupied in pitching tents and in other camp duties ; and when at night the new recruits retired to their beds of straw, under canvas roofs, they felt that they had begun a soldier's life.

On the 6th of June, Captain Gallup arrived in camp with forty men, followed on the 9th by Lieut. Henry Pearce, with twenty-five more men, which brought the battery up to the required standard of one hundred and fifty ; and the following order was issued :

HEADQUARTERS, TENTH R. I. VOLS.,
CAMP NEAR TENNALLYTOWN, June 8, 1862.

Special Orders No. 5.

Two commissioned officers and fifty privates are hereby detailed from Light Battery " L," attached to the Tenth Rhode Island Volunteers, for the purpose of bringing from Washington, the horses and equipments belonging to the battery. The regimental quartermaster will furnish the transportation necessary.

ZENAS R. BLISS,
Colonel Tenth R. I. Vols.

BENJAMIN F. THURSTON,
Adjutant.

On the 14th of June, a battery of six twelve-pounder guns (Napoleons), were received, and active drilling in the field began. Each of the three branches or "arms" of the military service had its distinguishing color ; blue for infantry, yellow for cavalry, and red for artillery. The body of the uniform worn by all was blue, — the trousers light, and the blouse dark blue. Artillerymen usually wore upon the front of their caps, a brass device representing two cannon crossed. A battery usually had six guns, was complete in itself, and in almost all cases served independently. In the case of the Tenth Rhode Island Light Battery, by order, it was numbered as Company L, Tenth Rhode Island Volunteers. Each piece of artillery, and each caisson, battery-wagon, etc., was drawn by four or six horses, with numerous drivers, one of whom rode the "nigh" animal of each pair. The officers and men diligently devoted themselves to duty and the Tenth Battery was soon ready for active service.

On the 23d of June, the battery received orders to move to Cloud's Mills, Va., to support a general advance of troops to the Peninsula, to join McClellan. The movement was made in a storm of rain, the battery being followed by a train of from fifteen to eighteen army wagons loaded with tents and supplies. As this was the first time the teams had been harnessed up, there was naturally considerable confusion and delay, which was aggravated by the increasing storm. Quartermaster-Sergeant Asa Lyman was hard at work in the rear, urging the line forward, with words of direction and encouragement. The battery had a lot of spare horses, which were ridden by men specially detailed for that purpose. As it crossed Long Bridge into Virginia, the rain and darkness increased. The spare horses became very unmanageable, as the men clambered into the rear of the army wagons for shelter, and still attempted to hold them; but with the sudden flashes of lightning, they began to break away, and disappear in the darkness. Lyman relates an amusing episode that occurred under his eye. "As I rode up from the rear, completely drenched, a vivid flash of lightning, illuminating earth and sky, revealed one of the battery men, on a rising knoll by the roadside, struggling with two horses, which were pulling in opposite directions. In his terror, the man was beseeching the Almighty to strike one of the horses dead, and relieve him of the responsibility. He declared, with an oath, that he couldn't ' hould ' but one baste, any longer." A considerable loss of horseflesh occurred on that dismal night—but it was more than replaced by foraging—so that a gain of one was reported at camp the following day.

The final halt was made at Clouds's Mills, near the camp of the Sixty-ninth New York,

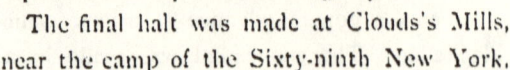

A Dismal Night

and the hospitalities extended to our men were very gratefully appreciated. The surgeon of that regiment drew very liberally for us from his hospital stores. It was real Irish hospitality given in full measure without stint or formality. The camp of the battery was located near Seminary Hill, commanding roads leading into Washington. Near by were the Sixty-ninth New York, the Thirty-second Massachusetts, and part of the Eleventh and Fourteenth United States Infantry, and three batteries of light artillery. The brigade was under the command of Colonel Bliss, of the Tenth Rhode Island Volunteers, acting-brigadier-general.

With such an environment, the Tenth Battery soon attained a most creditable degree of efficiency. An officer on the staff of Gen. Samuel P. Sturgis, commanding the division, paid it the compliment of saying that it had been selected by the General for a service, in which its efficiency would be thoroughly tested. The test of battle was not given but it is fair to say that the Tenth Battery was ready and willing to obey any call that could be made upon it. Immediately after the failure of the Peninsula

Lieut. Samuel A. Pearce, Jr.

campaign, under McClellan, it returned to its old camp, near Fort Pennsylvania, the headquarters of the Tenth Rhode Island Volunteers, relieving veteran troops for active service. During the absence of Captain Gallup, who was detailed on court martial duty in Washington, Lieut. Samuel A. Pearce, Jr., commanded the battery.

Our surgeon, Edward Carrington Franklin, rendered excellent service and was much esteemed by officers and men. He graduated at Trinity College, and studied medicine with Dr. A. H. Okie, of Providence, and later at the New York Medical College.

One death only occurred, during our term of service, and that by accident. Corp. James Flate was struck by the pole yoke of a limber, during an exhibition drill, and so badly injured that he died in four hours. He enlisted in New York as a detachment was passing through that city. He was faithful in the discharge of his duty, and by his social qualities gained universal favor.

The officers and men of the battery maintained very agreeable relations with their brother soldiers of the Ninth and Tenth Regiments. Col. Zenas R. Bliss, of the "Tenth" often honored the battery with a visit, and was always warmly welcomed. These pleasant relations have been continued and kept alive by annual reunions of the survivors of the Tenth Regiment and Battery.

During its term of service it acquired a proficiency in drill and artillery movements that excited the admiration of military visitants from Washington. Though it did not receive its "baptism of fire" as was confidently expected when it was ordered to an advanced position, the battery formed an important arm of the defence of Washington at a time when it became necessary to withdraw experienced troops from the fortifications around the city to reënforce the armies in the field.

At the close of its term of service, the Battery returned home in company with the Tenth, and shared the welcome which greeted their arrival. It was mustered out of service August 30, 1862. Some of the officers and men again volunteered, and made an honorable record.

In closing this brief sketch of the Tenth Battery, it is due to the men who originated and organized the Rhode Island National Guard, in 1861, to say that the promptness with which the men responded to this sudden call, was the result of patient and arduous military preparations to provide for just such emergencies as occurred in May, 1862. The Rhode Island National Guard maintained the efficiency of the militia companies, and enabled them to respond promptly in the time of need. In this regard special honor is due Col. James Shaw, Jr., its commander.

LIEUT. SAMUEL A. PEARCE, JR.,
Tenth R. I. Battery.

THE PROVIDENCE MARINE CORPS OF ARTILLERY.

LIEUT. SAMUEL A. PEARCE, JR.

The Providence Marine Corps of Artillery was the mother of ten batteries of light artillery, and the officers of this company assisted in the recruiting and drilling of these batteries during the War. By sending recruits to fill the depleted ranks they performed an important duty; and, it may be timely said, that the history of none of the Rhode Island Light Batteries would be complete without the history of the "Providence Marine Corps of Artillery."

It was organized in the year 1801, and is therefore one of the oldest military organizations in Rhode Island, and was the first militia light battery in the United States. It bears upon its roll of membership many of Rhode Island's distinguished citizens. Several of its former officers were chiefs of artillery, having regular army officers under them. Gov. William Sprague, Governor of Rhode Island, at the outbreak of the war, was a former commandant of this organization, and while holding his position as colonel developed the soldierly qualities which made Rhode Island's Governor conspicuous for his promptness in sending troops to Washington at the first call of the President of the United States.

In filling Rhode Island's quota, Governor Sprague conceived the idea of putting a regiment of light batteries into the field. These batteries were distributed in the armies of Virginia and the West, and made a proud record for themselves and in the great battles of the war.

Well may the old "Mother of Batteries" be proud of her children ; and long may her name be perpetuated by preserving the organization under its present charter.

An account of the visit of the "Marines" to Boston, in 1852, under the command of Col. Joseph P. Balch, taken from a Boston paper, may be of interest to the younger members of this company, and will show to some extent the character of the organization in which the war batteries were schooled.

"Boston, Saturday, September 18, 1852. Grand Review of the Marine Artillery of Providence, R. I., by His Excellency Governor Boutwell and staff, on Boston Common.

"Our artist has given us below a very correct view of this fine body of citizen soldiers, under command of Colonel Balch, as they appeared on Boston Common a few days since when reviewed by Governor Boutwell and suite. Did our space permit we should be pleased to give a detailed account of the review, but we must be concise. The artist has chosen the scene to depict the company as they appeared *à la* Sherman's Flying Artillery at full speed passing in review. It is a fact that the Providence Corps, as represented below, fired *one hundred* guns (notwithstanding a rain storm), in a second over six minutes with four pieces, while Sherman's Battery took seven minutes. The drill and discipline of the Marine Artillery was most excellent, and has infused a spirit among our own military that may result in the formation of a similar corps in Boston.

"The company was instituted and organized and the charter granted by the legislature of Rhode Island, under the name of the Providence Marine Corps of Artillery, in the year 1801. Upon the petition of the 'Marine Society,' 'praying for an act of incorporation for the purpose of perfecting themselves in the art military, and for the attack and defense of ships and batteries;' and one section of the charter provided that all the officers of the company should be chosen from the Marine Society; this provision has been modified from time to time and finally annulled. At the present time no connection with the Marine Society exists.

"From the time of their organization until the close of the war of 1812, the company was in a very efficient state of drill and discipline; the forts and preparations for the defense of the harbor of Providence during the war, were constructed under their direction. After this period, the interest in the company appeared to decline. New members, however, were admitted and the annual election held, that the charter might not be forfeited.

"In 1842, at the commencement of the 'Dorr Rebellion' a communication was addressed by the Executive to the several military companies of the State, requesting to be informed if in case of necessity, he could depend upon their services to aid in the preservation of *law and order*.

"Upon laying this executive communication before the company they at once took measures to render themselves efficient.

"Numerous accessions were made to their ranks, and during the campaign of 1842, the active roll of the company numbered about one hundred men. During this season, they uniformed themselves, and the next year assisted by the State erected a commodious stone building, which is occupied jointly with the State as the armory of the company and the State Arsenal.

"At this time the company were drilled and equipped as infantry. In 1847-48 the State furnished the company with their present battery and since that time they have drilled as light or flying artillery."

POEM.

Dedicated to the Tenth Battery Rhode Island Volunteers, before leaving their camp for home. By Lieut. Samuel A. Pearce, Jr. :

>Amid the joys that fill our every heart
>   At happy greetings from the loved at home,
>'T'is joy to feel that as true friends we part,
>   That so few shadows o'er our path has come.
>
>Days, weeks, and months we've shared each others lot,
>   And each his portion of the burden borne,
>And pleasant mem'ries linger round the spot,
>   Where rapidly those days and weeks rolled on.
>
>We leave this spot,—but not without a sigh,
>   For here we've counted many a happy day,
>Yet still we bid the moments swiftly fly
>   And hail the hour which sees us on our way.
>
>Safely returned we'll count our hardships sweet,
>   And looked for dangers but a calm repose,
>And ever as such friends we'll always meet,
>   And thus remain until our lives shall close.

Homeward Bound.

THE END—AT LAST.

FORT HILL, PAWTUXET NECK, R. I.,
July 4, 1893.

Comrades: Just a year ago the author wrote the introduction to this volume. To-day marks its completion. In the brief space during which it has been compiled there has been little opportunity for elaboration. It has been prepared one form of sixteen pages at a time, and an edition of six hundred copies printed.

No revision of the completed work has thus been possible, nor any opportunity afforded to leave out some irrelevant matter; but the writer has had the advantage of letting the plan of the book, so far as there is any, develop itself from month to month. It is made up of incidents furnished by a large number of comrades, who thus join the writer in bearing witness to the faithfulness of his record. From collections of old diaries, old letters, old newspapers and orders, he has had to puzzle out and piece together his material, but has at last, got together the needed facts, so far as it is now possible to discover them. He has sought by the liberal introduction of the spice of army life, to make the book entertaining, especially to the children of "the boys who marched in 'Sixty-two.'" On this account the volume has far outgrown his original purpose.

He gratefully acknowledges the assistance rendered from many sources, and the manifestations of deep interest, as the work has slowly yet surely progressed to the end. Whatever the reception which the critic of to-day may give to this book, it may be one of that class which Abraham Lincoln said people will read with satisfaction two hundred years hence, if fortunately a copy should be preserved so long in the Public Library.

It closes with brief sketches of the reunions of the Ninth and Tenth Rhode Island Veteran Associations, and a corrected roster of the Ninth and Tenth Regiments, and Tenth Battery Rhode Island Volunteers.

If by the perusal of these pages the comrades shall experience any added satisfaction for duty well performed in scenes of trial and danger, if in coming years it shall delight the hearts of their children, and children's children, to read the story of the eventful days when they put on uniform and hurried to the defence of the capital,—above all, if any impetus shall thus be given to the sacred cause of loyalty to our reunited country, then the desire of the writer will be abundantly satisfied.

WILLIAM ARNOLD SPICER,
Company B, Tenth R. I. Vols.

REUNIONS.

THE NINTH R. I. VETERAN ASSOCIATION.

NEARLY every year since the close of the War some of our comrades have held reunions to renew the old friendships of "Sixty-two."

The Ninth Rhode Island Veteran Association was organized in 1873, and has held twenty annual reunions up to the present time. The Association badge was adopted in 1875.

One of the most enjoyable gatherings was that at Silver Spring, on September 2, 1890, the twenty-eighth anniversary of the muster-out day. The following report has been preserved:

"Col. J. Talbot Pitman was reëlected president, and Hon. Harrison H. Richardson, of Nayatt, sergeant of Company H, secretary and treasurer. After the routine business was completed, the secretary, in behalf of members of the Association, presented to Colonel Pitman a gold badge, appropriately inscribed, embodying the State coat-of-arms, and military emblems, sug-

BADGE.
Ninth R. I. Veteran Association.

gestive of the recipient's rank in the service. In presenting the badge, Sergeant Richardson said:

"*Mr. President:* A few days ago I submitted for your approval the 'notice,' since issued, for this reunion, and possibly you may remember asking me 'what other important business besides the election of officers was therein referred to.' Perhaps my answer was hardly satisfactory, for I tried to evade the question.

"In truth, sir, I had been drawn into a conspiracy. A plot had been devised which would fail of success if you should get knowledge of it before we were ready to spring the mine.

"For some time past, members have felt that there was due to you from them some recognition of your untiring efforts to promote the success of this Association and to keep alive the spirit of comradeship among those who, twenty-eight years ago, shared with you the honors, as well as the toils and dangers of our hundred days' watch and ward over the city of Washington.

"Now, after the lapse of many years, as we recall the events of 'Sixty-two,' we can better understand the responsibility then weighing upon you as colonel, commanding the regiment, and there has come to us some appreciation of your patience with our imperfect, and sometimes none too earnest efforts to conform to military rule and discipline.

"We can now even remember with complacency that too previous fife and drum, which were wont to make such sad havoc with our early morning dreams. For surely the dulcet strains of the 'Reveille' were to be preferred to the clamor of the 'Long Roll,' which, at some midnight hour, we might have heard in our camp, if through our lack of vigilance the enemy had found an unguarded opening through our lines.

"So too, those daily drills, by squad, by company, and by battalion, sometimes irksome, especially to our cherished 'whangs' (army shoes), yet who shall say how much they may have had to do with our immunity from attack?

"These thoughts tend to impress upon us the sense of obligation to you sir, inasmuch as, in those days of our country's trials, your zeal in her service never abated, your vigilance never relaxed; and although ours was a bloodless campaign, yet to the Ninth Regiment belongs the honor of having faithfully performed all duties imposed upon it, and we can take pride in sharing that honor with our commander.

"*Mr. President:* Probably knowing how inadequate my words would be, to fittingly express their feelings towards you, the comrades have placed in my hands as a tangible testimonial of their regard, this badge, which in their behalf, I now present for your acceptance, in the hope that it may be found worthy to be worn by you upon all suitable occasions, in remembrance of the campaign of the Ninth Regiment in 1862, for the defence of the national capital."

Colonel Pitman responded with fitting acknowledgments, but was so completely taken by surprise, as to find it impossible at the moment to find words to suitably express his feelings. He fully appreciated the gift, and was very proud of the honor conferred upon him by his comrades of the Ninth Rhode Island Veteran Association.

Sergt. Harrison H. Richardson, of Company H, has filled the position of secretary and treasurer, with untiring zeal and fidelity since the organization in 1873.

The officers of the Ninth Rhode Island Veteran Association have been as follows:

Presidents.

Col. JOHN TALBOT PITMAN,   Lt.-Col. JOHN HARE POWEL.

Vice-Presidents.

Lt.-Col. JOHN HARE POWEL,   Capt. ROBERT MCCLOY,
Capt. HENRY C. CARD,   " JOHN A. BROWN,
" HENRY F. JENKS,   Lieut. FRANCELLO G. JILLSON,
Lieut. JOHN POLLARD,   " NATHAN D. BENTON,
" J. CLARKE BARBER,   " WILLIAM MCCREADY,
" RICHARD W. HOWARD,   " H. J. WHITAKER,
" GEORGE H. BURNHAM,   " WILLIAM R. LANDERS,
Adjt. HENRY C. BROWN,   Sergt. ENOS A. CLARKE,
Sergt. ROBERT S. BLAIR,   " JAMES F. MOWREY,
" JAMES B. STREETER,   Corp. JEREMIAH I. GREENE,
Corp. EDWARD P. LOWDEN,   " BENJAMIN B. MARTIN,
" SANFORD A. ROBBINS.   " HUGH O'DONNELL,
Priv. DARIUS COOK,   Priv. EDMUND BRAY,
" JOHN S. DAVIS,   " WILLIAM MASSEY,
" GEORGE CARMICHAEL, JR.,   " EDWARD H. BURDICK,
" JOSEPH BIGELOW,   " JOHN MCDEVITT,
" ANDREW CRUMLEY,   " WILLIAM J. MILAN,
" HENRY C. SAYLES,   " LUKE A. WOOD,
" CHARLES F. PIERCE,   " FRANK D. FISKE,
" STEPHEN A. PECK,   " HENRY A. BOWEN,
" ORLAND FREEBORN,   " JOHN H. STACY.

THE SOLDIER'S WELCOME.

BY MARY E. KILBURN, LONSDALE, R. I.

Welcome, thrice welcome, soldier friends,
  We give you hearty cheer,
We've watched and waited for this hour
  With mingled hope and fear;
We've missed you in our hearts and homes,
  Friends, brothers, sons and sires,
And now we shout that "Welcome Home,"
  Which trust and love inspires.

We lent you to "our holy cause,"
  To guard the nation's dome,
To keep the rebel hordes at bay,
  And save "fair freedom's" home:
And now your duty nobly done,
  We grasp with honest pride
Your sun-browned hands, that tell of toil,
  Near the "Potomac's side."

But in our joy we'll humbly raise
  Our grateful hearts above,
To Him whose guardian care has kept
  The objects of our love:
In sun, and in light and shade,
  His strong, protecting arm
Has been outstretched for your defence,
  To shield from every harm.

And while with happy hearts we sing,
  Oh let us not forget
The sorrowing and the suffering ones,
  Whose respite is not yet;
With loving hearts and ready hands,
  To cheer and to relieve,
We'll stand beside the soldier-boys,
  And comfort those who grieve.

And shall we not stand by our arms,
  And heed again the call;
Shall patriot blood forget to flow,
  And patriots fear to fall?
Oh, what are we, if land, and home,
  And liberty, and law,
Are weighed against our little life!
  (Prepare, then, for the war).

Our country! all we are to-day,
  And all we hope to be,
We gladly on thy altar lay,
  And consecrate to thee;
We ask not wealth, we ask not fame,
  This loan thy blessing be,—
United States may we remain,
  One land, one hope, one destiny.

Chorus:

Then while we shout a welcome,
  We'll sing in grateful lays
Of His kind love and tenderness,
  Who merits all our praise.

VETERAN ASSOCIATION.

THE STARRY STANDARD.

By Capt. J. McKinlay, Company D,
Written for a Flag-raising.

Behold your starry standard,
   Aloft in ambient air!
What heart so cold but rapturous throbs
   To see it floating there!
Be scorned the man who views the flag
   Of Valley Forge renown,
Who'd not resist the rebel arm
   Upraised to tear it down.

That flag:—beneath those streaming stripes,
   Your martyr'd fathers stood:
That flag they raised on Bunker Hill,
   And baptized with their blood:
We fling not forth defiantly,
   From towering spire and dome,
But rally round its hallowed shrine
   To guard fair Freedom's home.

Why are these starry ensigns raised
   To flaunt and flutter free,
Till towns appear like pennoned fleets,
   At anchor on the sea?
They're all unfurled to indicate
   That rebellion we detest,
And show the brave and loyal heart
   Within the nation's breast.

We court not war, with all the ills
    That follow in its train:
But order, law, and government,
    We surely dare maintain;
When mad, rebellious, wicked men,
    Would lawlessly break through
The glorious Constitution
    Your father framed for you.

Is there a heart with not enough
    Of patriotic fires,
To rally to the rescue, ere
    Loved Freedom's home expires?
Is there an arm so enervate
    That would not wield a blade,
To guard the Constitution
    Our noble fathers made?

Let Warren's gallant spirit now
    Inspire each sire and son;
Of every creed and nation,
    Let all unite in *one*!
Be party spleen and rancor drowned,
    In Union's swelling flood,
To save the glorious heritage
    Bought with our fathers' blood.

And may our patriot volunteers
    In triumph soon be seen,
Returning to their native home
    Of Perry and of Greene!
And though their war-worn features be
    With blood and smoke begrimm'd
May their flag stream forth triumphantly
    With all the stars undimm'd.

THE TENTH R. I. VETERAN ASSOCIATION.

BADGE—Tenth R. I. Veteran Association.

THE first reunion of the Tenth Rhode Island Veteran Association was held at Silver Spring, R. I., July 24, 1877. Col. James Shaw, Jr., was chosen president, and Adjt. John F. Tobey, toastmaster.

It was at the time of the labor riots in Pennsylvania, and the Providence *Journal*, referring to the Tenth reunion, said: "These are good times for veterans to be getting together. Possibly they may be wanted again, 'armed and equipped.'"

The Association Badge was adopted at the reunion in May, 1887, with the motto, "*Volens et paratus*," "ready and willing."

Its form, a spade, is suggestive of the shoveling done by the regiment on Battery Vermont, with the mercury at 100° in the shade. The badge also bears the date of enlistment, May, 1862, with the State anchor of hope. In the lower left hand corner is an infantry emblem, crossed muskets on a field of blue, and in the opposite corner an artillery emblem with crossed cannon on a field of red. The badge is supported by a gold bar with a military cap in the centre, marked 10, R. I. Vols. and Battery, the whole resting upon a ribbon of blue, with plain bar and pin at the top.

At the first reunion of the Tenth Rhode Island Veteran Association, His Honor Mayor Thomas A. Doyle, in responding to a toast, "The City of Providence," said: "The city is proud of this regiment, and of the alacrity with which it responded to the call of duty. We should keep our militia organizations strong."

Lieut. Samuel A. Pearce, Jr., followed with an original poem, which was received with much enthusiasm:

> As friends, as soldiers, aye, as brothers all,
> We here have met our camp-life to recall:
> To pledge our friendship in a friendly drink
> Of something mild, would surely have you think;
> To eat our rations in a Christian style,
> No *fierce guerillas* to molest the while,
> No *signal lights* far in the distance seen,
> No *anxious watchings* on the magazine.
> No Stonewall Jackson coming o'er the hills,
> No " grand round " escorts, no battalion drills,
> No balky horses, and no kicking teams,
> No bugle calls to wake us from our dreams;
> But here we are with hands and dishes clean.
> Plenty of napkins,—isn't it serene?
> . . . . .
> Though large our number there's an absent friend,
> Whose genial presence doth a sunshine lend:
> His name—you've guessed it: for I know you miss
> Our friend, companion, brother:—Colonel Bliss.
> Nine cheers for Bliss:—come, join me now,
> And drink the Colonel's health:—so, here's how!

On June 28, 1877, the Tenth regiment took part in the reception of President Rutherford B. Hayes, and the line was reviewed by him at Rocky Point, the Tenth being commanded by Capt. William E. Taber, Jr., of Company A.

The second reunion was held in Providence, in May, 1882, and the third in May, 1883, when Col. Zenas R. Bliss was present, and expressed his satisfaction at meeting his old comrades. He is still in the United States regular service. Hon. William A. James (formerly sergeant of Company A), speaker of the House of Representatives of the State of Illinois, was also present.

Since 1883 annual reunions have been held, nearly all on May 26th, the anniversary of the date of enlistment.

On the Fourth of July, 1887, the Tenth Rhode Island Veteran Association, William A. Spicer, president, participated in the ceremonies incident to the unveiling of the Burnside Equestrian Statue, on Exchange Place, Providence. Soldiers and citizens, State and city, joined in the tribute. The Providence *Journal* in referring to the presence of General Sherman said: "Other cities had interesting features in their celebration of the Fourth, but to Providence alone was reserved the best of all, William Tecumseh Sherman."

At the reunion of May, 1888, the steel howitzer, captured by the Tenth in 1862, was exhibited on the platform. It has since been placed with other memorials, in the museum of the Rhode Island Historical Society, Providence.

Quartermaster James H. Armington exhibited a sample of the "hard-tack" dealt out to the boys in 1862. He said according to the date thereon it was officially inspected in 1855.

The officers of the Tenth Veteran Association, have been as follows:

Presidents.

1877 to 1884. COL. JAMES SHAW, JR.
        1885. CAPT. AND EX-GOV. ELISHA DYER.
        1886. CAPT. WILLIAM E. TABER.
        1887. SERGT. PHILIP B. STINESS.
        1888. PRIV. WILLIAM A. SPICER.
        1889. SERGT. HENRY R. BARKER.
        1890. PRIV. WILLIAM A. HARRIS.
        1891. LIEUT. LEANDER C. BELCHER.
        1892. QUAR.-SERGT. ASA LYMAN.
        1893. SERGT. ALBERT J. MANCHESTER.
        1894. CORP. WILLIAM A. H. GRANT.

Vice-Presidents.

CAPT. WILLIAM E. TABER,
SERGT. WILLIAM H. H. BRAYMAN,
SERGT. PHILIP B. STINESS,
LIEUT. CHARLES F. PHILLIPS (president *pro tem*),
SERGT. WILLIAM STONE,
PRIV. ROBERT B. HOLDEN,
PRIV. WILLIAM A. HARRIS,
LIEUT. LEANDER C. BELCHER,
SERGT. ALBERT J. MANCHESTER,
CORP. WILLIAM A. H. GRANT,
CAPT. HOPKINS B. CADY,
CAPT. CHRISTOPHER DUCKWORTH.

Members who have served on the Executive Committee.

COMPANY A — Capt. William E. Taber, Lieut. Leander C. Belcher, Priv. Caleb C. Greene, Jr., Corp. Eugene F. Phillips, Corp. Albert C. Winsor.

COMPANY B—Corp. Nathan H. Baker, Corp. George T. Baker, Priv. William A. Spicer, Priv. James F. Field.

COMPANY C—Priv. George W. Lewis, Corp. Joseph W. Paddelford, Priv. Elisha W. Sweet, Priv. Edmund J. Munroe.

COMPANY D—Corp. William H. H. Brayman, Priv. S. Erastus Merchant, Priv. Levi L. Burdon.

COMPANY E—Lieut. Stephen H. Thurber, Sergt. William Stone, Corp. Ira R. Wilbur, Priv. Christopher A. Cady.

COMPANY F—First Sergt. Joel Metcalf.

COMPANY G—First Sergt. John B. Benson, Sergt. Albert J. Manchester, Musician John F. Parks.

COMPANY H—First Sergt. George A. Winchester, Sergt. Charles P. Gay.

COMPANY I—First Sergt. Henry R. Barker, Corp. Oliver S. Alers, Corp. Moses B. Chace, Corp. B. D. Hale.

COMPANY K—Corp. Joseph E. Handy, First Sergt. Munson H. Najac.

COMPANY L., *Battery*—Sergt. Philip B. Stiness, Priv. A. D. White, Quar.-Sergt. Asa Lyman, First Sergt. Amasa C. Tourtellot.

Staff.

COM.-SERGT. JAMES O. SWAN.

Secretary and Treasurer.

CORP. BENJAMIN F. PABODIE, SERGT. GEORGE A. WINCHESTER.

REUNION POEMS.

By Mrs. B. F. Pabodie,
Wife of Corp. Benjamin F. Pabodie, Company H.

The cherry snow had fallen, in the beautiful month of May,
The robins sung in the twilight,—on the purple lilac spray,
The grass was green in the meadows, in the freshening springtime life,
And we followed our peaceful duties, nor thought of the distant strife.
When early one sunny morning came a summons to our ears,
"The enemy threatens Washington, and we need more volunteers!"
The quick response from patriot hearts, our annals past will show,
Six hundred men, in scarce ten hours, had pledged themselves to go.
No time for preparation, scarce time to say farewell,
One night at home, with sorrowing friends, how fast the teardrops fell;
So thirty hours from the summons, all ready to meet the foe,
We started off for Washington, just twenty-six years ago.

How many of us remember the beginning of that campaign,
How we stood on Exchange Place, hours and hours in the midst of the pouring rain.
How they crowded us into the depot, and packed us into the cars,
But nought could dampen the courage of our valiant "Sons of Mars."
As through the long, long night we sailed, we talked of days to come,
And jest and jokes went freely round, for we dared not think of home.
What lay in the distant future, was hidden from every eye,
Suppose we never come back! What then? We have only once to die.
And so we traveled through the night and thro' the wearisome day,
With welcomes warm, and cheers and shouts in the cities along our way;
Then through the dust and mud we marched, till the fourth night settled down,
As we built our fires, and pitched our tents, on the hills near Tennallytown.

Then came the drill, and picket-guard, and the morning bugle call.
O, that getting up so early, 'twas the hardest trial of all!
Yet prompt to call we worked and drilled, and at night we took our ease,
As we gathered round the evening fires, that lighted up old Camp Frieze.
At length we were ordered to Fairfax, how gladly we hurried away,
On that long, hot march to Seminary Hill, for only three days' stay,
Not one of us wants to revisit that barren desert again.
Where the grasshoppers carried their rations, when they marched across the
  plain.
We hoped to have reached the battlefield, for courage there was no lack,
But a soldier's duty is " to obey," and the Tenth was ordered back.
'Tis hard no battles to recount, no skirmishes to relate,
But yet we know " they also serve, who only stand and wait."
So the old and veteran soldiers went forward to meet the foe,
While we guarded the forts around Washington, just twenty-six years ago.

More work, more drill, more " mounting guard," 'twas tiresome day by day,
But looking back, thro' the mist of years, it seems like nothing but play.
'Twas not for our pastime we tarried there, we felt whatever might come,
We were simply doing our duty for our country and our home.
Our patriotism no time can dull, nor trials make us forget;
Should the nation need us again, they'd find life in the old Tenth yet.
Alas! my brothers, those hours have flown, and the years have hurried past,
And sorrows many have sapped the strength which we thought would always
  last.
Our youth departed, our manhood fled, old age comes swiftly and sure,
There is little left for some of us, but patiently to endure.
The deeds we've done are not perhaps what we planned in our youthful
  dreams,
" Is life worth living," we sometimes ask, as we mourn o'er our shattered
  schemes.
Still one oasis in this bleak desert this festival night will show,
When we meet to talk of the pleasant times of twenty-six years ago.

OLD ARMY DAYS.

By Prof. W. Whitman Bailey.
Corporal Company D.

Dear fellow vets,
In such familiar phrase,
I now address my comrades of old days;
Yet as I think by no especial right,
I come before you on this festal night;
For, if you'll pardon what is scarcely meant,
A pun. I served my country by in-tent:
Still I remember in a mighty shower
Being " turned out " at some ungodly hour,
To walk before the Colonel's tent, and keep
The rebels silent while he went to sleep:
I often wonder as I think of this,
Whether our brave commander slept in Bliss,
For though a high wind blew with tempest's rack
And streams of water flowed adown my back
I guarded him so well that my relief
Forgot me for a while, much to my grief;
Perhaps to theirs: I will not here inquire
Lest I should stir some long-forgotten fire:
Speaking of fires, what a jolly thing
Those camp-fires were when Burdon used to sing:
Do the young soldiers of the present day
" See Nelly home " in that familiar way?
Or if they're modern " Titia's," are they still
Charmed by the glittering sword of Bunker Hill?
In nightly visions of a certain sort
I often find myself at this old sport,

And if a corporal called "attention" then,
I'd come bolt upright as I used to when
He'd turn us out at early reveille,
And talk quite loudly of our *corps d'esprit;*
Still plainer yet the captain's voice I hear,
Loud calling for some lusty volunteer,
To right his tent, or chop the wood, or go
To hunt up "System," in the realms below:
De mortuis nisi bonum hope I may,
And so about our grub I'll nothing say;
Except that hard-tack, when it's marked B. C.,
Is even now avoided still by me
As is that meat denominated junk,
And flung in hogsheads by the salted chunk;
Do I remember Fairfax and the clay,
In which we tried to drive our pegs one day?
Do I recall the march by night to town,
How cold we were, and how we washed it down
By something fluid, I will not say what,
Administered by the Colonel from a pot;
On that same night, or else I am a slave,
I stretched my full length on a barrel stave:
I wondered then, and even now can't see,
How I disposed of all my vertebræ;
My lucky comrades, made of sterner stuff,
Had fire, they said, and pies and food enough;
But now I'll order arms, and break my ranks,
To all my comrades I return my thanks;
I hope they'll pardon, if they don't agree
With a poor private once of Company D!

This brilliant effusion was followed by the ever popular song of "Seeing Nelly Home," by Burdon, of Company D.

Poem for the reunion of the Tenth Veteran Association, May 26, 1882.

BY SERGT. A. T. STARKEY, COMPANY D.

GLAD welcome to-night to the comrades assembled,
  Glad remembrance of those who in young manhood's strength,
Raised aloft their right hands as their country's defenders,
  And enlisted their names in the Rhode Island "Tenth."
Long years have passed by since we left our loved firesides,
  At fair Liberty's summons—her cause to defend:
The friendships we formed in the days of our service
  Were friendships for life, that shall never know end.
It was not given us on fair Liberty's altar
  To lay down our lives, as our brothers had done:
Had our country demanded,—not a soul would have faltered,
  Such was the spirit sublime, our comrades among.
How well I recall the events of the journey,
  The question our colonel, so gallant and true,
Asked De Wolf, who by looks was all of us junior.
  "My son, you look youthful: how old, boy, are you?"
"Twenty-four," says De Wolf. "O, ho!" says the colonel,
  "You'll do, my brave boy, put your name on the books:
I'll enter an item right here in my journal,
  You can't *always* tell a man's age by his looks!"
In the City of Brotherly Love behold our flirtations,
  The meal at "the Cooper Shop," ample and good;
The last ere we entered on Uncle Sam's rations
  And gave him our time for his clothes and his food.
Then the night march in Baltimore, through the street so historic
  Where the first brave martyrs to Liberty fell,—
The clank of our bayonets meeting the awnings,
  Our fears and our fancies we remember full well.
Then the strange disappearance of our friends in the darkness;
  As to right and to left they mysteriously fell

Down the dark, open cellar-ways left all unguarded,
   Till we all met at the station our adventures to tell.
Oh, the first meal at Washington, so rough and forbidding,
   With great chunks of meat, all gristle and fat;
How they flew through the air in that dining-hall dreary,
   Then the midnight alarm,—do you e'er think of that?
Our camp at Tennallytown, and the daily manœuvres;
   The return of Mauran, so triumphal and grand,
From his visit at home for his teeth's benefaction;
   His queer donkey-chariot and quaint driving-man.
" Poor darkness " was arrested for quitting his station
   Before the white tent of our Colonel so true;
To procure for himself a nice cold, creamy " ration,"
   Which he'd waited and longed for, who could blame him—could you?
The march over the river. So many crossed over
   Who never returned to glad Liberty's shore.
Our camp at old Fairfax—the return—and the journey
   To the Forts,—I've dreamt of them over and o'er.
Then our pathways divided, and each of our hundreds
   Lived a separate camp-life, and marched various ways;
At the fort called " De Russy," not far from headquarters,
   Company D of the Tenth whiled away the long days;
On the silvery banks of the creek near our camp-fires,
   With the cool water bathing our limbs day by day;
In the blackberry fields just over the river,
   We reveled at will, as the time wore away.
Till the day came at length when our campaign was ended
   With discharge from the service we had truly enjoyed,
Homeward bound every comrade now joyfully wended,
   To greet friends and loved ones, our footsteps employed.
Twenty years of success, as the world counts success;
   Twenty years of defeat, as the world counts defeat,
Have gladdened or saddened our swift-passing years,
   Since the days when as comrades we each other did greet.

Some have grown great in the eyes of the nation,
    Some have gone down in the race after wealth;
Some been content with a quiet vocation,
    Others been hindered by the loss of their health.
Till time with its hours of deep sorrow and pleasure,
    Rolling steadily on toward eternity's sea,
Has brought us at length to this festal reunion;
    And welcome, thrice welcome, the absent would be.
No, all are not here: some have ended life's history,
    Crossed o'er the dark river and entered Heaven's gate.
And while our paths widen o'er life's fleeting mystery,
    We shall all at one portal meet early or late.
Then may God keep us all through the rest of life's marching!
    May He prosper us all, give to one and all strength;
And may we, dear comrades, in all of our journeyings
    Ne'er forget the glad days of "the glorious old Tenth!"

THE TENTH BOYS.

POEM BY CORP. W. WHITMAN BAILEY,
Company D, Tenth Rhode Island Volunteers.

I know the Tenth boys, I am not mistaken,
    Though heads now are silvered, once auburn or brown;
Though shoulders are bent and knees may be shaken,
    Since pitching those "Sibleys" at Ten-ally-town.

'Tis all a delusion to treat them as older,
    Rheumatics? bronchitis? neuralgia? What then?
They *march* as they once did, aye, shoulder to shoulder,
    And "get there" precisely like average men.

VETERAN ASSOCIATION.

Their notes still are tuneful; just list to the singing.
　Is Burdon less musical now, than of yore?
He'll warble of "Nelly," the famed "Sword of Bunker,"
　And come up still smiling, to meet an encore.

Just happen to mention the Tenth has no glory,
　In view of yon howitzer, desperately won,
Dispute her proud title, the "regiment gory!"
　And seek your own quarters, for quarters we've none.

And so I repeat it and know it is truthful,—
　These comrades around me, despite what they say,
Are slender, erect and perennially youthful;
　Why! bless me! They mustered this very same May!

THE BOYS OF SIXTY-TWO.

By Sergt. T. A. Starkey, Company D.

Written for the Tenth Regiment Reunion, May 26, 1887.

[Air: "Auld Lang Syne," "The Sword of Bunker Hill."]

We gather here, this festal night,
　To clasp each comrade's hand,
To flash the beams of memory's light
　On days dark to our land;
To greet the present,—mourn the lost,
　To pledge our faith anew
To the cause for which we left our homes
　In eighteen sixty-two.

Long years have passed since first we met
   And we've grown old and gray,
And widely scattered are the boys,
   And some have passed away.
But thro' the years, where'er we've roamed
   Whatever we've found to do,
We've held in loving memory strong
   Those hours of sixty-two.

And could our days exceed in length
   The prophet's days of old,
The golden tale of those bright days
   To us will ne'er grow old.
The hours we passed on Southern soil
   With comrades tried and true,
Are treasured deep within the hearts
   Of the boys of sixty-two.

So, comrades, through the coming years,
   While life and strength endure,
We'll gather here with hearty cheer
   And friendship strong and pure.
And on each glad Memorial Day,
   Our comradeship renew:
That comradeship which made us one
   In eighteen sixty-two.

VETERAN ASSOCIATION.

A CAMP-FIRE.

By Corp. W. Whitman Bailey, Company D.

Our watchfire burns,
The soldier turns
To meet the friend of long ago:
The moments fly,
The years haste by,
But dearer doth each comrade grow.

We con once more
Our marches o'er,
We sing the songs we loved of old:
We grasp the hand,
Our hearts expand,
And closer to each friend we hold.

Can we forget?
Ah no! Not yet!
Despite our heads in rebel gray:
The fact is true,
We wore the blue,
And started hence the other day.

If comrades fell,
To them "farewell!"
And o'er them votive offerings place:
Recall the while
Each hero's smile,
And cherish his familiar face.

Remember, boys,
Beside the joys,
That duty calls us hence once more:
Our motto scan!
Let every man
Be "ready, willing," as of yore!

LOYAL EVER.

By Corp. W. Whitman Bailey, Company D.

Tenth Regiment Reunion, May 26, 1891.

Boys, though our hair be gray,
Yet shall this month of May,
Ever recall the day—
    Long, long ago,
When at our country's call,
Left we the college hall,
Business or trade, and all
    Marched on the foe.

Nor can we e'er forget,
How, though their cheeks were wet,
Maid, wife, or mother met—
    Sacred each name!
Though we might ne'er come back,
Better the battles' wrack.
Storm-blast and tempest's track,
    Honor than shame!

So then, with loyal pride,
Stood we, boys, side by side,
Comrades all, true and tried,
    So still we stand.
Gather we round about,
Fling wide "old glory" out,
Hail it with song and shout,
    God bless our land!

VETERAN ASSOCIATION.

AFTER DECORATION.

By Corp. W. Whitman Bailey, Company D.

Out in the pitying rain,
Leave we our dead again,
The gallant ranks of those
Who sleep beneath the rose.

Here where our children tread,
Lie the heroic dead,
For them nor shield nor name;
Their's is their country's fame,

Let every eye behold
Our starry banner's fold.
The dead did dare maintain,
It's glory without stain.

All that they had they gave—
Their victory, the grave,
For them 'tis mete to bring,
These garlands of the spring.

Our national poetry and song have been the offspring of mighty struggles and glorious achievements. These stirring melodies, every line bristling with patriotic devotion to home and country did much in preserving our National Unity.

In September, 1862, one of the darkest periods of the war for the Union, as the shadows of night fell upon the gory field of Antietam, but sixty miles away from our old camp at Fort Pennsylvania, a sick and wounded soldier in one of the hospitals, in a clear and strong voice, sung this song of victory at midnight :

> " Our flag is there! Our flag is there!
> We hail it with three loud huzzas!
> Our flag is there! Our flag is there!
> Behold the glorious ' Stripes and Stars ! '
> Brave hearts have fought for that bright flag;
> Strong hands sustained it, mast-head high,
> And, O, to see how proud it waves,
> Bring tears of joy to every eye!"

On the memorable 14th of April, 1865, just after the final surrender to Grant at Appomattox, and the fourth anniversary of the fall of Fort Sumter, by order of President Lincoln, the same old flag, lowered by rebellious hands in 1861, was raised again over the ruins of the fort. It was the writer's good fortune to participate in the ceremonies at Fort Sumter, and to be on the steamer which carried the news of the surrender of Lee, to the city of Charleston.

Arrived within hailing distance, we gave each ship, gunboat, and monitor, the good news, as we passed, upon which a scene of of the wildest enthusiasm followed, which quickly spread throughout the entire blockading squadron.

The sailor boys in blue crowded to the bulwarks, and, mounting aloft, manned the yards, climbing even to the main-tops, and, turning, swung their caps, and rent the air with their shouts.

"Hurrah! hurrah! hurrah! Lee has surrendered! Lee has surrendered! How welcome the tidings after the long struggle! 'Sweet after danger's the close of the war?'"

On the morrow, as we descended to the interior of Fort Sumter, we passed from the wall-steps to the platform near the new flag-staff, through a double file of navy boys in trimmest holiday attire. Here was assembled the great audience of five thousand soldiers, sailors and citizens, and we joined them in the stirring song of "Victory at Last," composed for the great occasion:

> For many years we've waited to hail the day of peace,
> When our land should be united, and war and strife should cease:
> And now that day approaches, the drums are beating fast,
> And all the boys are coming home: there's victory at last!
>
> The heroes who have gained it and lived to see the day,
> We will greet with flying banners and honors on the way:
> And all their sad privations shall to the winds be cast,
> For all the boys are coming home: there's victory at last!
>
> O happy wives and children! light up your hearts and homes:
> For see, with martial music "the conquering hero comes."
> With flags and streamers flying, while drums are beating fast:
> For all the boys are coming home: there's victory at last!
>
> *Chorus:*
> There's victory at last, boys, victory at last!
> O'er land and sea, our flag is free, we'll nail it to the mast:
> Yes, we'll nail it to the mast, boys, nail it to the mast,
> For there's victory, victory, victory at last!

Gen. Robert Anderson.

Gen. Robert Anderson, the hero of Sumter, then stepped forward and said: "I thank God that I have lived to see this day, and after four long years of war to be here to restore to its proper place this dear flag, which floated here during the days of peace. My heart is filled with gratitude to God, who has so signally blessed us, who has given us blessings beyond measure. May all the nations bless and praise the name of the Lord and all the world proclaim, 'Glory to God in the highest, and on earth peace, good

The Ruins of Fort Sumter in 1865.

will toward men!'" "Amen! Amen!" responded the vast multitude. Then the old veteran firmly grasped the halyards, and

"Forthwith from the glittering staff unfurled
The starry banner, which full high advanced,
Shone like a meteor streaming to the wind."

Thirty years have passed since that eventful day, and the precious remains of Robert Anderson, the hero of Fort Sumter, repose in the National Cemetery at West Point, but his noble character, and devoted service to his country, can never be forgotten.

From the smoke of Sumter day quickly arose the Sumter Club, whose anniversary it celebrates with "feast of reason, and flow of loyal soul." Among its treasures is the Confederate flag of Fort Moultrie, but nothing is so highly prized by the writer as the following note from the widow of General Anderson, in acknowledgment of a little pamphlet printed by the writer, entitled "The Flag Replaced on Sumter":

NEW YORK HOTEL, N. Y.,
December. 11, 1885.

MR. WILLIAM. A. SPICER, Providence, R. I.,
Rhode Island Vice-President Sumter Club.

DEAR SIR: Accept my thanks for your very kind letter and for your pamphlet which accompanied it. "The Flag Replaced on Sumter," both of which were forwarded to me from Green Cove Springs.

I often weep bitter tears that my dear husband and his services to his country at the moment of her greatest peril, seem so clean forgotten throughout the land; but now and then I am cheered by kind and pleasant words like yours, and I take heart again and my faith in God's promises and in my countrymen is renewed and strengthened. Be assured, my dear sir, that the effort of one of the youngest members of the Sumter Club to perpetuate General Anderson's "worthy name and fame" is fully appreciated and most highly prized by his widow and the mother of his children.

Yours very sincerely,

E. B. ANDERSON.

ROSTER.

THE NINTH AND TENTH RHODE ISLAND REGIMENTS AND TENTH RHODE ISLAND BATTERY, present the usual entertaining variety in their ranks, as to age, position, and occupation. The average age of enlistment, it is safe to say, was under twenty. Many of the recruits gave their ages more than they actually were, fearing that they would be rejected were the correct ages known. The author knows personally of several of his comrades who reported as eighteen who were barely sixteen. Every effort has been made to make the "Roster" as correct as possible.

ROSTER

OF THE

Ninth Rhode Island Volunteers.

FIELD AND STAFF.

Colonel.

JOHN TALBOT PITMAN.

Captain, First Rhode Island Detached Militia, May 6, 1861; mustered out Aug. 2, 1861; major, Ninth Rhode Island Infantry, May 26, 1862; lieutenant-colonel, June 9, 1862; colonel, July 3, 1862; mustered out, Sept. 2, 1862; lieutenant-colonel, Eleventh Rhode Island Infantry, Oct. 1, 1862; mustered out, July 13, 1863.

Lieutenant-Colonels.

JOHN T. PITMAN. (*See Colonel.*)

JOHN HARE POWEL.

May 26, 1862, mustered in; originally served as captain Co. L; June 9, 1862, promoted to major; July 3, 1862, promoted lieutenant-colonel; Sept. 2, 1862, mustered out.

Majors.

JOHN T. PITMAN. (*See Colonel.*)

JOHN HARE POWEL. (*See Lieutenant-Colonel.*)

GEORGE LEWIS COOKE.

Originally served as first lieutenant, Co. L; detached as regimental quartermaster; July 3, 1862, commissioned and mustered in as major; Sept. 2, 1862, mustered out.

Surgeon.

LLOYD MORTON.

Assistant Surgeon.

HENRY KING.

Chaplain.

N. W. TAYLOR ROOT.

Adjutant.

HENRY C. BROWN.

Originally served as second lieutenant, Co. A; June 2, 1862, promoted adjutant.

Quartermasters.

GEORGE LEWIS COOKE. (*See Majors.*)

WILLIAM MCCREADY, JR.

Regimental quartermaster from May 26 to July 3, 1862.

Sergeant-Major.

ROBERT FESSENDEN.

Quartermaster-Sergeant.

ALFRED O. TILDEN.

Hospital Steward.

HENRY E. TYLER.

Commissary Sergeant.

HORACE G. MILLER.

Served as sergeant, Co. H; June 9, 1862, appointed commissary sergeant.

COMPANY A.

Captain.

ROBERT MCCLOY.

First Lieutenant.

ALBERT W. TOMPKINS.

Second Lieutenant.

HENRY C. BROWN.

June 2, 1862, appointed adjutant.

Sergeants.

Oliver H. Perry,
Arnold F. Salisbury,
George Morris,

John R. Anderson,
Joseph P. Farnsworth,
Charles C. Crocker.

Corporals.

Frederick Schneider,
Thomas H. Holmes,
Daniel H. Johnson,
John McKelvey,
William H. Chace,

George Schneider,
Alfred Jerauld, Jr.,
Henry M. Stetson,
Simeon B. Ramsbottom.

Privates.

William Bartlett,
Samuel A. Bennett,
Zephaniah Bennett,
Jubal Blount,
Edmund Bray,
†Charles E. Buffum,
George N. Burlingame,
George Burns,
William A. Carter,
Henry H. Clark,
Joseph H. Clark,
Darius Cook,
Patrick Coyle,
Israel F. Crocker,
Alonzo Crowell,
John Cullen,
Joseph D. Davenport,
John S. Davis,
John T. Fanning,
Ferdinand A. Follett,
Thomas Forrest,
Albert Fuller,
Ferdinand A. Gardner,
John Glancy,

Michael Goodwin,
Stephen A. Grover,
Thomas Hallowell,
Henry L. Hammond,
William Hay,
John Hayward,
Thomas H. Holmes,
Daniel A. Hopkins,
William J. Hughes,
James A, Kelley,
William H. Kelley,
Thomas J. Kennedy,
Henry Kimpton,
Edward Knight,
Augustus A. Leach,
John E. Lee,
Thomas Locking,
Thomas Locklin,
John T. Lowden,
John H. Lundy,
Peter Lyme,
Aldine Manier,
William Massey,
Charles H. Mathewson,

† Minor; discharged, July, 1862.

RHODE ISLAND VOLUNTEERS.

John McCabe,
Peter McCabe,
Patrick McCusker,
John McGinnity,
David McKelvey,
Daniel B. McKenna,
Amaziah B. Merchant,
Peter Merchant,
Hugh Muldoon,
George W. Newell,
Thomas Norris,
William O'Donnell,
John Ramsbottom,
Patrick Ready,
James Riley,
George A. Roberts,
Richard Roberts,
A. Sylvester Rounds,

Alonzo F. Salisbury,
Thomas Sawyer,
George B. Sharples,
James R. Sherman,
Edward Shuttleworth,
Lewis F. Slocum,
William H. Slocum,
Patrick Starrs,
William Stewart,
Ansel L. Sweet,
Charles I. Sweet,
Roger Tattersall,
Oscar Thayer,
John Trainor,
Nathaniel Walker,
Thomas Wheeler,
James A. Williams,
Sylvanus C. Wilson.

COMPANY B.

Captain.
HENRY C. CARD.

First Lieutenant.
J. CLARKE BARBER.

Second Lieutenant.
JAMES McDONALD.

Sergeants.

William R. Lewis,
Thomas Place,
James H. Perrigo,

James M. Holmes,
Amos L. Burdick.

Corporals.

John Tweedie,
Nathan J. Crandall,
Edwin R. Cottrell,
Peleg D. Sisson,

Joseph Richmond,
James A. Sisson,
William F. Hawkins.

Musicians.

Pardon Babcock,

Daniel B. Jackson.

Privates.

Andrew J. Allen,
Joshua Allen,
William D. Babcock,
John W. Barber,
T. Stanton Barbour,
Uriah Baton,
George Bellamy,
Andrew Bray,
Edward C. Brown,
E. James Buddington,
Thomas A. Buell,
Edward H. Burdick,
Thomas T. Burdick,
William H. Burdick,
George Carmichael,
Thomas H. Champlain,
Stephen Coleman,
William T. Collins,

James A. Congdon,
John P. Crandall,
Edward G. Crandall,
William Davenport,
Daniel Donovan,
John Ecclestone,
James A. Edwards,
Charles H. Eldred,
Charles H. Gavitt,
Horace P. Gavitt,
Dean Gould,
Courtland T. Hall,
Joseph Haywood,
William Horsfall,
Daniel B. Jackson,
William Jackson,
James Johnson,
Milton P. Johnson,

RHODE ISLAND VOLUNTEERS.

T. W. Johnson,
William Johnson, Jr.,
David Kenneth,
Moses D. Kinkade,
Edmund R. Langworthy,
George E. Leonard,
George W. Livsey,
John McAvoy,
Thomas McLean,
James McNulty,
J. Howard Morgan,
Nathan E. Nash,
George P. Neugent,
Isaac Partelow,

Horace L. Peckham,
James M. Pendleton, 2d,
George A. Richmond,
Gilbert S. Roach,
Everett A. Schofield,
Nathan S. Sheffield,
John Surber,
Francis W. Taylor,
Charles W. Thompson,
John P. Trant,
James L. Ward,
Richard Welch,
John B. Wells,
William H. Wells.

COMPANY C.

Captain.

JOHN A. BOWEN.

First Lieutenant.

GEORGE A. SPINK.

Second Lieutenant.

WILLIAM H. POTTER.

Sergeants.

John C. Potter,
William C. Nichols,
Horace Remington,

Crawford R. Williams,
Allen E. Keech.

Corporals.

Nathan B. Whipple,
Lewis G. Arnold, Jr.,
John Devlin,
George C. Gilmore,

John Remington,
Hugh O'Donnell,
Jonathan R. Weaver,
*Hollis Taber, Jr.

Musicians.

George R. Tourjee,

Horace H. Woodmancy.

Wagoner.

Henry H. Roberts.

Privates.

Albert Arnold,
Edward P. Baker,
William H. Baker,
Nathaniel G. Ball,
John J. Battey,
Allen H. Bennett,
Jesse Bicknell,
Joseph Bigelow,
Samuel E. Bowen,
Peter Brown,
William B. Browning,
Daniel W. Cady,
Peter Carroll,
John Carey,
Joseph P. Cornell,
George W. Dawley,
William H. Dimond,
James F. Fanning,
Thomas Farmer,

Cornelius Franklin,
Charles C. Gardner,
Peter Goodness,
William Hunt,
Thomas Hughes,
Zephaniah Jenkins,
John D. Jordan,
Zebulon Londeau,
Thomas Lindsay,
James Malaney,
George Matteson,
John McArthur,
James McDonnell,
Patrick McMann,
Joseph Miller,
Charles Morris,
Henry Nichols,
Michael Noon,
William H. Northup,

* Died August 13, 1862, in hospital.

Felix O'Donnell,
Frederick Owen,
John O. Neill,
William O'Neil,
Robert Platt,
Henry Peagot,
Charles H. Prew,
Harrison Provost,
John Quigley,
Samuel J. Randall,
Patrick Reagan,
Ambrose P. Rice,
Henry H. Roberts,
Lewis Roberts,

Elisha Sherman,
Elisha O. Sherman,
Francis Smith,
Michael Spellacy,
George A. Spencer,
Lewis T. Spencer,
William C. Spencer,
Edward Tathroe,
Joshua W. Tibbitts,
William H. Tucker,
Oliver T. Wilbur,
John Wilson,
Alonzo G. Wood,
Warren Young.

COMPANY D.

Captain.
JOHN McKINLAY.

First Lieutenant.
JOHN POLLARD.

Second Lieutenant.
WILLIAM McCREADY, JR.

Sergeants.

William T. Crawford,
Thomas McCarthy,
Israel Arnold, Jr.,

Robert S. Blair,
William T. Gildard.

John McFadden,
Joseph R. Stafford,
Samuel C. Lomas,
Horatio Giles,

Alfred Hough,

Uriah M. Adams,
James Aigan,
Robert Arnett,
Noah A. Ashworth,
Jonathan M. Bass,
George Birchell,
Thomas Boyd,
James Boyle,
James Brennan,
Samuel Briden,
Alonzo Colvin,
Lyman Colvin,
William H. Cory,
Andrew Cramley,
Thomas Crumley,
George Davis,
Daniel Devlin,
George H. De Wolf,
Peter Dolan,
Luke Duxbury,
David Fogarty,
Patrick Freeman,

Corporals.
Thomas Meagher,
Ferdinand Haskins,
Christopher T. Geldard,
John Crumlay.

Musicians.
Charles E. Greene.

Privates.
Matthew Green,
William Greenlese,
David Glover,
Robert Hall,
Thomas Hall,
Alexander Harkness,
Michael Hafferin,
John Hollingsworth,
Daniel Hoyle,
James Jackson,
James H. Jolly,
Walter Loudergan,
John McCaffrey,
Michael McCormick,
Neil McCourt,
John McDevitt,
Michael McKern,
Cornelius Moninihan,
Hugh McMullen,
†Benjamin North,
John North,
James O'Brien,

* Discharged for disability June 23, 1862.

RHODE ISLAND VOLUNTEERS.

Henry O'Neil,
James Parker,
Thomas S. Parker,
James Pollard,
Thomas Quinin,
William Rankin,
Orrin G. Rawson,
Alexander Ritchie,
William J. Root,
John Ryan,

John Schofield,
Almon C. Shorey,
James Smith,
Patrick Smith,
James Stewart,
Walter S. Sutcliffe,
James Wood,
James White,
Olney Whipple,
Richard J. Whittle.

COMPANY E.

Captain.

ISAAC PLACE.

First Lieutenant.

PHILIP D. HALL.

Second Lieutenant.

NATHAN D. BENTON.

Sergeants.

Fenner Colwell,
George W. Haradon,
Trowbridge Smith,

George H. Johnson,
Joseph Miett, Jr.

Corporals.

Byron S. Thompson,
William T. Brooks,

Martin G. Cushman,
Henry E. Baker,

David Dines,
James Jaques,

Samuel Preston,
Gilbert A. Thompson.

Musician.

Albert Beverly.

Privates.

Moses A. Aldrich,
Cyrus R. Bennett,
Henry A. Bennett,
Jacob Butterfield,
George W. Buxton,
Willard D. Colwell,
Marcus M. Cooke,
James Demick,
†Edmund Esty,
George B. Evans,
William H. Fuller,
John Gallagher,
Frederic C. Gove,
Alexander Henderson,
Thomas Hughes,
Thomas W. Irons,
George H. Johnson,
Martin G. Lyons,
Walter Mather,
William J. Milan,

Thomas Pryor,
John Regan,
Robert Sandford,
Joseph Sedgwick,
Osborne M. Southwick,
Enoch Spencer,
Thomas B. Spooner,
Dustin D. Stevens,
Augustus R. Steere,
James Sullivan,
John Sullivan,
Winfield S. Thompson,
Alexander Tongue,
Charles F. Tifft,
Joseph Wilmouth,
George Wilson,
Thomas D. Wilson,
Hiram Wood,
Joseph M. Young.

† Discharged as a minor, July 9, 1862.

RHODE ISLAND VOLUNTEERS.

COMPANY F.

Captain.
JOHN M. TAYLOR.

First Lieutenant.
RANDALL HOLDEN.

Second Lieutenant.
RICHARD W. HOWARD.

Sergeants.

Edward F. Steere,	Jeffrey G. Davis,
Benjamin Hill,	Henry P. Babson,
Moses Brown,	George T. Lamphear.

Corporals.

William F. Hill,	James Bushee,
James R. Read,	Stephen P. Steere,
S. Wildes Coggeshall,	George T. Lamphear,
J. Phillips Pond,	Delondo Bennett.
John E. Whipple,	

Musicians.

David Spencer,	Daniel Baxter.

Privates.

William Atchison,	Wilcox Barber,
Henry W. Ballou,	Daniel Barney,
Charles Ballou,	†Stephen L. Barney,
Lillibridge Barber,	George Blackington,

† Discharged for disability, Jan. v, 1862.

Daniel Brayton,
Thomas Britton,
George Britton,
Charles Bowers,
William T. Brown,
John Burns,
Alfred Crandall,
Frank P. Chace,
Oliver H. Clark,
Charles Colvin,
George R. Congdon,
Henry N. Cook,
William R. Cornell,
Benjamin Cottrell,
William Davenport,
Albert Davis,
Cortes A. Darling,
Michael Fleming,
Samuel K. Gardiner,
†Richard Gibney,
Samuel Graves,
Thomas B. Greene,
Edward Harvey,
Sylvanus C. Holbrook, Jr.,
Thomas L. Hopkins,
Albert F. Howard,
Alfred A. Jackson,
Samuel C. Jenckes,
Arnold Jennerson,
George C. Johnson,
Thomas Johnson,
Jesse D. Keach,
Edward King,
Mosier Lock,
Bernhard Morris,
George A. Nichols,
John Niles,
Rufus H. Northup,
†John O'Brien,
Thomas Owen,
H. B. Perry,
B. Ray Phelon,
Elisha Place,
William Price,
Henry Price,
G. W. Henry Pollard,
George B. Pollard,
William H. Rice,
Richard R. Richmond,
Nelson Searle,
Simon G. Sherman,
Thomas Sipple,
Otis W. Smith,
Thomas L. Smith,
Javis Smith,
George Smith,
James E. Spencer,
George W. Spencer,
John T. Spencer,
Otis Spencer,
Edward F. Steere,
†Alonzo P. Stone,

† Discharged as a minor.

RHODE ISLAND VOLUNTEERS.

William Taylor,
Henry B. Terry,
B. Greene Tew,
Robert W. Townshend,

B. Egbert Vaughan,
Jerome Weaver,
John Westgate,
Edward J. Wilbur.

COMPANY G.

Captain.
CHARLES L. WATSON,

First Lieutenant.
FRANCELLO G. JILLSON.

Second Lieutenant.
HENRY J. WHITAKER.

Sergeants.

Austin J. Scott,
James B. Streeter,
William T. Smith,

Enos A. Clarke,
Daniel E. Wilcox.

Corporals.

Horace A. Scott,
James A. Sweet,
William P. Davis,
A. Sayles Clarke,

George H. Baker,
Edwin W. Whipple,
Sanford A. Robbins,
George W. Thayer.

Musician.
William M. Goff.

Privates.

Jenckes Bartlett,
Allen F. Baxter,
Alba Bellows,
Asa Bennett,
George W. Bolton,
Charles W. Bradford,
Henry W. Brown,
Charles A. Burlingame,
Alexander Campbell.
Albert Carey,
Edwin Carter,
Christopher Carter,
Charles A. Chase,
Foster H. Clark,
Henry Congdon,
Aaron Congdon,
Edmond Congdon,
Timothy Curran.
John H. Durgin,
Caleb Freeman,
Irving Gaskill,
Oscar F. Gifford,
Abraham Greaves,
John Green,
Richard Green,
William Henry Harrison,
Thomas Healy,
George J. Hendrick,
Terny Hogan,
Albert Hudson,
William A. Jenckes,
Thomas Judge,
Samuel Longley,
George Law,
Alexander Levine,
Thomas Lewis,
Luke Lynch,
William E. Mason,
Samuel Parrish,
Hiram Parker,
Charles A. Pierce,
George S. Potter,
Thomas Prior,
Thomas Riley,
Henry C. Sayles,
Marcus L. Smith,
Horatio I. Stockbridge,
Patrick O. Sullivan,
Thomas Sullivan,
James Swindles,
Isaac S. Tanner,
Benjamin Tourtellott,
Joseph H. Wheelock,
Luke A. Wood.

COMPANY H.

Captain.
HENRY F. JENKS.

First Lieutenant.
FRANK ALLEN.

Second Lieutenant.
GEORGE A. BUCKLIN.

Sergeants.

Edmund Crocker,
Horace G. Miller,
Latimer LeFavour,

Charles E. Adams,
Ambrose P. Rice,
Harrison H. Richardson.

Corporals.

George P. Grant,
Edward P. Lowden,
Alanson P. Wood,
Edward Thayer,

Joseph Harrison,
W. C. Benedict,
Richard Eldredge, Jr.,
Jabez W. Pitcher.

Musician.
George F. Olney.

Privates.

Lyman A. Aldrich,
William T. Arnold,
John H. Almy,
Frederick A. Baker,

George F. Ballou,
Stephen J. Ballou,
Phanuel Bishop,
Jerome D. Bliss,

Horatio N. S. Booth,
†Charles D. Bray,
Joseph A. Brown,
Andrew A. Buckley,
Charles H. Bullock,
Frank H. Carpenter,
Charles E. Carpenter,
David E. Cash,
George H. Cole,
Warren F. Cook,
Henry Crocker,
Robert E. Curran,
†Byron E. Daggett,
Benjamin A. Dennis,
John H. Eaton,
David L. Fales,
James H. Fairbanks,
Stephen F. Fisk,
Frank D. Fisk,
George H. Foster,
David A. Gage,
William H. Gardner,
Luke Glancy,
Joseph B. Gooding,
Thomas A. Gregson,
*Richard Gridley,
Albert F. Howe,
Charles A. Ide,

George T. Jeffers,
Pardon Jenks, Jr.,
Edwin Leach,
Charles A. Mathewson,
Walter Merry,
George Murphy,
Charles W. Nickerson,
Edward A. Patt,
Henry N. Pervear,
Stephen A. Peck,
Charles F. Pierce,
Henry A. Pierce,
Jabez W. Pitcher,
Joseph Rice,
Robert Saunders,
Joseph W. Seagraves,
Frank S. Shove,
William H, Slocum,
Smith Tattersall,
William G. Thurber,
†Tate Timony,
Frank M. Tyler,
Percival D. Warburton,
Henry H. Welden,
Hamlet Wheaton,
John F. Whiting,
Charles D. Wood,
Anthony G. Wood.

† Discharged as a minor.
* Discharged on surgeon's certificate.

RHODE ISLAND VOLUNTEERS.

COMPANY I.

Captain.
SAMUEL PEARCE.

First Lieutenants.
GEORGE LEWIS COOKE,
WILLIAM H. SURGENS.

Second Lieutenants.
WILLIAM H. SURGENS,
HORACE G. BARRUS.

Sergeants.

Horace G. Barrus,   Charles H. Rounds,
Samuel B. Cole,   Haile Turner,
Luther Cole, Jr.,   James A. Manchester.

Corporals.

Jeremiah I. Greene, Jr., Peleg Bosworth, Jr.,
Caleb S. Carr,   Isaac Gorham,
Frederic A. Driscoll,   Thomas F. Marion,
George L. C. Wheaton,   Benjamin B. Martin.
Nathaniel T. Sanders,

Musicians.

John W. Hubbard,   Samuel D. Maxwell.

Privates.

John P. Abbott,   A. C. Aldrich,
Albert J. Adams,   Joseph W. Aldrich,

William A. Arnold,
Isaac Barnum,
John Booth,
William Booth,
Henry A. Bowen,
William Bradshaw,
Mark P. Brown,
John H. Buffington,
Charles H. Bullock,
Robert H. Bullock, Jr.,
Henry T. Burr,
Norman G. Burr,
Elijah Calland,
William Champlin,
Thomas Clarke,
Thomas Clifford,
Edwin J. Collamore,
Robert Crowther,
Thomas A. Curran,
Willard B. Drown,
James B. Drown,
James F. Follett,
George C. Franklin,
Nathaniel W. Gushee,
George Guyette,
Charles D. Horton,

George H. Hunter,
R. H. Johnson,
James H. Johnson,
John Kelly,
Wilson Little,
Theodore Medbury,
William H. Myers,
Galen F. Nichols,
Thomas W. D. Peck,
James E. Peck,
Allen P. Peck,
Joseph Price,
Robert Ridgwell,
Eugene I. Roffee,
Matthew Ryan,
John P. Salisbury,
Jeremiah Sheehan,
A. J. Shurtleff,
*Joseph N. Simonds,
Walter F. Thompson,
Winfield S. Tompkins,
James E. Viall,
George W. Walker,
John R. Wheaton,
Barton J. Whipple,
William Williams.

* Died September, 1862, at Warren, R. I.

COMPANY K.

Captain.
JAMES R. HOLDEN.

First Lieutenant.
WILLIAM H. GARDNER.

Second Lieutenant.
GEORGE H. BURNHAM.

Sergeants.

Albert B. Streeter,
George H. Abbott,
James F. Mowry,

George H. Allen,
Ambrose L. Atwood.

Corporals.

William C. Clark,
Samuel B. T. Crandall,
Alonzo A. Greenman,
Daniel J. Viall,

David Briggs,
George W. Allen,
Thomas Johnson.

Privates.

*Sylvester B. Arnold,
William Ash,
William Baker,
George B. Bromer,
Job Butler,
Sanford Buxton,
Joseph C. Clarke,
John Cooney,
Patrick Coyne,

Patrick Fanning,
Peter Gormley,
William Groves,
Joseph A. Green,
James Haggett,
James Hughes,
David W. James,
James Kelley,
Patrick Kennedy,

* Died August 2, 1862, in hospital.

William W. Maxon,
Joseph Mechling,
Robert F. Northup,
George Nye,
Nathan T. Oatley,
John R. Oatley,
Welcome A. Potter,
Harry A. Richardson,

George W. Richmond,
Jesse W. Richmond,
William H. H. Swan,
John M. Taylor, Jr.,
Brightman Tucker,
Nehemiah Watson,
Isaac Westcott,
William Young.

COMPANY L.

Captains.

JOHN HARE POWEL. (*See Lieutenant-Colonels.*)
BENJAMIN L. SLOCUM.

First Lieutenant.

WILLIAM R. LANDERS.

Second Lieutenant.

WILLIAM H. KING.

Sergeants.

Edmund W. Fales,
Lance De Jough,
George H. Tabor,

William M. Minkler,
Thomas S. Nason.

Corporals.

Sumner Lincoln,
William L. Pfeiffer,

Schuyler Van Renssellaer,
William C. Rogers,

RHODE ISLAND VOLUNTEERS.

Frank Morgan, William S. Slocum,
Sigourney B. Goffe, Benjamin A. Peckham.

Musicians.

Cassius M. C. Freeborn, Christopher Gladding.

Privates.

Theodore Almy, Henry T. French,
Samuel Babcock, Michael Garrick,
William H. Barber, John E. Goffe,
Alexander N. Barker, John Gould, 2d,
Henry B. Bateman, Robert W. Gould,
Thomas Blacklock, George B. Harrington,
Edward T. Bosworth, Henry I. Hudson,
James M. Brown, James Melville,
Benjamin T. Brown, John L. Nason,
George M. Brown, Michael O'Brien,
George F. Boone, Jefferson O'Riley,
Charles G. Burnett, David Peabody,
William F. Barlow, Alexander Peckham,
Truman Burdick, Charles T. Prouty,
Thomas Campbell, Randall Pullen,
Robert W. Chappell, John Ramsden,
Samuel Clark, Ferdinand S. Read,
William E. Coggeshall, Frank Rice,
Daniel C. Denhan, Henry Ridell,
James Dewick, Edward R. Seagur,
Theophilus C. Dunn, Albert G. Sherman,
John B. Durfee, Thomas W. Sherman,
Benjamin B. Durfee, James Simmons,
John Fludder, Edmund D. Slocum,
Orland Freeborn, John H. Stacy,

Edmund Stanhope,
Frank M. Swan,
John W. Tayer,
John E. Tabor,
Edward H. Tilley,
William S. Vose,

John Vicars,
William W. Wales,
Nicholas A. Wilkey,
Edward V. Wescott,
Thomas Young.

ROSTER

OF THE

Tenth Rhode Island Volunteers.

FIELD AND STAFF.

Colonels.

ZENAS R. BLISS.

Military Record from 1854 to 1863.

He was appointed a cadet at West Point in 1850 by the Hon. Nathan F. Dixon, of Rhode Island. Graduated in 1854. Was appointed a brevet second lieutenant in the First Infantry and ordered to Fort Duncan, Texas; served there till June, 1855; was transferred to Fort Chadbourne, Texas, and was adjutant of the battalion en route to that post. Was promoted second lieutenant, Eighth United States Infantry, and ordered to Fort Davis, Texas, and served there till 1857 or 1858, most of that time in command of a detachment of mounted infantry and engaged in scouting for hostile Indians. Was transferred with company to Fort Hudson, Texas, and to various other posts on that frontier till 1860, when he was promoted first lieutenant, and ordered to the command of his company and the post of Fort Quitman, on the Rio Grande. From 1856 was in command of a detachment of mounted infantry, and also served in command of a company, and the posts of Forts Hudson, Clark and Quitman, and as post quartermaster, commissary and adjutant at various posts.

In March, 1861, while in command of Fort Quitman, he received orders to march to San Antonio, Texas, for the purpose of being transferred to the North. He abandoned the post and marched about forty miles, when he received orders to await the arrival of Colonel Reeve, Eighth Infantry, who was on the march to the coast with other companies of the regiment. He returned to his post, and on the 5th of April joined Colonel Reeve's command and marched to San Antonio, Texas, a distance of about six hundred and fifty miles. On the 9th of May, 1861, when they were about fifteen miles from San Antonio, they were met by a large force of over two thousand men, under rebel Gen. Earl Van Dorn, consisting of a regiment of infantry, one of cavalry, a battery of six pieces of artillery and an independent company of about one hundred men. On leaving their posts they had been led to believe they were to be transferred to the North, and were ordered to take only sufficient ammunition to protect themselves from the Indians, and to take rations from post to post. When met by the rebels they had not, according to their orders, more than ten or fifteen rounds of ammunition per man, and only one day's rations. An unconditional surrender was demanded, and Lieutenant Bliss was ordered by Colonel Reeve to inspect the rebel troops, to see if they were well armed and equipped, and to count or estimate the number of men After some difficulty he did so and made his report that they were well armed, etc. They had previously captured the arsenal at San Antonio, and supplied themselves from the stores there. A council of war was held, of which Lieutenant Bliss was not a member, and the command was surrendered. He was a junior first lieutenant, and had nothing to do with the surrender any more than any private, but was held as much responsible for it as any one. No officer who was with the command at the time of surrender was promoted during the war, though several of them received the strongest recommendations for promotion for gallantry and good conduct on frequent occasions.

He remained a prisoner of war at San Antonio till February, 1862, when he was ordered to Richmond, Va., for exchange. There were but three left of the officers captured in May, the others having succeeded in getting North on parole. On their arrival in Richmond they were shut up in the negro jail and remained there till April 5th, when they were exchanged, having been held prisoners of war eleven months.

In May, 1862, he was appointed colonel of the Tenth Rhode Island Volunteers and served with it till August, when he was appointed colonel of the Seventh Rhode Island and remained colonel of it till honorably mustered out after the close of the war. He commanded the regiment on the Fredericksburg campaign, and at the first battle of Fredericksburg, and was recommended by all his superiors for promotion to the rank of brigadier-general, for gallantry and skillful handling of his regiment under fire.

In 1863 he went with the corps to Kentucky and thence to Vicksburg and Jackson, Miss., on the campaign after Johnston, and at the conclusion of it was recommended, first in the corps, for promotion to the rank of brigadier, and his promotion, with others, asked for by General Grant. But he did not receive it. He returned with the corps to Kentucky, and started for Knoxville with the corps in the winter of 1863 and 1864, but at the request of General Ammen, commanding the district or department, he was ordered to the command of the District of Middle Tennessee, and remained in command of it till the corps was withdrawn from Tennessee. It was an important command. He had a large post and several regiments, and protecting about two million rations for Sherman's army and a large extent of country. At the end of the campaign he was again recommended for promotion to the rank of brigadier-general, but did not get it though all others recommended did.

He went with the corps to Annapolis, Md., and was assigned to the command of the First Brigade, Second Division, Ninth Army Corps, and commanded in the Wilderness, where he was brevetted for gallant and meritorious services. He was in command of the brigade to Spottsylvania, where he was injured by his horse jumping on him in crossing a stream in the night. He commanded the brigade at the mine which was constructed by a regiment of his brigade, and at the explosion of the mine and ensuing battle, and received a very complimentary letter from his division commander, Gen. Robert B. Potter. He remained in command of the brigade to some time in the early fall when he was obliged to take a sick leave. After being absent sick some weeks, he was placed on light duty on a board of officers, as president, and remained on that duty till the close of the war in the following spring.

After being mustered out of the volunteer service he was on recruiting service, and in command of Schuylkill Arsenal and Fort Porter, N. Y., till May, 1866, when he went with his company to South Carolina and was assigned to the command of the district of Chester, in that State. He was Acting Assistant Commissioner of the Bureau of Freedmen and Abandoned Lands, provost judge and provost marshal, etc., and had charge of all the civil and military business of that district. In August he was ordered on recruiting service, receiving the detail for having served longer in the field during the rebellion than any officer in his regiment In August, 1867, he was promoted major of the Thirty-ninth Infantry, and commanded the posts of Jackson Barracks, Forts Jackson and St. Philip, and Ship Island, Miss., till 1870, when he was transferred with the regiment to Texas, and commanded the posts of Forts Duncan, Clark, Stockton, Davis and Bliss, and for more than a year the regiment. In 1878 he was ordered on duty in command of the principal depot, general recruiting service, David's Island, New York Harbor, and having been promoted lieutenant-colonel of the Nineteenth Infantry, he was in 1880 ordered to the command of Fort Hays, Kansas. In 1881 he was transferred with the regiment to Texas, and commanded the post of Ringgold Barracks. In 1882 he went on sick leave and at the expiration of it returned to Texas and commanded Forts Duncan and Clark, and for more than a year the regiment, till in 1886 he was promoted colonel of the Twenty-fourth Infantry, and has commanded it and the posts of Fort Supply, Indian Territory, and Fort Bayard, New Mexico, to the present time.

Colonel Bliss has been in command of an independent organization, district, brigade, regiment or post since 1860, except for about six or eight months, and has not been absent from his regiment on detached service but once since 1867, and has served longer on the southwestern frontier than any officer ever in the service.

JAMES SHAW, JR.,

Colonel and Brevet Brigadier-General.

Entered service as lieutenant-colonel, Tenth Rhode Island Volunteers, May 26, 1862; promoted colonel, Aug. 6, 1862, served in defences of Washington; mustered out by reason of expiration of term of service, Sept. 1, 1862. Re-entered service as lieutenant-colonel, Twelfth Rhode Island Volunteers, Dec. 31, 1862; served with Ninth Army Corps before Fredericksburg, at Newport News and in Kentucky, and with General Carter at Somerset, Ky.; mustered out, expiration of term of service, July 29, 1863. Went before "Casey's Board," passed as colonel, being the fifth of that grade out of 700 examined, and was appointed colonel, Seventh United States Colored Troops, Oct. 27, 1863; joined for duty and assumed command, Nov. 12, 1863, at Camp Stanton, Md. Served continuously with the regiment or in command of the forces to which it was attached, as follows: Commanding post at Jacksonville, Fla, and brigade on expeditions to Cedar Creek and Camp Melton; commanding First Brigade, Third Division, Tenth Army Corps, Aug. 13 to 21, Aug. 25 to Sept. 25, and Oct. 26 to Dec. 4, 1864; commanding First Brigade, Second Division, Twenty-fifth Army Corps, from and after Dec. 4, 1864; commanding Second Division, Twenty-fifth Army Corps, Feb. 21 to March 13, 1865; commanding sub-district of Victoria, Tex., from Jan. 16, 1866, to Feb. 21, 1866; commanding Central District of Texas, Feb. 21 to May 9, 1866. Contusion on head from rifle ball in action, Sept. 30, 1864. Brigadier-general by brevet "for meritorious services during the war," to date from March 13, 1865. Discharged with the regiment at Baltimore, Md., Nov. 16, 1866.

RHODE ISLAND VOLUNTEERS.

Lieutenant-Colonels.

JAMES SHAW, JR. (*See Colonel.*)

WILLIAM M. HALE.
Promoted from captain, Company I, August 11, 1862.

Majors.

CHARLES H. MERRIMAN.
(Acting till June 9, 1862.)

JACOB BABBITT.
Killed at the first battle of Fredericksburg, Va., December, 1862.

Adjutants.

BENJAMIN F. THURSTON.
(Acting till June 9, 1862.)

JOHN F. TOBEY.
Served as first lieutenant Company K.

Quartermasters.

JAMES H. ARMINGTON.
(Resigned July 19, 1862.)

WINTHROP DE WOLF (acting).

CHARLES W. ANGELL.
First lieutenant and quartermaster, July 25, 1862.

Surgeon.

GEORGE D. WILCOX (major).

Assistant Surgeon.

ALBERT G. SPRAGUE (first lieutenant.)

Chaplain.

A. HUNTINGTON CLAPP.

Sergeant-Majors.
JOHN F. TOBEY.
(Acting till June 9, 1862.)
EDWARD K. GLEZEN.

Quartermaster-Sergeant.
LYSANDER FLAGG.

Commissary Sergeant.
JAMES O. SWAN.

Hospital Steward.
CHARLES G. KING.

COMPANY A.

Captain.
WILLIAM E. TABER.

First Lieutenant.
JOSEPH L. BENNETT, JR.

Second Lieutenant.
LEANDER C. BELCHER.

Sergeants.

William A. James, Sullivan H. Dawley,
Pembroke S. Eddy, Daniel D. Bucklin.
Ambrose R. Peck,

RHODE ISLAND VOLUNTEERS.

Corporals.

William W. Thompson,
Albert C. Winsor,
George W. S. Burroughs,
Joseph Smith,
Joseph C. Cheetham,

Eugene F. Phillips,
Caleb C. Greene, Jr.,
Godfrey Greene, Jr,
John H. Johnson.

Privates.

William H. Aldrich,
†Frank H. Angell,
*William F. Atwood,
Henry B. Barrows,
Joseph E. Blake,
Nathan S. Blake,
William T. Brown,
John Buchanan,
Robert Charnley,
Daniel E. Corey,
Isaac Dakin,
Charles H. Dexter,
William H. Dingwell,
Barnard M. Eddy,
John Farrell,
Franklin B. Ham,
Frank T. Hazlewood,
†William H. Heath,
Wendell P. Hood,
†James B. Horton,
John H. Johnson,
†John Larramore,
Edwin Morse,

Inman A. Mowry, Jr.,
†James Murphy,
Michael O'Connell,
Ebenezer Peck.
Joseph S. Phipps,
Silas W. Plimpton, Jr.,
Ashael Potter,
Adam Pomfret,
†Owen H. Quinland,
James Redfern,
Charles H. Saunders,
John Shawcross,
Henry B. Shearer,
†Eben Thing,
Orlando P. Thompson,
Reuben L. Thornton,
†John Torrance,
George R. Waite,
John A. Waite,
Lewis C. Whittier,
†Frank H. Williams,
Charles Wilson,
Luther T. Winslow.

* Died at Georgetown hospital, June 20, 1862.
† Discharged as a minor, July 8, 1862.

COMPANY B.

Captain.

ELISHA DYER.

May 4, 1842, adjutant-general, State of Rhode Island; honorably discharged, May 4, 1847; 1857, Governor of the State of Rhode Island; 1861, captain, Fourth Ward Company, First Regiment Rhode Island National Guard; May 26, 1862, mustered in captain, Co. B, Tenth Regiment Rhode Island Volunteers; Sept. 1, 1862, mustered out of service.

First Lieutenants.

SAMUEL H. THOMAS.
(August 11, 1862, promoted to captain Company I.)

WILLIAM C. CHACE.

Second Lieutenants.

WILLIAM C. CHACE.
(August 11, 1862, promoted to first lieutenant.)

CHARLES F. PHILLIPS.
(August 11, 1862, promoted from first sergeant Company B.)

Sergeants.

Charles F. Phillips,	Charles L. Stafford,
Henry B. Franklin,	Eben W. McGlaulin,
Nathaniel B. Chace,	George T. Baker.

Corporals.

Samuel W. Church,	Barnabas J. Chace,
Nathan H. Baker,	Addison W. Goffe,
John Tetlow, Jr.,	John B. Kelley,
William P. Vaughan,	Charles H. Scott.

Musician.

Edward M. Gage.

Privates.

Frederick Alexander,
Samuel A. W. Arnold,
Joshua M. Addeman,
Charles H. Anthony,
Thomas Burlingame,
De Forest Brown,
John G. Browning,
James W. Blackwood,
William W. Bliss,
Horace K. Blanchard,
†Jesse M. Bush,
Charles H. Clarke,
Charles M. Corbin,
Charles C. Cragin,
William P. Cragin,
James T. Cook,
Forrest F. Emerson,
James F. Field,
George M. Fanning,
†Byron Harris,
Edwin B. Fiske,
Frank Frost,
Henry G. Gay,
Charles B. Greene,
Charles T. Greene,
Francis Gould,

George W. Handy,
†William H. Hawks,
Robert B. Holden,
John S. Holmes,
Charles E. Hosmer,
†David Hunt, Jr.,
Enoch F. Hoxie,
†George A. Jenckes,
George P. Kenyon,
Joseph W. Lake,
Charles M. Latham,
Henry S. Latham, Jr,
Dean S. Linnell,
Richard P. Lobdell,
Benjamin T. Marble,
*Matthew M. Meggett,
Charles S. McCreading,
William H. Moffitt,
James Nicholson,
Charles E. R. Page,
†Allen G. Peck,
Addison Parker, Jr.,
John F. Pierce,
Owen S. Pond,
Thomas T. Potter,
Samuel H. Pratt,

* August 18, 1862, died in hospital, Fort Pennsylvania, D. C.
† July 8, 1862, discharged as a minor.

Samuel G. Rawson,
John A. Reynolds,
Dana B. Robinson,
George W. Robinson,
William W. Salisbury,
Livingston Scott,
Orville B. Seagrave,
Thomas J. Smith,

George H. Sparhawk,
*William A. Spicer,
Franklin A. Steere,
†Frank F. Tingley,
†George E. Thompson,
James R. D. Thompson,
Benjamin W. Wilbour.

COMPANY C.

Captain.

JEREMIAH M. VOSE.

First Lieutenant.

JOHN E. BRADFORD.

Second Lieutenant.

CALEB B. HARRINGTON.

Sergeants.

Henry N. Stevens,
Daniel B. Rodman,
Amos G. Thomas,

Harry D. Perkins,
Joseph W. Padelford.

* July 1, 1862, detached on special service at General Pope's headquarters.
† July 8, 1862, discharged as a minor.

RHODE ISLAND VOLUNTEERS.

Corporals.

Joseph W. Bradford,
William C. Angell,
Joshua Hunt,

Caleb E. Thayer,
William B. Durfee.

Musician.

†Joshua H. Thomas.

Privates.

William Allen,
John Atkinson,
Ezra Bisbee,
James Bowden,
†William T. Boyden,
Edward L. Brown,
John A. Brown,
†Thomas A. Brown,
Charles R. Burke,
James E. Campbell,
William B. Durfee,
George Eagan,
Jerome B. Farnum,
John H. Gardner,
Ellis T. Hayward,
Albert F. Hoxie,
John L. Hussey,
Gilbert A. Irons,
Nathan Jacques,
Isaac C. Kendall,
John E. Kenyon,

Daniel E. Kiley,
William H. Leonard,
George W. Lewis,
Theodore F. Lewis,
Rice A. Miller,
Edmund J. Munroe,
Thomas B. Munroe,
George A. Pettis,
George P. Rose,
Frank Seamans,
Stephen A. Shaw,
Silas Sherman, Jr.,
Henry H. Steadman,
Elisha W. Sweet,
George L. Thurber,
James Tomman,
William Tremble,
John H. Tyler,
James H. Waterman,
Andrew J. Williams,
Ferdinand A. Williams.

† July 7, 1862, discharged for disability.

COMPANY D.

Captains.
CHARLES H. DUNHAM.
(Acting till June 8, 1862.)
WILLIAM S. SMITH.

First Lieutenants.
JAMES H. ARMINGTON.
(Resigned July 19, 1862.)
WILLIAM S. SMITH.
(June 8, 1862, promoted to captain.)
WINTHROP DE WOLF.

Second Lieutenants.
WINTHROP DE WOLF.
(July 25, 1862, promoted to first lieutenant.)
CHARLES W. ANGELL.
(July 25, 1862, promoted from private.)

Sergeants.
Thomas A. Starkey,
Charles S. Mathewson,
Edward W. Brown,
Thomas F. Tobey,

†Samuel R. Dorrance,
Daniel Bush,
William H. H. Brayman.

Corporals.
Howard O. Sturges,
Henry A. Foster,
George H. Daniels,
Edward N. Gould,

Philip Kelley,
Brockholst Mathewson, 2d,
Frederic Buttendorf,
Edward K. Thompson.

† July 15, 1862, discharged on surgeon's certificate.

RHODE ISLAND VOLUNTEERS.

Privates.

Edward Aborn,
George W. Adams,
Nelson W. Aldrich,
Willard J. Allen,
Frederic J. Armington,
†William Whitman Bailey,
Alfred H. Barber, Jr.,
James H. Barney,
George B. Barrows,
George B. Binney,
George D. Briggs,
Samuel T. Brown,
Herman Buttendorf,
George Bucklin,
Levi L. Burdon,
John G. Burrough,
John H. Cady,
Henry T. Chace,
Edward C. Clarke,
Peleg Clarke, Jr.,
Harry Castello,
Eben B. Crane,
Samuel S. Davis,
Charles H. DeWolf,
J. Halsey DeWolf,
John K. Dorrance,
James D. Dougherty,
Henry P. Eldridge,
James M. Flagg,
Charles O. Giles,

Albert E. Ham,
Henry A. Hamilton,
William A. Harris,
Frederic H. Hedge, Jr.,
Charles H. Hidden,
William H. Hubbard,
Lucien E. Kent,
George W. Kennedy,
Albert B. Kimball,
Henry J. Levalley,
Thomas Livingston,
Hugh McGovern,
Norman N. Mason,
Frank S. Mead,
S. Erastus Merchant,
Joshua Mellen,
James Morning, Jr.,
Elisha C. Mowry,
Charles K. Newcomb,
William R. Okie,
Edward S. Parker,
Robert H. Paine,
J. Haradon Peck,
John Pitman, Jr.,
John Anson Price,
John M. Richmond,
Christopher Rhodes,
John R. Sisson,
Herman C. Stillwell,
Charles M. Smith,

† July 15, 1862, discharged on surgeon's certificate.

John E. Smith,
John R. Smith,
†Solomon Smith,
Edward K. Thompson,
Robert Thompson,

Joseph Ward,
George C. Webster,
*Charles H. Wildman,
William L. Wickes.

COMPANY E.

Captain.
HOPKINS B. CADY.

First Lieutenant.
STEPHEN THURBER.

Second Lieutenant.
MOSES O. DARLING.

Sergeants.

John A. Jeffrey,
Raymond W. Cahoone,
Ray G. Burlingame,

William Stone,
Frank Holden.

Corporals.

Orsmus A. Taft,
Isaac S. Burke,
Joseph C. Whiting, Jr.,
Welcome B. Darling,

J. Collins Gould,
Nathan T. Robinson,
Ira R. Wilbur,
William A. H. Grant.

* July 1, 1862, detached on special service at General Pope's headquarters.
† July 15, 1862, discharged on surgeon's certificate.

Musician.

Amos B. Sherman.

Privates.

Samuel S. Baker,
John Bishop,
James B. Brogden,
Chauncey Brown,
Joseph R. Burrows,
†Arthur Burt,
Charles H. Burt,
Christopher A. Cady,
Walter D. Colwell,
Lewis E. Davis,
Samuel Dunkerly,
John F. Durfee,
James A. Foster,
Joseph B. Hayward,
William H. Henshaw,
†Edwin Herrick,
Michael Hickey,
Joseph H. Horr,
Theodore Horton,
George W. Horton,
Henry H. James,

†F. M. Johnson,
Daniel Kelly,
†A. W. Ladd,
George W. Lindsay,
Thomas A. Manchester,
†C. W. Mason,
Edward T. Nichols,
†Henry W. Pearce,
Ellery W. Price,
John Russell,
John Sawyer,
Job W. Sherman,
William H. Sherman, 2d,
William Simmons,
Charles A. Sweet,
Nathan J. Sweetland,
Charles J. Tourtellott,
Gilbert P. Vallett,
William H. White,
Henry A. Wellman,
Henry S. Yarwood.

* July, 1862, discharged as a minor.

COMPANY F.

Captain.

BENJAMIN W. HARRIS.

First Lieutenant.

ORVILLE P. JONES,

Second Lieutenant.

GEORGE W. FAIRBANKS.

Sergeants.

Joel Metcalf, Jr.,
Charles A. Barbour,
Charles H. Worsley,

Charles G. Ingraham,
George T. Bowen.

Corporals.

William E. Thurston,
Samuel A. Whelden,
William W. Crandall,
Charles E. Carnes,

Thomas H. Shannon,
Andrew Greenhalgh,
James Ferguson,
William H. Luther.

Privates.

John Buckley,
George N. Capron,
Michael Carlin,
James Collins,
James Curran,
John Drugan,
Patrick Fay,
Joseph Field,

John Goud,
William D. Gardiner,
James Hanney,
John Hannifen,
Edward Healey,
George C. Luther,
John McDonnell,
James McElroy,

Samuel Meegan,
Peter Mullen,
William Mullen,
John Niles,
Andrew O'Hare,
David O'Hare,
Charles O'Neil,
William Platt,
Seaman Pattinson,
James W. Randall,

Michael J. Ryan,
John Rouch,
Joseph Simons,
Simon Smith,
Henry Sherman,
Solomon Taylor,
Charles E. Tetlow,
James Welch,
Henry Zuill.

COMPANY G.

Captain.
ALBERT CRAWFORD GREENE.

First Lieutenant.
JAMES H. ALLEN.

Second Lieutenant.
EBEN BURLINGAME.

Sergeants.

John B. Benson,
Philip C. Gray,
Edmund W. Hawkins,

Albert J. Manchester,
Andrew J. Dexter.

Corporals.

Charles H. Allen,
George Crittenden,

Charles F. Northup,
Franklin Cooley,

Charles H. Jordan,
William C. Thurston,

Asahel H. Harris,
James A. Peckham.

Musician.

John F. Parks.

Privates.

George M. Adams,
George F. Aldrich,
Thomas W. Angell,
John R. Atwood,
Stephen A. Barry,
Henry N. Brown,
Henry R. Brown,
Greenleaf D. Brown,
Isaac Brown,
Joseph E. Brown,
Gustavus B. Burlingame,
Hiram Brand,
John R. Burke,
David R. Campbell,
Patrick Cashman,
George Chace,
George Chatterton, Jr.,
Richard Clarke,
James Doran,
William W. Eddy,
Erwin S. Eggleston,
Pardon B. S. Fords,
George W. Franklin,

†Frederick A. Fry,
Albert L. Greene,
Samuel H. Hopkins,
Erastus M. Hunt,
William G. Hynds,
Royal E. Jones,
George Kellogg,
Frank R. Lewis,
‡Albert A. McDougald,
John E. Mathewson,
Dennis McLaughlin,
Lewis A. Medbury,
Frank B. Mott,
Thomas E. Noonan,
Benjamin F. Nicholas,
George W. Nicholas,
Charles E. Osborne,
Allen Paine,
Arnold J. Paine,
Charles H. Philbrick,
Benjamin E. Phillips,
Stephen Phetteplace,
Stephen W. Poole,

† June 24, 1862, discharged for disability.
‡ June 9, 1862, discharged as a minor.

RHODE ISLAND VOLUNTEERS.

William H. Poole,
Henry Schoch,
Benjamin Scott,
Albert W. Sprague,
Daniel Sullivan,
John W. Taylor,
George H. Tyler,

Lewis O. Walker,
John Warner,
Samuel S. Warren,
Alonzo Whipple,
James C. Whipple,
Reuben Wickes,
Preston D. Yerrington.

COMPANY H.

Captain.
CHRISTOPHER DUCKWORTH.

First Lieutenant.
NICHOLAS B. BOLLES.

Second Lieutenant.
WILLIAM H. MASON.

Sergeants

George A. Winchester,
Edward C. Kendall,
Henry G. Lillibridge,

Alfred Baker,
Charles P. Gay.

Corporals.

Charles H. Beadle,
Benjamin F. Pabodie,
William T. Hovey,
Alphonso W. Martin,

George A. Kendall,
Albert G. Knowles,
James A. Bucklin,
Charles A. Kimball.

Musicians.

William E. Dickerson,   William J. Tilley, Jr.

Privates.

James Annis,
Job Armstrong,
Bradford W. Bennett,
William A. Brown,
William A. Brownell,
Frederick G. Chaffin,
Henry Clark,
Warren F. Clemence,
William H. Crins,
John H. Dodge,
Albert E. Fuller,
Mark Hartsine,
William H. Hedley,
Joshua M. Hunt,
Charles H. Jackson,
Robert Knight,
Benjamin Lewis,
John E. Larned, Jr.,
Almy Mathewson,
Alonzo Mathewson,
William H. Mathewson,
William B. Pierce,
Henry Read,
Henry Reinwald,
Charles A. Remington,
Albert F. Remington,
George F. Sheldon,
Edwin A. Smith,
William H. Thornton,
Edwin I. Thurber,
Edward Updike,
†George Williams.

COMPANY I.

Captains. (*See Lieutenant-Colonel.*)

WILLIAM M. HALE.

SAMUEL H. THOMAS.

(August 11, 1862, from first lieutenant Company B.)

First Lieutenant.

CHARLES H. MUMFORD.

† July 7, 1862, discharged as a minor.

RHODE ISLAND VOLUNTEERS.

Second Lieutenant.

PETER ALEXANDER REID.

Sergeants.

Frank R. Dennis, Henry R. Barker,
William T. Luther, Daniel E. Barney.
John R. Allen,

Corporals.

John W. Greene, Benjamin D. Hale,
Moses B. Chace, Thomas N. D. Reynolds,
Frederic A. Studley, Oliver S. Alers,
Frederic S. Luther, Charles W. Howe.

Musician.

Edwin R. Burr.

Privates.

John G. Alers, Charles Gerlach,
Fenner R. Allen, George W. Grant,
William H. Ayer, William F. Green,
Leander Baker, James S. Griffin,
Horace E. Barker, George G. Gunn,
James G. Brown, George B. Hale,
Horace R. Butts, George W. Harris, Jr.,
Matthew A. Chace, Thomas W. D. Horton,
Richard J. Chappell, †Charles E. Millard,
Charles F. Church, Cornelius W. Miller,
Robert Dickerson, †George W. Mereweather,
George Foster, Thomas Moore,
Joseph Garrett, James M. Munroe,

† July 7, 1802, discharged as a minor.

Charles W. Peck,
John F. Peck,
Edward B. Peck,
John F. Paine,
George Pepall,
James W. Presbrey,
George H. Pike,
William H. Pullen, Jr.,
Frederic Roberts,
Charles E. Ross,

Daniel O. Sullivan,
Charles A. Schuler,
Henry P. Tillinghast,
William Toye,
William H. Trenn,
Pardon Wilbur,
Chauncey C. Williams,
Albert W. White,
Samuel Y. Weaver.

COMPANY K.

Captain.
G. FRANK LOW.

First Lieutenant.
JOHN F. TOBEY (adjutant).

Second Lieutenant.
WILLIAM G. PETTIS.

Sergeants.

Munson H. Najac,
William A. Wilson,
James E. Blackmar,

Sylvester Martin,
Nathan S. K. Davis.

Corporals.

Frederick W. Ellis,
James F. Davison,

James F. Mason,
J. Bradley Adams,

John D. Edgell,
Jesse P. Eddy,

Zephaniah Brown, 2d,
Joseph E. Handy.

Privates.

Israel M. Bullock,
Mathew Blanchard,
Benjamin Briggs,
James P. Brown,
Benjamin H. Case,
Edison C. Chick,
John S. Chick,
Frank A. Church,
Amos Cross,
John B. Davison,
Edgar J. Doe,
Thomas Farrell,
Amasa R. Goffe,
§Stephen P. Greene,
John B. Hanna,
Daniel H. Helme,
Benjamin H. Hemminway,
John J. Holmes,
John C. Hopkins,
Stephen A. Horton,
William C. Ives,
Walter M. Jackson,
Willis B. Jackson,
Reuben W. Johnson,
Gilbert A. Kenney,
George H. Kenyon,
Frank A. Love,
De Witt C. Mathewson,

Carlo Mauran,
Frederick McCausland,
†J. Wilson McCrillis,
George H. Messer,
Samuel N. Mitchell,
Henry L. Place,
Albert B. Pond,
Harris H. Potter,
Horatio N. Reynolds,
‡Charles E. Rhodes,
Henry W. Robinson,
Lewis L. Sagendorph,
George W. Shaw,
Elisha Smith,
Daniel Sullivan,
Charles D. Thurber,
Frank H. Thurber,
George K. Tyler,
William H. Underhill,
Levi C. Walker,
A. Fuller Warren,
George W. Welden,
Charles S. White,
Thomas G. Whaley,
William C. Witter,
Charles D. Wilbur,
William H. Young.

* June 7, 1862, discharged as a minor.
‡ July 7, 1862, discharged as a minor.
§ Discharged as a minor.

ROSTER

OF THE

TENTH LIGHT BATTERY RHODE ISLAND VOLUNTEERS,

(Company L.)

Captain.
EDWIN C. GALLUP.

First Lieutenants.
Senior. SAMUEL A. PEARCE, JR.
Junior. FRANK A. RHODES.

Second Lieutenants.
Senior. AMOS D. SMITH, JR.
Junior. HENRY PEARCE.

Hospital Steward.
CHARLES W. CADY.

First Sergeant.
AMASA C. TOURTELLOTT.

Quartermaster Sergeant.
ASA LYMAN.

Sergeants.

James S. Davis, Jr.,	George W. Paton,
Henry W. Brown,	Stephen G. Luther,
Calvin J. Adams,	Philip B. Stiness, Jr.

Corporals.

John L. Remlinger,
Henry A. Guild,
Smith F. Phillips,
Nathaniel F. Winslow, Jr.,
Ephraim Greene,
John P. Dow,
Charles H. Starkey,

Alphonso Bennett,
Henry A. Boss,
Isaac S. Andrews,
*James Flate,
James M. Harrison,
Liscomb C. Winn.

Artificers.

William Almy,   Charles J. Noonan.

Musician.

Daniel F. Read.

Volunteer Surgeon.

Edward Carrington Franklin.

Privates.

George H. Adams,
Robert Aldrich,
George Aldermick,
Smith A. Alexander,
Henry H. Almy,
Thomas Atwood,
Henry C. Bailey,
Samuel Bailey,
Edwin H. Barnes,
Norman K. Barnes,
William A. Bates,
George H. Baxter,
Alfred A. Bicknell,

Horatio N. Billington,
Frederic D. Bliss,
William J. Booth,
William A. Bragg,
William B. Briggs,
Gardner K. Browning,
Henry A. Burchard,
Frederic L. Burden,
Frederic Campbell,
Donald Cameron,
Joseph Carroll,
Thomas Chace, Jr.,
John Carvey,

*August 8, 1862, killed by accident near Fort Pennsylvania.

Frank W. Cole,
Nelson G. Cole,
Elijah D. Collins,
James Cruikshanks,
James Crook,
Edgar A. Cummings,
George Cummings,
James Curran,
Bethil Curtis,
Charles Dougherty,
Joseph D. Dow,
Aaron Duxbury,
Ezekiel Emerson,
Joseph R. Elsbree,
Mitchell J. Fagan,
Mitchell A. Feeley,
Edson D. Foilett,
Joseph A. Fowler,
Thomas H. French,
Smith Goodspeed,
Frederic W. Granger,
George W. Greene,
Patrick Gleason,
Edward P. Harney,
David Hart,
Henry N. Hopkins,
James F. Hopkins,
J. Ray Hopkins,
Daniel H. Horton,
Gideon M. Horton,
Mitchell F. Holden,
Patrick Herren,

William H. Harvey,
William Jenkins,
William F. Johnson,
George P. Johnson,
George Kearney,
Patrick Kelly,
Willard A. Knight,
William Londaigon,
Timothy McCarthy,
Joseph McClellan,
Patrick McGettrick,
Peter McCready,
Peter McDermott,
Prescott Miller,
George F. Munroe,
Patrick Murphy,
Henry Myers,
Matthew Meehan,
Hugh McGuire,
John McCarty,
Ambrose A. Newbert,
Ellery Northup,
Francis Perkins,
Duty Place.
James C. Potter,
Oliver A. Potter,
Thomas H. Ray,
Jason B. Reynolds,
Albert Richards,
Henry A. Remington,
Isaac Riley,
George Robinson,

RHODE ISLAND VOLUNTEERS.

Myron Rounds,
William A. Ryan,
Augustus Read,
John Schaab,
Matthew Scott,
Henry L. Shippen,
William Somerville,
William Southers,
George Stone,
Charles N. Sheldon,
John Stewart,
Henry J. Stewart,
John Taylor,
Israel O. Taylor,

Henry Tucker,
Stephen D. Tucker,
William L. Tyrrel,
Daniel R. Tennant,
William Turner,
Brayton Vallett,
Stillman W. Wade,
Allen T. White,
Alpha B. White,
David H. Wright,
James Wood,
William E. Woodworth,
Patrick Welch.

TILLINGHAST'S ASSEMBLY ROOMS,
PROVIDENCE. R. I., May 26, 1893.

At a meeting of the Tenth Rhode Island Volunteers and Battery Veteran Association, held this evening, upon motion of Comrade Charles F. Phillips, the following resolutions were unanimously adopted:

Resolved, That a vote of thanks be tendered to Comrade William A. Spicer, as an acknowledgment of the satisfactory manner with which he has performed the arduous duty of editing and compiling the History of the Ninth and Tenth Regiments Rhode Island Volunteers, and Tenth Rhode Island Battery.

Resolved, That a special copy of the new Regimental History, suitably bound and inscribed, with these resolutions inserted, be presented to Comrade Spicer by this Association.

Resolved, That a committee of three be appointed by the President to carry into effect the foregoing resolutions.

President Albert J. Manchester appointed as this committee Charles F. Phillips and William A. H. Grant, of the Tenth Regiment, and Philip B. Stiness, of the Tenth Battery.

Upon motion, Comrade Harrison H. Richardson, of the Ninth Regiment, was added to the committee.

Attest:
GEO. A. WINCHESTER,
Secretary.

RESOLUTIONS.

PROVIDENCE, R. I. Oct. 21st 1893.

At a meeting of the Joint Committee on Publication of the Ninth and Tenth R. I. Regiments Veteran Association, Comrade Henry F. Jenks, of the Ninth Regiment Association, was appointed Chairman, and William A. H. Grant, of the Tenth Regiment Association, Secretary.

Comrade William A. Spicer, the regimental historian, reported that he had completed the work assigned him by the Committees on Publication, and had now the pleasure of presenting them with a copy of the History.

Comrade Harrison H. Richardson, of the Ninth Regiment Committee, said he had no doubt but that the history now completed would receive the hearty endorsement and approval of the comrades, as it had of the Committee on Publication, and offered the following resolutions:

WHEREAS, Comrade William A. Spicer has brought to a successful conclusion his labors as Editor of our Regimental History, and has produced a volume which, while not recording any thrilling feats of arms, presents a graphic picture of life in the camp and on the march, as described by the Boys in Blue of '62; therefore,

Resolved, That the thanks of our several Associations are due to Comrade Spicer for the patient persistency displayed in his search for material, and the skill with which he has woven the threads of his narrative, as well as for the careful discrimination displayed in the production of a book which may find its welcome in the family circle, or the public library, as well as at the camp-fire; and,

Resolved, As a further testimonial of our appreciation, that Comrade William A. Spicer be, and he is, hereby appointed Treasurer, to receive and to disburse all funds appropriated or coming from the sale of books, reporting as required to this committee, or its successor.

The above resolutions were unanimously adopted.

HENRY F. JENKS, Chairman.
W. A. H. GRANT, Secretary.

Oct. 21st, 1893.

A LETTER FROM CHAPLAIN CLAPP.

THE following letter from Chaplain Clapp, of the Tenth, has been received since the completion of the history. On account of its general interest to the comrades, it is printed in this separate form to accompany the book.

NEW YORK, December 15, 1893.

MY DEAR SPICER:

I greatly rejoice in the new proof of their good sense which our comrades of "the Ninth and Tenth Rhode Island" have shown in selecting you as their historian, to make lasting record of our varied experiences in the days of the Rebellion. A glance, which you have kindly allowed me, at the proof sheets of your volume, more than satisfies,—it delights me, with the taste, discrimination, and truthfulness with which you have executed your delicate task. That you deserve well of us all, I know from personal observation, so far as your story of the campaign of the Tenth and our companion battery is concerned, and I cannot doubt your equal faithfulness in what you have said of our sister regiment. The record is an honorable one. True, we whose service was limited to that campaign cannot claim to be survivors of bloody battlefields. We have no scars to show in token of the sharpness of rebel sabres or the true aim of rebel rifles. We may not in old age shoulder our crutches and show how fields were won, but "the boys" whose loyalty you so well commemorate, did faithfully the one work to which they were so suddenly called in that serious emergency. They defended the capital from threatened invasion at a most critical time. They prevented the execution of a rebel plan, the carrying out of which by the enemy would have been disastrous in the extreme, and when unexpectedly ordered to the front for closer and more deadly contact with the foe, not a man of our inexperienced and comparatively untrained force held back. No one grudged the discomfort of that weary march to "Seminary Hill," which gave us the privilege of facing the Marshall House, and in loving memory of the "gallant Ellsworth," singing with a *vim* not often put into the words :

      "Down where the patriot army by Potomac's side."

And following it with :

      "John Brown's body lies a'mouldering in the grave,
      But his soul is marching on."

Had not superior military wisdom returned us to our forts and batteries near Washington, and sent toward Richmond better seasoned men in our stead, the Rhode Island boys would have gone into battle with a courage and efficiency not inferior to those of the bravest whose names are enrolled as having deserved well of their country. This is proved beyond dispute by the careers of many officers and men, who, after honorable discharge from the Ninth and Tenth, enlisted in other regiments and served to the end of the war, or till they were called up higher to receive the recompense of the loyal and the brave.

You have wisely given prominence to the bright side of the picture, but it need not be said that there were many serious hours in our three months' campaigning — hours spent in hospital tents beside sick comrades, several of whom came near to death, but were mercifully restored — thanks to the Great Physician, and to the marked skill and care of our worthy surgeon. Alas, that it did not avail to keep back from the grave the brave and youthful Atwood, Meggett, and Walker, whose memory your volume so faithfully embalms, and whose brightest record is on high. My own memory brings back also many hours spent with Rhode Island's wounded boys from other regiments, whom frequent inquiries brought to light in the various hospitals in Washington, and whom it was a melancholy pleasure to serve by communicating with their parents, wives, or other friends at home. Last of all shall I ever forget that long anxious homeward ride with our uncomplaining sick, on couches extemporized from unscrewed backs of car seats — patient sufferers whom it was an indescribable relief to hand over to the care of their loved ones at home.

Serious also, but to me most pleasant, were the daily seasons of Scripture reading, prayer and song, at headquarters, and the Sabbath services held there, and at as many of the forts and batteries as could be reached on the back of "Fanny," the chaplain's mare. Many a brief informal address delivered from her saddle was most respectfully listened to by "the boys," drawn up in a hollow square, and headed by the officer in charge. Not one unpleasant incident, not even a look of disrespect marred those hours of worship. A somewhat wide observation convinced me that those regiments were very rare in which were enrolled so many cultured, self-respecting gentlemen, as were found among the officers and privates of the Ninth and Tenth Rhode Island.

Colonels Bliss, Shaw and Hale; Surgeon Wilcox; Adjutants Thurston and Tobey; Quartermasters Armington and DeWolf; Captain Elisha Dyer, Ex-Governor of our State, and eminent in all civil, educational, social and religious circles; and scarcely less known in City and State, the entire list of captains whose companies numbered men eminent in professional life, with college graduates and undergraduates, many of whom now ad[orn] a high post of honor — have we not just occasion to be proud of them?

Never will the writer forget his first introduction to the genial Colonel Bliss whom he had not the good fortune to know before meeting him at Camp Frieze. Governor Dyer led the humble chaplain, verdant enough in all military matters, up to the stalwart soldier, saying : "Colonel, I beg to your acquaintance my friend, Rev. Mr. Clapp, our chaplain, whom you will be glad to know." "Well," said the colonel, his face wreathed in smiles, "I've been twelve years in the army and you are the first chaplain I ever had about me. I don't know what to do with you." "Never mind," was the reply, "You'll soon learn; we shall be the best friends in the regiment, and you'll not know how to do without one." "Good!" said the colonel; "He, sergeant, put up the chaplain's tent next to mine; and, chaplain, I want you to come into my mess." Into that tent and mess the chaplain went, the friendships formed there with the staff largely helped him in bringing good influences upon the young and inexperienced in the ranks, and have been matter for pleasant memories in the years that have since rolled by.

If this note were not already too long, I would like to tell our comrades of an incident that befell their chaplain on a hot, pitchy dark Sunday night, between nine and ten o'clock, on the way back from Battery Vermont to Fort Pennsylvania. Unable to see a yard ahead your chaplain laid the reins upon Fanny's neck, and thinking of his home and parish, had, without knowing it, reached the front of Secretary Stanton's house; just then, on account of repeated rebel threats (but without our knowledge), guarded by a detail of troops. Suddenly, hoarsely sounded in the chaplain's ear, from a mounted soldier at his side, till then unseen and unheard, "Halt! Who goes there?" "Friend, with the countersign," was answered with a trembling voice. "Advance, friend, and give the countersign." The countersign was whispered. "The countersign is wrong. Come with me to the captain of the guard." For a few minutes the chaplain believed himself to be in rebel hands, but reined faithful Fanny up at the guard tent. In answer to the captain's questions, he gave his name and "pedigree" as chaplain of the Tenth Rhode Island Volunteers, and in proof thereof, produced from his pockets a handful of letters so addressed. Scanning the chaplain's face by a lantern's light, the captain allowed that it didn't have a rebel look — but the wrong countersign, how was that? At length it dawned upon the captain's mind. "Oh, the Tenth Rhode Island boys are not in our division, and their countersign is not ours! You may pass on, sir!" And the chaplain did pass on with a far lighter heart than he had known for half an hour or more.

You know that unfortunately the duties of my position here, since 1862 have kept me from meeting with the survivors of the Tenth in their annual reunions — a deprivation which I have most deeply regretted. Had I ever permitted to be with you, I think I should have earlier made a confession of an act of indiscretion of my country's laws of which the boys of the Tenth would never have suspected their chaplain, and of a sacrifice in behalf of the United States Treasury for which he has never had due credit. A private of the Ninth, after that regiment had gone over the east fork of the Potomac, being seriously ill, sent word of his desire to see his friend, the chaplain of the Tenth. "Fanny" took the chaplain and mail in the mail wagon to the capital, where it seemed best to let her rest for a few hours before going back to Tennallytown. So the chaplain foraged for "a good and fast saddle horse," but the stable keeper said he could furnish only a small, pacing mare, "gentle and easy-going," he said, "but unable to make more than six miles an hour at her best." The chaplain mounted, and the little creature ambled quietly along Pennsylvania avenue on our errand of mercy. Presently a loud peremptory shout was heard from the rear, but attracted little notice. It was heard again and shortly again, but without a thought that it was meant for the innocent chaplain, till a big, rough, mounted policeman came alongside, grabbed the pacer's rein, and, in a wrathful voice, asked: "Why didn't you stop when I challenged you?" Confession of ignorance as to the meaning of the shouts was humbly made, but the officer growled: "Come along with me." And sure enough, the chaplain was haled before a police justice and accused of *fast driving* in the streets of Washington, contrary to the laws of that great city. The chaplain told the judge his story, rehearsing with affecting sincerity the words of the pacer's owner as to the six-mile-an-hour limit of her speed. Begging to be allowed to go to his sick friend in the Ninth's camp, he was finally allowed to do so, on his pledging his word to present himself at the court on his return. He did so present himself, bringing along the stable keeper, who retold the story of the pacer's six-mile limit. But all would not avail. The treasury was at a low ebb, the policeman was angry, and a strong swearer, and the justice thought that "a fine of *five dollars* would be about right!" It was paid, and the sacred streets of the capital were avenged for having resounded to the rattling feet of a pacer rushing along their surface at the rate of six miles an hour!

When you meet again our comrades you may tell them the story, which for obvious reasons I kept from them in camp. They may smile at it now as long and as loudly as they choose.

And do not fail to assure them of my sincere regard, my gratitude that I was allowed to share with them our brief campaign, my lasting memory of their many kindnesses, and my earnest prayers for their best welfare here and for their final blessedness in the eternal Kingdom of the Prince of Peace.

    Always cordially yours,

        A. HUNTINGTON CLAPP.

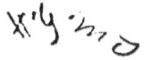

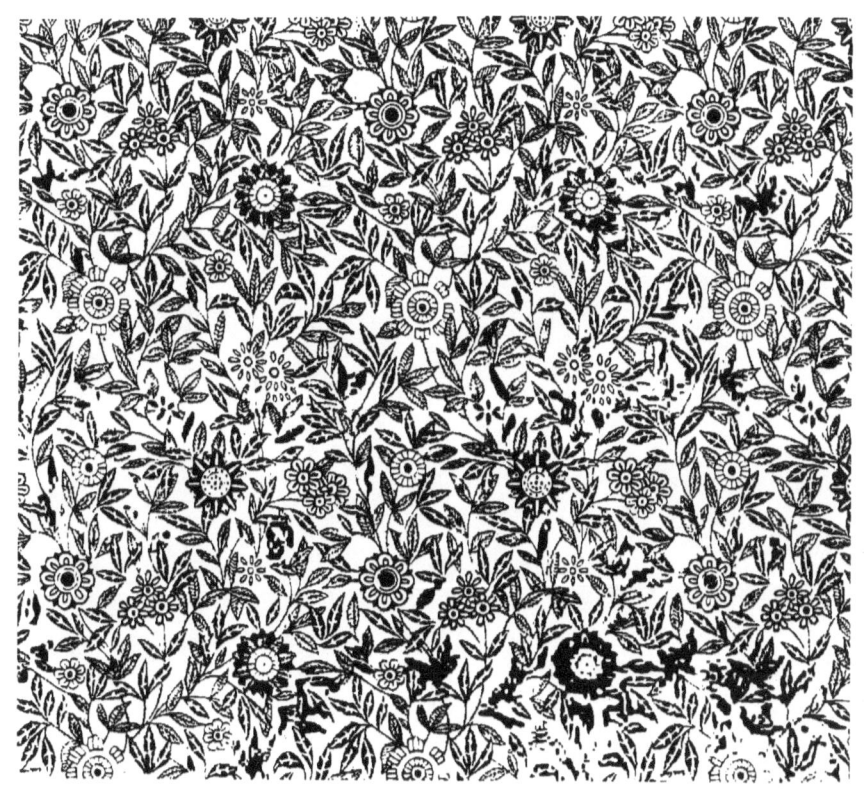

www.ingramcontent.com/pod-product-compliance
Lightning Source LLC
Chambersburg PA
CBHW030548300426
44111CB00009B/894